The Bully Around The Corner

The Bully Around The Corner

Changing Brains – Changing Behaviours

David Halstead, M.Ed.

This book is dedicated to all those boys and girls, men and women who took their own lives because they decided the bullying they were experiencing was so denigrating and so debilitating *they could no longer go on living.*

This book is further dedicated to the boys and girls, men and women who have never reached their potential or who are struggling daily to *overcome the detrimental affects of being bullied.*

Lastly, this book is dedicated to all those educators, parents, community workers and leaders who have made it a personal mission to make positive inroads into resolving *this soul destroying behaviour.*

∿ ∿ ∿ ∿ ∿ ∿ ∿ ∿ ∿ ∿

A special dedication to my wife Peggy, for her tireless support, to our children who are making a difference in their respective communities and to our grandchildren, those present and those yet to come hoping they may *be spared the damages caused by bullying.*

The Bully Around the Corner:
Changing Brains – Changing Behaviours

Author: David Halstead, M.Ed
ISBN: 0-9731650-2-2

Published by: Brain Power Learning Group
22 Beaulynn Cove, Winnipeg, Manitoba
Canada
R3T 5G4

Cover Design and Layout: Relish Design Studio Ltd, Winnipeg, Manitoba, Canada
Printed by Kromar Printing, Winnipeg, Manitoba, Canada

TABLE OF CONTENTS

Title		Page

PREFACE

This book is written to be of assistance to school administrators, teachers and other school personnel, police officers, social workers and parents who are committed to do all the small and large things necessary to make their schools and communities safer, more personally enriching and assist children to become socially responsible citizens.

The title *The Bully Around the Corner* was chosen to speak to both the literal and figurative presence of bullying.

Literally there are bullies who are in those shadows waiting to do some harm. Some of these bullies lurk around their victims locker, in or near the washroom at breaks or in the midst of a group. The victims know who they are, where they are most of the time and what they will try to do.

Figuratively there is the subculture of bullying the bigotry, class or group status, clique entitlement and thought processes engendered by mental health and developmental deficits.

Regardless bullying is a mind set, it is a lifestyle which provides the bully with some level of satisfaction and the victim one or more levels of harm. But both are being victimized by this behaviour.

Why would I take several years to write this book, to develop and deliver workshops for teachers and others. It is because I, like most of you, have been bullied at some time in my past and it wasn't fun. In addition I have spent over forty years as an educator with the past seven plus years studying the latest brain research to try to understand the developmental aspects of human behaviour. My research reveals the following.

◆ Our behaviour is the result of integration of our genetics, pre and post natal environments and those things we have learned consciously and non consciously.

◆ Although we like to view ourselves as highly cognitive, rational beings we are controlled to a considerable extent by the emotional regions of the brain and other non cognitive brain areas which will be explained later in this book.

◆ The neural networks formed within our brains determine who we are and the behaviours we display.

◆ The brain does not change quickly. **This is not a quick fix book.**

◆ Each child's brain goes through several synaptic growth spurts with periods of active refinement which may continue up to age 29 or so. Children are not adults in tiny clothes nor are teenagers equipped with fully mature brains.

◆ Every brain is unique. Every child presents his/her own state of being. **One size (solution) will not fit all.**

◆ The good news is that most children will, with appropriate programming, be able to adopt socially acceptable behaviours and live as responsible citizens.

◆ However, the children who have been severely damaged will challenge the system at every turn and regrettably a few may never be able to live socially acceptable lives. This is a reality.

I am often asked the question, "Why is bullying such a big item these days when it has always been with us? My answer is this. As we become more and more conscious of the injustices experienced by women, children, people of colour or creed or whose gender orientation is other than the "norm," we clearly see these injustices as wrong and counter to the standards of a civilized society. We also are recognizing and accepting that bullying is unacceptable and harmful to the bully, the victim and the community at large.

OUR CHANGING SOCIETY

In traditional cultures, which thrived in small villages, a child grew up being the responsibility of the entire village which often was their extended family. In addition the child was responsible to each other member of the village. Perhaps this was the golden age of social brain development. The industrial revolution and global migration changed all that.

From the mid 1800's to the middle of the 20th century there was a triumvirate responsible for the social development of the child. The family, the church and the school all operated in collaboration to fashion an educated and social child.

In the last fifty or so years the family and the church have become less relevant entities in the lives of many children and the schools have, by default, taken on the role of all previous partners.

Today's families are under a great many pressures. Some of these are self inflicted and others are the result of workplace and community instability. Fortunately, there are many great families in every income strata who are doing everything in their power to provide good homes for their children.

But there are homes in every income strata which for one reason or another are not able to provide for the child's cognitive, emotional and material needs. Some of these homes are very transparent, others are known only when there is a domestic dispute which ends up in a murder-suicide or a mother and her children hiding in a women's shelter. But these are like the visible part of an iceberg. Hidden below the surface are a multitude of homes where children are abused or simply survive within the emotional disharmony of their home. We never really know what goes on behind the closed doors of most of the homes in our school area. We hope for the best but must always be willing to respond, as necessary, when conditions are less than optimum.

Church attendance in many regions has fallen dramatically in the last fifty years. Many children are no longer hearing the religious stories or are not active in a range of church sponsored children's and youth groups. Even staff within school systems which are nominally church centred report that although the children hear the words of compassion, charity and acceptance they are unable to convert these words into respectful actions.

Lastly, the principle focus of this book is to give the reader an increased understanding of the complex nature of bullying, a vast number of possible strategies and from this information choose to develop programs which will meet the specific needs of the children.

BULLYING IS MORE THAN A LEARNED BEHAVIOUR

It is widely accepted that bullying is a **learned behaviour**. This may, in large part, be true only if we accept a broad understanding of "**learning**". However, a learned behaviour is usually far more difficult to change than an erroneously learned mathematical fact. For example, should a child learn that 3+3=5 it will probably not take very much work on behalf of the teacher and the child to correct this bit of learning.

In the case of a bullying behaviour, it is likely there are emotional and multiple other memories formed which support the bullying activity and may not respond to traditional therapies or **one off commands**.

In addition, there is always the possibility that a child's bullying behaviour starts from frustration, anger and fear and the child will lash out at the first object, animal or human within range. This act may not be altogether random and it is likely the child will select another child who is less likely to fight back to be the target.

The bully often learns from this behaviour that it is rewarding, even comforting to beat up some defenceless soul.

None of the above explanations or arguments are of interest to the victim. He or she is being victimized and needs your help to make this stop.

As you proceed through the book I sincerely hope that the information you find will be helpful in dealing with individual students and developing school practices that will make your school and community safer and the lives of all students happier and more productive.

NOTE: There is a relatively new school legal thought process called Constitutive Criminology which is proposed by Stuart Henry and Dragon Milovanovic.

Crime is defined as "**the harm resulting from humans investing energy in harm producing relations of power.**" from an essay by Jeanne Curran and Susan R. Takata, **this sounds a lot like bullying to me.**

CHAPTER 1
INTRODUCTION

WHAT IS BULLYING AND WHY SHOULD WE CARE?

The definitions of bullying include. Bullying is:

* is **a repeated "one-way" set of unprovoked, physical, psychological and sexual harmful interactions** directed by the bully at a less powerful victim.

* a **socially disruptive pattern** of behaviour where one person or a group of persons deliberately choses to overpower and/or control another person through physical, psychological or sexual abuse.

* an **imbalance of power**, whereby a bully, for his/her personal gain, routinely abuses one or more victims.

* the **repeated harassment** (a criminal activity) of physical, emotional or sexual, health-endangering mistreatment of another person (the Target) by a cruel perpetrator or perpetrators (the Bully or Bullies).

* something you do when you are angry at the world and there is no one to listen to you. (This reactionary definition was given by a young teenager who was being held in a youth correction centre.)

BULLYING CONCEPTS

Bullying as a criminal activity

Bullies physically, psychologically and sexually assault their victims. They steal or damage the property of others. They denounce, defame and otherwise slander their victims. Their actions cause victims to withdraw from society, to commit suicide and in smaller numbers commit homicide.

Bullying as a mental health issue

Bullies have a serious negative affect on the mental health of their victims. **Also many bullies are individuals who are suffering from some level of brain under development (developmental deficit) and/or a mild to a severe mental disorder.**

Bullying as a lifestyle

Bullying should also be seen as a life style. It is a coping strategy, a habit, a consistent way of life, so ingrained in their psychological make up that many find it difficult to stop even when they acknowledge this as a problem.

Bullying is addictive

Practically every time a bully intimidates or physically harms another person the bully receives a "hit." They **are further rewarded** for their activities by the applause from a group of unthinking, supportive peers.

In either case the brain's pleasure zone is being activated.

Victims

Virtually every one can become the victim of a bully.

Bullies

* directly or indirectly **kill people.**

* cause intense short and long term psychological damage to their victims.

* **steal the self respect and human dignity of others.**

* have an insatiable need for power over others. They bear little or no regard for the physical and emotional well being of their victims. They make and enforce rules which serve their own self interest.

* are cowardly in their acts.

* come in both sexes, all age groups, all religious affiliations, all income groups and all cultures.

NOTE: There is not a single concept which would describe each and every bully

COMMON CHARACTERISTICS OF BULLIES

Of course each bully will not have all the characteristics.

Bullies:

Are:

- Control freaks.
- Deceitful and manipulative.

Have:

- Shallow self esteem.
- Narcissistic, ego centred feelings.
- Cognitive and emotional memories of being bullied.

Hold:

- Deeply embedded racial/bigoted beliefs.
- Superficial personal values.

Possess low ability:

- To feel valued by significant others.
- To manage anger.
- To manage impulses.
- To value the rights of others.

Lack:

- Emotional attachment with parent(s).
- Empathy towards another's pain.

Limited:

- Academic performance.* *See note*
- Social monitoring skills.
- Social consciousness.
- Social conscience, remorse or empathy.
- Drive to develop play and work skills.
- Willingness to accept responsibility.

Possess:

- Weak, full spectrum, language skills.
- Lower than average workplace skills.
- Fear of taking calculated risks.

Present:

- Early behaviour problems.
- Unhealthy obsession with certain persons.
- Fascination with anti social acts.
- Low natural response in the brain's pleasure reward zone.

NOTE: Academic performance is a relative term. In fact many bullies are academically performing at or above the mean. However, many are unwilling to push themselves to achieve higher grades and others are annoyed that their sense of entitlement is being usurped. Solid academic performance does not always translate into social responsibility.

Cautionary Notes:

1. Virtually all persons have moments when they display one or more of the above characteristics.
2. Even when a person displays one or more of the above, the intensity may vary from fleeting to deeply ingrained.
3. Bullying can be simply cognitive misbehaviour or it may be driven by a range of environmental cognitive-emotional influences, may be the activity of a very disturbed mind or a combination of all three.
4. Bullying is not an easy problem to understand or resolve.

BASIC BRAIN FACTS ABOUT BULLIES.

BRAIN FACT # 1

The brains of childhood bullies are generally operating in a survival mode specifically in areas of their emotional self including feeling that they are not respected.

BRAIN FACT # 2

The untreated brains of childhood bullies will likely be unable to cope with adult life in a socially acceptable and productive manner.

BRAIN FACT # 3

Many untreated conduct disordered bullies will develop adult anti-social personality disorder.

BRAIN FACT # 4

The brains of bullies have a high likelihood to become addicted to one of more chemical substances.

CHAPTER 2
PURPOSE

This book is about **hope, about chance, about understanding, about change, about responsibility, about structure and about solutions.**

♦ The **HOPE** is that we can make a better world for all children who are attending our schools or living within our communities. This hope is extended to the troubled children who bully, to their victims and those who standby and watch. In fact all of these groups are victims and many are destined to never fulfill their potential unless sound, proactive and reactive interventions are applied to the problem of bullying.

♦ **Chance** is ever present in our lives. But although chance can never be controlled in an absolute sense, chance can be modified. We have a better chance of having healthy bodies if we eat right, exercise properly and otherwise take care of ourselves. We have a better chance of having healthy active brains if we follow certain practices, are the benefactor of "good" genes and have experienced an invigorating, positive environment. We can positively increase our chances of living a safe and productive life if we avail ourselves to the best education available. **We can affect our chances for good or evil. We need to find ways to increase the chances for the bully, the victim and the bystander** to have productive lives.

♦ **Understanding** Research in neuroscience through the use of the most advanced imaging devices and complex chemical analysis, is providing a better understanding of how the brain functions under a variety of conditions. This **understanding** will increase our chances to find solutions.

What are the functions of the various regions of the brain? What roles do the 70+ neurochemicals play in facilitating brain activity. What makes us happy?

What makes us sad, angry or fearful? What gives us the ability read faces, interpret vocal tones and understand humour? How do our brains grow and develop?

The new data is giving us greater insight into understanding the nature of the brain of all persons including the "bully." It is important to gather this data and distill it into formats which will allow practitioners, in all settings, to better understand, to educate, to remediate and to develop appropriate, proactive programs.

♦ **Change** is the key to success. **Education is the most significant change process we will ever encounter** but your experience repeatedly tells you that the brain often resists change. However, if change is introduced in manner which is safe, supportive, stimulating, repetitive and provides clear vision then the brain will likely be receptive. **Teachers are change agents.**

This will not be an easy assignment. This problem will not go away with the application of a simple solution or by itself. **There is no quick fix.**

Any law enforcement officer who has served in an area for any length of time can, almost to a person, predict which young person will end up having serious conflicts with the law. Not only that, he/she can usually predict the kinds of problems these children cum adults will have.

- ◆ The **responsibility** for meeting the needs of troubled children, with developmentally dysfunctional brains, **does not rest solely with the school and the classroom.** It rests also with the social services programs, the public health services, the law enforcement agencies, the various government policy making bodies, the religious community, the service clubs, the arts, culture and sports communities and most importantly with the parents themselves.

  "It takes a village to raise a child." Children who are cared for by "A Village" are given the support and direction so critical for their short and long term development.

  All elements within every structure of every community must be devoted to the elimination of bullying. It must be stressed again and again that schools cannot be left alone to fight this serious menace to the well being of children, their families and society in general.

- ◆ **Programs:** We must develop a complex array of programs which take into account the full nature of bullying, the structure of these "bullying brains" and gain the support of those in our community, province or state who have the interest and power to affect change.

CHAPTER 3

HISTORY OF BULLYING AND A NEW VISION

For far too long the act of bullying and the bullies themselves have not been considered as serious impediments to our society.

Bullies have always been feared but they have been endured.

In the old western movies the bully was the bad guy with the black hat who was usually shot by the good guy, wearing a white hat or the town vigilante mob "strung him up" close to the end of the movie. **Nearly every one cheered.** Sometimes the bully was the rancher who harassed the farmer, vandalized the farmer's property, cut the farmer's fences, drove his livestock off and burned his crops.

Often this bully was admired, at least at the outset, and had a following mainly because he seemed so powerful. **Fear often creates friends.**

For far too long bullies have been accepted as a normal part of society. In the movie *It's a Wonderful Life*, old man Potter is a bully. So was the drunken marine Sergeant who marched his platoon into a swamp where about half of them drowned. So is the husband who routinely beats and otherwise abuses his wife and his

children. **The corporate world has provided a refuge for many a bully.** The male or female executive who fires people simply because he or she can is a bully. The administrator who favours some employees and harasses others regardless of their respective value to the organization is a bully.

Schools have been plagued by bullies for generations. These include:

The big kid that waits around the corner of the school and robs or beats up younger, smaller kids.

The female student who initiates gossip about another female student for the purpose of controlling that student.

The kids who are using cyberspace to ridicule and torment other children.

Stereotypes have confused the issue and limited our thinking.

The **stereotypical bully** is the big, tough kid who has more brawn than brains, but knows that by using violence, intimidation and street cunning he can gain a certain level of self satisfaction and perhaps grudging respect.

The **stereotypical victim** was the "98 lb weakling" who was repeatedly getting sand kicked in his face. He wants to rid himself of the bully and plans to do so after completing a body building program, which was advertised on the back pages of comic books. In real life after months and years of torment the "98 lb weakling" still doesn't amass a huge muscular frame but he might secure a gun which he brings to school or the work place and takes out his revenge on his tormentor. **Or what happens all too frequently is he kills himself because his life has become unbearable.**

Girls are bullies too.

The above two stereotypes were males. The stereotypical belief was that girls didn't bully and that most of the victims were cowardly, timid boys.

These beliefs were and are **wrong, wrong, wrong.** Both males and females bully and both males and females are bullied. For far too long we have underestimated the nature of the violent, vengeful female in our society. Because of this we have not appreciated the damage caused by the female bully largely because we misinterpreted that aspect of her behaviour as nonviolent and not dangerous or it is often the case the bullying is not noticed.

A RENEWED VISION AND RESULTING MISSION

We all must become responsible. Virtually everyone has been bullied or knows a bully or has had to deal with a bully in the school yard, inside a family, at the community centre or the workplace. Bullies and bully like behaviours exact an enormous social and financial cost to all affected. **We all have a stake in reducing the number of bullies in the world and the carnage they wreak upon society.**

We must **also** eliminate the **lonely teacher** syndrome from the equation. It must not only be the concerned teacher who tackles the problem of the bully but the whole school and the whole community must become active partners.

The **good news** is that in the last 10-15 years many societies and countries have come to realize that bullying is not only uncivilized it is causing serious problems for both the bully and the victim. Researchers have begun to analyse the nature of bullying and the devastating short, long and terminal effects that bullying has upon the victims and the bullies themselves.

CHAPTER 4

MYTHS ABOUT BULLYING

There are many myths about bullies and the bullying process. These stem from a general lack of understanding about the nature and consequences of bullying. In addition, bullies are not interested in being discovered and having their behaviours denounced.

These myths, however, do great disservice to the victims, the bullies and others in their midst.

1. **Bullying** is simply **a playing out** of our natural competitive instincts. **"The strong get stronger while the weak get weaker and may not survive."** This is an extremely unhealthy view of competition. This view may also lead to violations of the law.

   * A bully who robs a bank while brandishing gun certainly takes advantage of unarmed bank employees, mostly females, who stand the risk of being killed, wounded or severely traumatized by the event

   * A 130 pound boy who steals a 70 pound boy's lunch money is certainly not operating in a natural competitive environment

   * Students who continuously torment another student because that student has a speech impediment, a learning disability or wears old clothes are hardly being competitive on an even playing field.

2. **Bullying is nothing more than two people settling a dispute on the playground, street or in a sporting event.**

   A couple of years ago I was attending the birthday party of a friend. One of the other guests an, older gentleman, asked what I did and when I told him I gave workshops on the Nature of the Brain of Bullies etc. he replied "In my day bullying wasn't a problem, we just went out behind the school and had it out".

   This has nothing to do with bullying. This is simply two, more or less equal kids settling a dispute although perhaps not in the most civilized way.

In such cases the assumption exists that either person could win, but in the case of bullying **the bully always wins.**

3. **"Sticks and stones may break your bones but names will never hurt you." This is wrong and very often dead wrong.**

   Psychological abuse is every bit as damaging and, in fact, may have longer lasting effects than cuts and bruises. I can recall a 35 year old man from a small rural community who left school immediately after his 16th birthday due to the intense and unrelenting bullying by others within the school. To this day, nearly 20 years later, whenever he encounters one or more of his former tormentors, he leaves the store or crosses the street. His life has been permanently put on hold intellectually, emotionally and vocationally as a result of the years of bullying he experienced while attending school.

   Teasing vs taunting. "Are we are getting too caught up in the normal teasing that goes on between children?" The question is one of intent and equality. Does the teasing have a reciprocal aspect as one would expect between equals? Or is the "**teasing**" one way and have a meanness or demeaning quality to it? In the first case it is teasing in the second it is **taunting** ie. verbal harassment.

4. **Bullying is an activity which is the domain of boys.**

   The stereotypical bully is the beefy boy with a scowl on his face. This stereotype is the reality in many instances but he is not the only bully. Boys get tagged with this image because bullying is associated with physical intimidation or physical violence. The male bully is more likely to steal your money, punch you in the face, knock you off your bike, even steal your bike or otherwise vandalise your property. **But girls also bully.**

5. **"Nice" girls don't bully.**

   The definition of **nice** is open to interpretation. Yes, "**nice**" girls can and do bully as well as many other girls. "**Nice**" girls will bully in a vicious manner, in order to, establish and maintain their position within a social circle. Their style of bullying is almost a mirror image of their male counterparts. They use verbal assaults, innuendo, gossip and relationship shunning as their preferred weapons of choice.

Only in the last few years have we seen a significant increase in females being engaged in physical abuse of other females.

6. **Bullying is pretty much restricted to the lower social economic classes ie. rich kids do not bully.**

   While the reasons for bullying may vary from social class to social class the acts of bullying occur across the socio-economic spectrum. This has been so for generations. A reading of "Tom Brown's School Days," clearly attests to the fact that wealth and prestige are not conditions that inoculate children against becoming bullies.

7. **Bullying is simply part of growing up. Kids will grow out of this phase.**

   If only this were true! It is true, a number of bullies will eventually come to grips with their counterproductive behaviour through increased mental capacity, social maturity and increased social awareness. But **studies have repeatedly shown that upwards of 60% of school yard bullies have a criminal record by age 25.**

   NOTE: A sad commentary of our society is that we are unwilling to spend money adequately diagnosing ands treating mental health illnesses or development issues of school age children but we will spend huge sums of money to keep these individuals, as youth or adults, in jail.

8. **Victims can stop the bullying process by just facing up to the bully.**

   There is a poster about which reads. "**You have never known fear until you have had to face up to a bully.**" As has been mentioned before and will be mentioned again throughout the material, bullies do not fight fair. Victims are selected because the bully deems them to be vulnerable. In military terms, the victim is a soft target.

   Now this does not mean that all victims shy away from their tormentor. Some are able to correctly size up the situation and apply one of their own strengths to resolve the issue. Others have brought knives and guns to school to balance the equation. They do this only after they have been tormented,

harassed, beaten, robbed or even raped. The victim who seeks revenge is a very dangerous person.

All too often it is the **revenge driven victim** who commits the horrible final act of violence and it is he/she who receives the massive public wrath. The bully or bullies are allowed to go free.

Think about the bullies at Columbine High, in Taber, in Whitewood, in Mission, in Ottawa and the countless other bullies in every other school or community. **When are they held responsible for their actions? Seldom!**

9. **Bullies will stop their bullying activities if an authority figure tells them to do so.** This information appeared on a TV documentary and a recent newspaper article about bullying. How wrong could this person have been? Another comment that is often made by school principals "**Don't let me catch you doing that again.**" The bully will agree but under his/her breath mutters. "**That's right you'll never catch me again.**"

   Sure there are some kids who have the capability to change their ways as the result of a reprimand but they are more the exception than the rule.

10. **Bullying is a learned behaviour and can be "unlearned" quickly. (Very Important)**

    For some this is true. **BUT** most bullies are meeting some psychological need by controlling and traumatizing others. Hence their brains have become **cognitively and emotionally hardwired to bully.** They have limited understanding of these needs nor the tools to meet them in socially acceptable ways.

    Experts in childhood psychology report that the progress made in working with children with Conduct Disorder or similar environmentally and/or genetically induced conditions is slow and perilous. The major impediment aside from the cognitive and emotional damage the person has experienced is the unwillingness of the person to understand that he/she has a serious problem now or will have in the future.

11. **Bullies are naturally aggressive, fearless individuals.**

    In fact most bullies are cowards. They rely on size, age, numbers or some other advantage before they embark upon a bullying exercise. One of the latest cowardly acts being carried out by bullies is **Cyberbullying** where the bully uses Instant Messaging, e-mail from anonymous sites, or the use demeaning websites. Victims are reporting that messages are extremely vile, degrading and threatening and the perpetrator is anonymous.

Cyberbullying is becoming a horrific new and dangerous phenomena. The technical challenges to manage this outrageous and grievous activity are immense.

Cyberbullying truly reveals the cowardly nature and developmental deficits which typifies bullies.

12. **Bullies are good leaders.** While bullies actually aspire to leadership their destructive behaviour patterns make them ineffectual leaders. Unfortunately this behaviour pattern is often not recognized by staffing selection panels and many bullies are promoted well beyond their capacity to perform.

Bullies in leadership:

- have difficulty establishing group unity, in fact they will knowingly play employees off against each other.

- tend to be self centred and have difficulty allocating authority.

- are uneven with their performance reviews or criticism. Some employees are favourites and other employees are targeted for abuse.

- target able employees because these employees have more expertise and are far more productive than the bully manager.

- seldom listen carefully to the concerns of the employee, they are prone to yelling and discounting the employee.

- are not trusted by their subordinates.

- are extremely unlikely to assist in the development of an anti bullying program for their school, branch or company.

NOTE: They often have lower than average abilities to organize an event or gain the active participation of colleagues or other employees. A comment about one bully was that "He couldn't organize a drunken party in a brewery."

13. **Bullies are not found in community service managerial/leadership positions in education, religion, sports or health care.**

This is untrue. Some aspects of bullying are seen as seen a strong leadership qualities. See myth # 12 above and Adult Bullies within our Schools in the Appendix I.

14. **A bully's bravado is a reflection of their intellect, skill set and other abilities.**

Youthful bullies bully to achieve a level of personal or social status while adult bullies, particularly managers, bully in their attempt to maintain their position.

In actual fact most physical bullies are of only average ability. Psychological bullies tend to reveal better than average academic performance. Many bullies are fearful of seriously attempting training because they feel they will either fail or have only limited success. Bullies, as students, are less likely to risk in class and are also unwilling to let others risk in a safe climate.

15. **Increasing the amount of religious teaching or religious based "values" education will automatically reduce the amount of bullying in a school.**

In principle this should be true, but some religious teachings have strong discriminatory overtones concerning gender roles, gender orientation, race and other religions to name a few. In such cases the bully feels increasingly justified in his/her attacks on others because, from a religious perspective, the victim is a person of lesser value or status.

16. **Society's approval of "bully like" behaviours in certain situations actually means that bullying is an acceptable behaviour.**

In certain sporting activities, intimidation or intent to injure are the responsibilities of "role" players. Often these players have few other skills.

Another example is the business executive or government official who prides him/herself on making the tough decisions especially those decisions relating to dismissing employees.

17. **There are no adult bullies in schools.**

Unfortunately this is also untrue.

When I am giving workshops I repeatedly hear of school administrators, teachers, coaches and support staff who use bullying tactics to maintain control or to otherwise exercise power within the school environment. **Fortunately, I also am aware of the thousands of other teachers and administrators who are extremely capable educators who do not resort to bullying.**

See: Adult Bullies within our Schools Appendix I.

CHAPTER 5

OVERRIDING BRAIN FACTS

BRAIN FACT #5

The primary purpose of our brain is to ensure our survival.

The amount of energy our brains can devote to **learning of cognitive, social and kinesthetic skills is inversely proportional** to the amount of energy our brains must devote to survival.

NOTE: Children raised in environments which are full of stress, trauma, danger and/or neglect will be less likely to develop the relative gray matter so necessary to becoming a academically or socially competent.

BRAIN FACT # 6

Our brains define us.

They define how we interact with others, our level of empathy, our capacity for love or hate and our ability to be socially and personally responsible for our actions.

NOTE: Every action or reaction that we take or will ever take is the result of our brain's response to given stimulation.

BRAIN FACT # 7

Our brains define our world.

Is the world safe or violent, caring or hateful, full of challenge and hope or full of oppression and despair?

NOTE: This assessment is the result of combining cognitive and emotional memories and mental wellness.

BRAIN FACT # 8

Every brain is unique.

Each brain is "**a complex aggregation**" of neural networks resulting from the developmental interplay of our genetics, our pre and post natal environments and all our conscious and non-conscious learning experiences.

NOTE: This applies equally to the academic superiority of the genius and the behaviour of a troubled or dangerous child.

BRAIN FACT #9

The output capacity of every brain is dependent upon the maturity of its individual networks and their ability to integrate information and existing knowledge.

*NOTE: Remediation or skill development can only be achieved when teaching and training are introduced at the upper levels of the child's **current capacity**.*

BRAIN FACT #10

Each brain is a conglomeration of continuums.

For example, every brain is somewhere on the "mathematics continuum," the "empathy continuum," the "pleasure/reward continuum," the "hit a tennis ball continuum" etc.

NOTE: The good news that there is always some point of strength from which to begin remediation. It is important to always work from the student's strength.

Success breeds success.

BRAIN FACT # 11

The brains of children within the school setting are all at various stages of emotional, cognitive and kinesthetic development.

It cannot be assumed that all or most children of a certain age will be at the same or similar developmental level in any of the above key areas.

NOTE: It is important to recognize that the brains of educators assigned to work with children are also significantly different in terms of intellectual capacity, skill level and social conscience.

NOTE: It is equally important to realize that a teacher's capacity in language is significantly more advanced than that of most students and even more so than that of students who have or are experiencing severe stress or trauma.

BRAIN FACT #12

The neural networks of children's brains are still under construction as many synapses are being made "permanent," axons are being myelinated , unused neurons and synapses are being pruned or reassigned and neural networks are being further integrated. Well used synapses with their axons and dendrites "glued in place" are considered to be hardwired.

The positive side is that these brains are becoming more efficient and effective at gathering and processing new information and creating new knowledge.

The negative side is that these still developing brains are vulnerable to short and long term damage due lack of stimulation, sexual, emotional and physical abuse and the use of street drugs.

BRAIN FACT # 13

It is not until a person reaches twenty plus years of age that both hemispheres become equally active in the processing of language.

This implies that most children within the school system are unable to effectively combine the logical language processing of the left hemisphere with the more global or holistic language processing of the right hemisphere.

NOTE: The implication is that frequently adults and children are not communicating. The still developing brain is less likely to fully comprehend the verbal, written or implied messages being delivered by an older, more developed brain.

The reverse is also true. Many adults have difficulty processing the language and thought constructs of children and adolescents.

BRAIN FACT # 14

The thought processes of the brains of children and most early adolescents tend to be concrete in nature.

These, still to be, developed brains do not have the capabilities to understand nuances, inferences, tonal inflections or intuitive projections.

The more dysfunctional child is more likely to be concrete in his/her thinking patterns and the less likely to be able to accurately to assess the intent of verbal statements, facial expressions and body language.

BRAIN FACT #15

It is estimated that a child's intelligence can be changed by +/- 20-25 IQ points by the environment the child has the good or bad fortune to live in.

Brains which have had their development delayed as a result of low stimulation, limited language exposure, living in stressful, dysfunctional environments will tend to show low **functional IQs.** These children will appear to be handicapped in academic and social settings and more problematic in the school environment.

NOTE: Any brain which consistently experiences significant stress may suffer neural paralysis or neural death in the hippocampus. The left hippocampus has been shown to have shrunk by 26% and the right hippocampus by 22%. This will cause short or long term memory loss depending upon the intensity and duration of the stress.

BRAIN FACT #16

The neural "cognitive and emotive conditioning" developed early in life can play a significant role in determining the nature of future information the brain may accept later in life.

Neural networks built while the brain is flooded with stress chemicals associated with fear, anxiety, anger and hate can become "hardwired" to over react to the world in unproductive or counterproductive ways.

BRAIN FACT # 17

Approximately 40-45% of all children DO NOT form strong emotional attachments with a significant adult. These children not only fail to bond, their brains sense betrayal and tend to switch to "survival mode."

BRAIN FACT #18

Some bullies have been shown to have a lower than average number of dopamine receptors in their pleasure zone/reward systems.

This may be a genetic and/or environmentally induced condition. This increases their need for more exaggerated forms of stimulation including street drugs.

BRAIN FACT # 19

Sexually abused girls suffer dramatically altered neural development patterns.

Outcomes include: early physical and sexual maturity, unusual hormonal reactions, impaired immune functions, high arousal states, sleep disorders, nervousness, depression and anxiety.

CHAPTER 6

BULLIES: WHO ARE THEY?

BULLIES:

- are likely children cum adults who have an underdeveloped or damaged frontal lobes and limbic brain areas. (Most male bullies have lower than average testosterone levels and lower verbal intelligence.)

- may be genetically predisposed to violence.

- may be acting out both conscious and non-conscious learning.

- **It is a fact**, few bullies become well without moderate or intensive treatment.

BULLIES LIVING BEYOND THE SCHOOL YARD

- **Bullies inside the family.** It is estimated that 8-16% of all prospective fathers will physically, emotionally and sexually abuse the mother of their unborn child. They do this because they cannot afford to lose control of this woman to another person even an unborn child.

- **Bullies in jail.** The self obsessiveness, lack of caring, impulsive nature, low cognitive and/or language skills and unwillingness to be socially responsible are the basic ingredients for criminal behaviour.

- **Bullies in the workplace.** The vast majority of workplace bullies are unproductive, counterproductive, technically incompetent and frequently use subterfuge to **maintain** their place within the organization.

- **Coaches.** Coaches who are bullies are extremely problematic. They may place extreme emphasis on winning, verbally and physically abuse players, force players to play injured, berate players for being "sissies", or having "no guts", openly encourage hazing rituals and model other dysfunctional behaviours.

BULLIES IN THE COMMUNITY

- may commit road rage and other driving infractions, impulsively physically assault other persons.

- (Males) frequently commit date rape.

- within a marriage are prone to physically and emotionally abuse their spouses and children. Those who are addicted to alcohol are extremely dangerous marriage partners.

CHAPTER 7

NINE BULLY TYPES

NOTE: There is no one kind of bully nor is there one kind of bullying activity.

NOTE: The following descriptions are designed to help you identify bullying activity and also help you to determine the approaches you might use to remediate the situation. A bully may present more than one of these "types".

NOTE: A word of caution. There is no such thing as a good bully. All bullies cause their victims to suffer incredibly. However, some bullies are more responsive than others to recognizing their behaviour and to accept remedial therapy.

1. BORDERLINE BULLY

The borderline bully is ever present in classrooms across our nations. This is the child who normally acts in a socially responsible manner, is caring of other students, is cooperative and often has positive profile in the classroom. But from time to time this child acts out in an unpredictable, uncharacteristic, mean spirited manner to one or more students.

The bad news is that this child could be any child within the classroom.

The good news is that this child will likely respond well to even a modest remediation program.

BRAIN FACT #20

A brain's primary operating area, at any given moment, is dependent upon the stress/trauma it is experiencing.

A low level of stress allows the frontal cortex to be fully engaged, more stress will result in greater interaction between the frontal cortex and the limbic area. The most extreme form of stress, outright terror, results in purely reflexive responses directed by the brain stem.

NOTE: It is important to recognize that children go through a range of mental and physical developments, in a haphazard and sporadic fashion. Therefore, on any two consecutive days a teacher is faced with a slightly different

class. This of course does not include mood changes brought about by personal or family illness, the arrival of a new sibling, the reconstitution of the family, changes in the families economic stability etc. All of these factors plus many others can impact on even the most mature and best natured child.

Observed Behaviours

♦ Individual is generally considerate of other students.

♦ Is often seen teasing and being teased by a circle of friends.

♦ Normally plays and works well with all or most students.

♦ Recently is seen to be more actively teasing individuals who are not part of normal friendship circle. There is very little, if any, reciprocal teasing.

♦ The teasing may have moved into a more aggressive taunting format.

♦ Jostling in the hallways is taking on a more aggressive tone but only with certain students.

♦ Individual seems to be trying to impress specific classmates.

♦ Individual seems to be a bit "edgier" than normal.

Analysis of behaviour – A Possible Check List

♦ Other students have experienced a growth spurt and student feels left out.

♦ Student may have less well developed social skills at this moment.

♦ Current family issues may be causing student stress.

♦ Student may be experiencing unusual difficulty in one of more subjects.

♦ Student's giftedness may be causing frustration.

♦ Student is being bullied by another student.

2. THE "LEARNED" BIGOTED BULLY

BRAIN FACT #21

Recent MRI studies of amygdalae of individuals viewing images of Black and White faces showed greater Blood Oxygen Level Dependent (BOLD) activity when viewing a picture of a person whose face was a different colour than that of the viewer.

NOTE: At first glance this may suggest that the brain is naturally biassed. BUT! Further analysis showed that the BOLD activity corresponded to the relationship the viewer had with people of a different skin colour. A good relationship resulted in a lower BOLD reading and vice versa. The brain can be taught to discriminate and has the capacity to "automate" under given circumstances.

NOTE: The relationship is acquired and enhanced through either direct or vicarious experiences.

Bigotry is a defensive action usually motivated by fear and learned hatred. It is designed to preserve **"one's rightful place"** in the hierarchy of society and to ensure that others stay in **"their place."** A current buzzword is **entitlement.** Some children and adults feel they are **entitled to a place in the sun** regardless of whether or not they have made any attempt to earn that place.

NOTE: We used to play a game in our school yard, especially in the late Fall or late Winter. We would build a mound of snow and then try to be the person at the top of the mound. The person at the top of the mound would tease the other kids with."I am the King of the Castle and you're the dirty rascal."

The other kids would try to de-throne you, as it were.

Bigots constantly strive to be the king (or queen) of the castle because they believe that is their rightful place. In this case this is not a game! Bigots are always fearful, perhaps even paranoid that others will dethrone them. Bigots learn these attitudes from parents, older siblings, other relatives and members of their own cultural group by both example and direct instruction.

The principal tenant of a bigots belief system is that others are lesser human beings, **do not deserve respect** and in fact others should be denigrated at every opportunity.

The stereotypical bigot is the uneducated, "unwashed hick" from the country, but bigots can be found in religious communities, amongst university personnel, professional associations and virtually every cultural group throughout the world. The key to bigotry is intolerance supported by ignorance.

Again bigots strive to keep others in "their place."

Observed Behaviour

* "You can't be our friend because you are..............."

* Name calling using the gutter language, denigrating racial slurs.

* Isolating a child of another race, creed, colour.

* Ridiculing dress, food, accents and cultural practices.

* "How come **they** win all the scholarships?"

* "If I ever catch you dating a..................."

* "Watch out, they'll soon have all the good jobs."

* They get the good grades because they "Suck up to the teacher."

* If there are only a few students of another group, they may be singled out for special negative attention.

* Cliques and gangs often form around racial groupings.

  NOTE: Children who are bi-racial are often shunned by members of both races.

Analysis of Behaviour – A Possible Check List

It is important to know the community structure. Who are the traditional power brokers? Who are the new "kids on the block"? Where are they in the power structure?

Cliques and gangs may be formed for protection purposes and have no criminal intent.

School yard clashes along cultural lines.

* Strong religious biases within the community at large.

* Separations in the student body by culture and school programs. Does one group dominate in one area and another in another area. Who are the strong students?

NOTE: It is important to realize that bigotry will emerge even if all the students are from the same racial, cultural and creed based group. There are always family economic differences, slight variations in hair and skin colour and people who live on the "other side of the tracks or the other side of town".

Examples: I lived in West Africa for two and a half years and bigotry between clans and skin tones was rampant. In another case I was told that children of a large First Nations Community use the N. word to put down children whose skin tone is darker than average. A young woman with dark hair who was born in South America of Caucasian parents told about coming to Canada as a child and being called a Mexican by her mainly blond haired classmates who were from her own culture.

3. "LEARNED" AGGRESSIVE BULLY

Throughout our society there exists a dominant mind set which defines one's self on **superficial exterior criteria.** The Baby Boomer slogan of "**Whoever dies with the most toys wins**", the corporate world which "**Bottom Lines**" every thing even at the expense of product quality, consumer expectations and employee loyalty or the world of professional sports where "**Winning is the only thing**" creates in our minds and the minds of our children the idea that life is simple. We can quantify everything. Other expressions common in today's vocabulary include **Win at any Cost, Losing is for Losers, Rules are for Referees, Look After #1, and Might is Right.** These learned values have become central to the thinking of many adults and children.

BRAIN FACT #21

It takes time and energy to develop any skill or piece of knowledge. There are seldom shortcuts, but good teaching, good coaching and plenty of practice can expedite the process. BUT the brain will not learn unless it does the work.

Observed Behaviours

- The big, strong but under skilled athlete who intimidates smaller but more skilful players. An example is the "goon player" on the hockey team.

- The student who throws a temper tantrum after losing a game or scoring low on a test.

- The student who blames others for the loss. He/she targets the coach, the referee, other team mates or the teacher. But seldom accepts responsibility.

- The parents who verbally and on occasion attacks the referee, the coach or even other parents when their child is playing a game.

Analysis of behaviour – A Possible Check List.

- The student/athlete feels his or her value is highly dependent upon the outcome.

- The students/athletes who feel they must win to receive **recognition** from their parents.

- The students/athletes who are reticent to practice or study but still want to win or do well.

- The teacher or coach who overemphasizes the need to win as the "only acceptable outcome."

- Parents who derive their personal value vicariously from the accomplishments of their children.

- The children who value themselves based on their clothes, entertainment devices and the vehicles they drive to school.

4. "CONUNDRUM" BULLY

In every school there are number of children who, on the surface, seem to have it all. They are attractive, not lacking for material things, get decent to good grades, seem to have friends, have aspirations, good social, athletic and leadership skills but still bully other students. They are **conundrums** because they don't seem to fit any of the common stereotypes of bullies. This may be because the common stereotypes are not necessarily accurate or all encompassing.

It should also be remembered that what we see on the outside is not necessarily representative of what is going on in the inside. Far too many children or adolescents are experiencing difficulty coping with their personal development, their self concept and the expectations which parents and others place upon them.

There may also be an under current of domestic turmoil within their family. It is not uncommon for these individuals to "**put on brave face**" or to "**play a role.**" This is what they want us to see.

However, when they bully they are doing so because bullying helps them meet some need.

Observed Behaviour

- They are unexpectedly observed taunting a classmate who is outside the "circle of friends" or being over zealous during "Frosh Week," or repeatedly making snide hurtful remarks about another student.

- They are observed trying to "put down" the top students in the class. They may be trying to get these students to "taper off".

- They are observed using their leadership roles as a way to reward friends and to isolate other students.

- They seem to be letting their grades drop.

BRAIN FACT #22

The cognitive – emotional balance which we call authentic self esteem cannot be bought, successfully role played for a long period of time or provided by someone else. It must be developed personally and over time.

Analysis of Behaviour – A Possible Check List

- They may be feeling overwhelmed by parental expectations or personal responsibilities.

- Their brains may not be maturing in a fashion which allows them to be as productive as some other students.

- There are things happening inside the family which are unsettling.

- They don't have the energy to always "play the role."

- In adolescence boy-girl relationship issues often challenge the cognitive and emotional maturity of most teens.

- The question of sexual orientation is a major and unsettling concern for teens.

  NOTE: Adolescent males may force themselves to be unnecessarily aggressive and uncaring to make sure that others do not see them as "gay."

5. "STATUS BULLY" BULLYS FOR LAUGHS AND "APPLAUSE"

The **status bully** is often an male student between the ages of 8-15. His style of harassment is a combination of physical "practical jokes" and verbal abuse. The victims are generally smaller and for some reason not well liked by a majority of students. While there is a power trip associated with this level of bullying the real reward is the approval provided by both a close circle of friends and the uncaring adulation provided by the "audience of bystanders".

BRAIN FACT # 23

Applause will raise the dopamine level in the reward circuits of the brain.

NOTE: These bullies are frequently seen as popular. They have a circle of friends, they love to "kid around", they are kind of flashy and they appear not to take life too seriously. They present nuisance problems for teachers and other school staff.

Observed Behaviour

- Generally moves with friends.
- Stuffs kids into lockers.
- Knocks kid's books to the floor.
- Trips kids in the hallway. (Have a nice trip?)
- "Washes" kids faces with snow.
- Insults fellow students about their size, sexuality, clothes etc.
- Tries to make himself look like a hero.
- Tends to strut.

- Bullies in a very public manner.

  NOTE: Victims are highly traumatized because the abuse is so public and they also feel the ridicule from the non supportive bystanders.

Analysis of Behaviour – A possible check list

- Perhaps this bully is a member of a school team, which automatically provides a group of friends.

- Schools which strongly identify themselves with one or two sports teams germinate this type of bully.

- Bully tends not to be a strong student either by choice or neurological development.

- Bully's use of humour could be considered "developmentally delayed."

- Bully's talents may be in areas other than the school's normal curriculum offerings.

- Bully sees the school more as a social gathering place than an institution of learning.

- Bully may have support within the community due to general good nature and being a "fun loving kid."

6. "SOCIAL POWER" OR RELATIONSHIP BULLY

There is more than one way to hurt, dominate and traumatize another human being and to make that individual feel so unworthy that he/she will think about or actually commit suicide.

The relationship bully uses social power to psychologically demean their victim, usually of the same age and gender. This tends to be more of a female style of bullying. There are no bruises, no bloody noses just hurt and badly damaged feelings.

The strategies include shunning, rumour mongering, selecting friends for prestige not friendship, verbally abusing "friends" or chosen targets and using intimacy for control purposes.

The physical structure of relationship bullying often involves concentric circles, Rosalind Wiseman writes that there is the Queen Bee at the centre and groups of Wannabees in other circles. Others describe the core group as the "princesses", others call them witches or some similar name. There is a long list. No matter what these groups are called there is a person who is the leader and a surrounding group or groups of supporters.

The person at the centre invests a incredible amount of energy to maintain her position. The emotional energy she directs at others is not for the purposes of establishing friendship but rather for maintaining control, status and power. **Entitlement** seems to play a

role in this bullying style. It is also believed that these individuals have **not** formed supportive emotional relationships with one or more of their parents.

The leader is always under stress to maintain position and it is not unusual to find these leaders in their mid to late teen years turning to alcohol and other drugs to help cope with their emotional needs.

We, as humans, are social animals. There rests the basis for the power of relationship bullying. People are vulnerable because they want to belong. Girls are more at risk because they place great value on relationships.

BRAIN FACT # 24

Studies are showing that girls who do not bond with at least one parent are more likely to use relationship bullying strategies. They are limited in their ability to form close emotional relationships with others.

NOTE: This lack of bonding may be instrumental their delayed development of both a social consciousness and a social conscience

Observed Behaviour

A great deal of relationship bullying is conducted beneath a teacher's radar level. The comments, the looks, the eye rolls, the shoulder shrugs appear to the "non involved" as pretty innocuous stuff. But both the victim and the bully know exactly the intent of the message.

- Two or more girls have formed a small clique.

- This clique has its own jokes, eye rolls, shoulder shrugs etc.

- These gestures of distain are uniformly directed at specific students.

- The "other" students may be disadvantaged in some way or may be in other power relationships.

- If the "in" group numbers five or six there will likely be small and rotating changes in membership certainly at the periphery.

- In some school situations there may be more two or more groups and some girls will cycle their membership between groups.

- The leader of a group may have her heart set on a particular male student and will go ballistic on any girl he is seen talking to. Oddly enough the guy may have no interest in the "Bully Girl."

It is not uncommon for individuals to be "expelled" from the group in a very direct manner.

NOTE: It is then you, the teacher, will get a visit from that girl's mother complaining about "How mean these other girls are to her daughter." It is important to restrain yourself from laughing aloud or blurting out "Well she had it coming. I guess she knows how some of the other girls feel."

Analysis of Behaviour – A possible checklist

- Children raised in an "Avoidant Attachment" environment are inclined to control in a relationship bully manner.

- Children living in homes where social status is based on material possessions, appearance, belonging to certain clubs or holding certain student positions.

- Children who have felt neglected.

- The child is seeking revenge for some real or imagined injustice. Such as another girl getting the top mark in the class, making the cheerleading squad or being selected for a prestigious spot on the squad or talking to a boy she considers is hers.

- The child has had limited ability to feel empathy for others.

- The child who is trying to impress a parent by being "popular."

- The child wants to control a level of social interaction.

- The child is extremely focussed and exhilarated by her position of power.

- The control of others enhances this child's self identity.

NOTE: Donna Davis, a school counsellor writes "That the girls who are cheerleaders, members of a dance class or female students in or vying for student government are highly likely to be relationship bullies".

7. "IMPULSIVELY AGGRESSIVE" BULLY

This bully can be extremely dangerous and unpredictable. In street jargon, these individuals carry a "chip on their shoulder"

NOTE: Bullying is something you do when you are angry at the world and there is no one to listen to you. (This definition was given by a young teenager who was being held in a youth correction centre.)

BRAIN FACT # 25

Their amygdalae are hyper vigilant. They are in permanent survival mode and they are prone to being easily offended or threatened by a range of stimuli.

Most of these stimuli would be viewed as trivial by others. They over react. They may also be living with a considerable amount of repressed anger.

Observed Behaviour

- Angers easily and often.

- Responds physically to accidental bumps in the hallway.

- Can't stand people looking at him/her.

- Keeps people on edge.

- "Goes crazy" when losing.

- Takes anger out on defenceless individuals.

- Views criticism or suggestion for improvement as personal attacks.

- Uses anger to control others.

- Displays reading and writing problems.

- Expresses anger through profanity and physical aggression.

Analysis of behaviour – A possible check list

- ADHD, ODD, FAS, Bi-polar Disorder.

- Depression and brain trauma.

- An unfortunate combination of genetic, environmental and learning influences including above normal levels of testosterone.

- A dysfunctional family situation.

- An underachieving student.

- Possesses a low level of language skills.

- Becomes negatively stimulated by the school environment.

- Has experienced abuse/victimization.

  NOTE: Girls who have been sexually abused can be volatile and extremely physically violent.

- Lives daily with "super heated" amygdalae.

- Has lived in a variety of foster homes.

- Has no or limited anger management skills.

- Unable or unwilling to identify the source of his/her anger.

- May be abusing steroids. (Check out "roid rage" on the INTERNET.)

8. "PERSONAL POWER" BULLY

The behavioural pattern of the personal power bully includes **deliberate** actions to intimidate or injure, an obsession to carry out these actions on specific people and a low sense of both social consciousness and social conscience.

NOTE: While all bullying activity should be seen in the realm of criminal behaviour the personal power bully removes all doubt.

BRAIN FACT # 26

The cingulate gyrus may be genetically predispositioned or environmentally altered and allows the individual to becomes fixated on particular individuals and/or actions.

NOTE: Individuals with this condition are likely to be undeterred by rules, admonitions or court orders.

NOTE: Stalkers, including those who track down and often murder ex lovers or spouses, are examples of such individuals.

Observed Behaviour

- Tends to obsess on certain kids.
- Plans an attack or attacks.
- Harasses victim on a daily basis.
- Routinely steals lunch or lunch money.
- Vandalizes personal property including another kid's lunch.
- Uses extortion.
- Steals or destroys homework.
- Forces able students to perform poorly.
- Seriously disrupts classes.
- Language skills are usually limited, reading and writing skills well below grade level.
- May give indication of being obsessed with weapons and certain violent movie roles.
- Older students frequently smoke, binge drink and use other drugs to enhance social prowess.
- Is known to the police, for shop lifting, vandalism and other misdemeanours.

Analysis of behaviour – A possible check list.

- Low level of active dopamine receptors on the brain's reward system.
- Low authentic self esteem.
- Has experienced abuse or severe physical punishment.
- One parent who has an addiction or other mental health problem(s).
- Overactive cingulate gyrus.
- Believes he/she "owns" the other person.
- Low social skills, interacts only with similar students.
- Lower than normal testosterone levels. Uses bullying to enhance sense of self.

9. "SOCIOPATH" BULLY

The Sociopath bully is the "**complete**" bully who is an extremely dangerous individual. These bullies are psychotically self obsessed to the extent that they act entirely for their own purposes. See: *Conduct Disorder.*

Observed Behaviour

- Limited to nil social conscience.
- Has "High Self Esteem?"
- Displays narcissistic tendencies.
- Virtually no empathy for victims.
- Has extreme difficulty with responsibility.
- Cold and calculating.
- Feels justified.
- Appears exhilarated when committing the offence.
- Vandalizes property including setting fires.
- Intimidates and terrorizes teachers.

BRAIN FACT # 27

MRI scans of Conduct Disordered individuals have revealed that their right temporal lobes are smaller than those of "normal" persons.

NOTE: Some of the functions of this lobe are to be able to read the emotional messages in faces, distinguish between tonal qualities in voice and read body language.

BRAIN FACT #28

SPECT scans show lower activity in the frontal and temporal lobes of the Conduct Disordered person.

Analysis of behaviour – A possible check list

- ADHD and Oppositional Defiant Disorder.
- Severe underdevelopment of and/or damage to the frontal and temporal lobes.
- Genetic predisposition towards violence, depression, alcoholism and low activity pleasure zone.
- Low levels of adrenaline and serotonin.
- Low levels of testosterone.
- Extensive childhood abuse.
- Traumatic life experiences evoking intensely violent emotional memories.
- Environmentally induced genetic damage.
- Pre and post natal exposure to nicotine.
- Narcissistic tendencies or Narcissistic Personality Disorder.

CHAPTER 8

HOW DO BULLIES SURVIVE?

Bullies are not without guile and "street smarts."

They are adept at:

- lying and cheating. Bullies have limited appreciation for the truth or fair play.

- being insincerely nice (slimy) to the people when it is in their best interest to do so.

- aligning themselves to a like minded group to increase their power base.

- blending into society. Society is still wrestling with the concept of the bully as a dangerous and damaging person. All too often they think of him or her as a jerk who must be tolerated.

- denial: Most bullies will adamantly deny that they have committed any transgression.

- intimidation: Bullies intimidate people into compliance.

SCHOOLS CAN CREATE EXCELLENT ENVIRONMENTS FOR BULLYING

- School staff may be under skilled on the nature of bullying and are overwhelmed with myriad of other matters.

- Students must come to school. The bullies have a ready made, captive audience. It is like a buffet (lunch) of victims.

- School administrations fail to set up a bully free school with educational, supervision and corrective action programs. For example, some new schools are now being architecturally designed to eliminate hidden corners etc.

- Some schools have policies on bullying but have no programs to handle the matter

- Some school staff are bullies and will resist the establishment and implementation of anti-bullying programs.

AN OVERSTATEMENT BUT A TRUISM

One of the most effective antidotes to bullying is having the bully, through his or her own efforts, **become successful in a socially acceptable manner.** This results in increased knowledge, increased self and social awareness, increased brain development and increased authentic self esteem.

CHAPTER 9

IS BULLYING ON THE RISE?

This question is also often asked in my workshops. The research would seem to support that incidents of bullying are increasing.

TWENTY FIRST CENTURY STRESS AND TENSION

There are a number of reasons to help explain why this is happening. Bullying is often a stress or survival related response to a dysfunctional environment. The levels of stress and disorder in families today is on the rise for a variety of reasons. In her book "**Why is everyone so** *cranky*?" C. Leslie Charles identifies ten "C" trends: **Compressed Time, Communication Overload, dis-Connectedness, Cost, Competition, Customer Contact, Computers, Change, Coming of Age, Complexity. TEN C's = Increase in Stress.**

The Reverend Dale Lang, who lost a son in a high school shooting speaks of two key elements fuelling the angst that tends to spawn violent aggressive children. He speaks of "**Instant Gratification**" and "**Extreme Self Centredness**."

Martin Seligman writes of these matters when he condemns the shallowness of the "Self Esteem Movement" that is almost a religion for the Baby Boomer generation. He also denounces their desire to feel valued for their "Toys." Seligman writes that we can't receive self esteem from others or by things, but can only gain it through our own emotional and cognitive growth and well being.

THE INCREDIBLE VIOLENCE ON TV AND VIDEO GAMES

Hardly a workshop goes by without a participant commenting on a child in his/her school who is completely captivated by instruments of violence and violent acts. Some of these children are in kindergarten.

The media industry frequently conducts studies to which reveal that there is no connection between TV violence and street crime. However, the fact remains that the most vulnerable children are the ones spending the most time watching TV with little or no supervision or debriefing.

BRAIN FACT #29

The neural networks of the brain are formed in accordance to the nature of the real or virtual inputs the brain receives.

For many children their major mental stimulation, areas of meaningfulness and moments of novelty are derived from TV, violent TV and video games.

A recent study shows a direct relationship between the number of hours watching TV and bullying behaviour.

In addition to the time a child spends watching TV reduces amount of time available for the child to learn social consciousness and develop a social conscience through interaction with other children and adults.

Further more, video games which involve skill building such as aiming a gun or a killer ray device at a human like target can severely restrict the mental processing of certain players to distinguish between real and virtual persons. In one extreme case, an adolescent became extremely proficient at a game which involved killing virtual humans with one shot. In real life he killed eight people with eight shots.

CHAPTER 10

BRAIN DEVELOPMENT OF A BULLY (AN OVERVIEW)

There is little, if any evidence, that a person awakes one morning and decides to become a bully or another type of violent or aggressive person. Being a bully is normally NOT a cognitive decision!

The process of becoming a bully is one which takes a number of genetic, environmental and learning interventions. It is the brain, not the right elbow or the left big toe that directs and controls the bully's cognitive and emotional aggressive anti-social behaviours. A bully's brain is a dysfunctional brain caused by some serious deficits in genetics and/or in development. It is therefore imperative that we understand why certain brains produce bullies.

The following research based data details probable developmental aspects from the time just before fertilization until the present stage of a child's life.

THE FACTOR OF GENETIC CHANCE

Although it has been known for some time that, except for identical twins, we are all genetically different. Having the same mother and same father does not guarantee siblings an equal shot at the same genes. Each parent is the product of many gene combinations. Which genes that are part of a given sperm cell or are designated to a specific ovum is largely one of chance although there are roles played by dominant and recessive genes and other related factors.

THE ENVIRONMENT – CONTROLLED CHANCE

While it is largely by random chance that a child receives a specific genetic trait. It is by **controlled chance** that a child is exposed to a specific environment or set of environments. While every child has a unique set of genes, it is also true that each child is cocooned in its own special environments which shape and reshape the brain. Not even the brains of identical twins, living in the same general environments, will receive identical environmental stimulation. Parents and other caregivers are critical and have it within their power to create positive or negative environments.

"Environmental characteristics are defined as supports, controls, models and expectations that are thought to be meaningful to the (child) juvenile."–*p.29 Michael Slavkin, Firesetting: An Exploratory Analysis*

LEARNING: CONSCIOUS OR NON-CONSCIOUS

Learning, either conscious or non conscious, is the third major force. Learning is not restricted simply to the establishment of cognitive or emotional skills but also affected by the impact each plays upon the other.

BRAIN FACT # 30

Every brain activity is multifaceted. Even learning something as simple as 2 + 2 = 4 will involve several brain areas at the minimum and others depending upon the complexity of the learning process.

BRAIN FACT #31

Seldom does any "cognitive" learning take place without emotional input or the establishment of a related emotional memory.

THE BRAIN'S BUILDING BLOCKS

The following highlights contributing factors which may or may not restrict the normal development of a child's brain.

Pre-genetics

♦ Alcoholic men and men who smoke heavily produce damaged sperm. Should one of these sperm fertilize the ovum there is every possibility a damaged zygote will be formed. Learning disabilities, attention problems are thought to be possible outcomes. It is known that children of alcoholic fathers are on average 1/3 lb. lighter at birth than the norm.

♦ Males who use alcohol, tobacco, solvents, marijuana and cocaine run the risk of reducing their sperm count, increasing the number of deformed sperm and reducing their level of fertility to the point of possible infertility.

- Cocaine molecules may be transported on the sperm and enter the egg at the time of fertilization.

Genetics

Chromosomes

- Determine our physical sexual characteristics.

- Carry our genetic makeup which will then be the designer blocks for further development.

- Contain about 25,000 genes.

Violent Behaviour

- An enzyme on certain genes on the X chromosome determine one's propensity for violent behaviour. Approximately 33% of males and 16% of females possess this enzyme.

- It is now known that genes can be permanently altered by highly stressful, violent environments.

- **Genes will do everything it takes to duplicate themselves and survive. In animal studies this has lead to intense rivalry between members of a species for maintenance of the genetic inheritance.**

- The enzyme Monamine Oxide-A (MAO-A) is known to break down neuro chemicals, primarily noradrenaline, and serotonin. One's natural level of MAO-A is predetermined genetically.

- The level of noradrenaline in the brain is largely determined by genetics, the environment and the levels of MAO-A.

- Low levels of noradrenaline may precipitate planned, methodical levels of violence. High levels of noradrenaline may lead to impulsive violent acts.

Alcoholism

- Genes determine our ability to metabolize alcohol. Persons, especially adolescent males, with a high metabolizing enzyme are more inclined to become alcoholics while environmental factors are more influential in adult alcoholism.

  NOTE: A Japanese study showed that 95% of adolescent males identified as alcoholics possessed the high metabolizing enzyme.

Serotonin Levels

- Serotonin levels initially seem to be set by genetics. Low serotonin levels and/or a reduced number of serotonin receptors may lead to aggressive behaviour and depression.

- Low serotonin levels may be a contributing factor to some forms or aspects of ADHD.

Obsessive Disorders

- Obsessive Compulsive Disorder (OCD) is a severe, familial condition that affects approximately 2% of the population. The way OCD is inherited is not clearly understood, but researchers believe it involves multiple genes.

- Persons suffering from OCD tend to have an overactive, underperforming Cingulate Gyrus which may and may not be a genetic trait.

Narcissism and Narcissistic Personality Disorder

BRAIN FACT # 32

Narcissism is not so much the basis of the "narcissistic personality disorder" of psychiatry as it is a natural, heritable character trait. "In fact, narcissism has certain parallels with a second personality trait that we identify as aggression." *Narcissism: A Genetic Trait–A.M Benis, 2004*

- Narcissistic individuals can become extremely aggressive should they feel that their "self importance" is not being recognized or appreciated by others.

- Narcissistic Personality Disorder affects about 1% of the general population and 2-16% of the clinical population.

Depression

BRAIN FACT # 33

A propensity for depression is carried on the genes of approximately 50% of the population. Fortunately, most do not succumb to the illness because the aggravating environmental conditions are not present.

Attention Deficit Disorders

BRAIN FACT # 34

It is now believed that a significant proportion of classic ADD and ADHD is inherited.

- It is thought that the genetic aspect of ADD and ADHD is polygenic in nature.

NOTE: There are many reasons why children and adults have problems with paying attention. Daniel Amen in Healing ADHD has identified six and has suggested treatment for all.

Intelligence

BRAIN FACT #35

The brain of every child is genetically predisposed to gather information, process it and build complex knowledge networks each in its own unique manner.

BRAIN FACT # 36

Although it is natural to conceptualize intelligence as strictly cognitive it is important to understand that we also possess an emotional intelligence and the two intelligences are integrated.

PRE-NATAL ENVIRONMENT

Fetal Alcohol Spectrum Disorder FASD

- ◆ A mother who consumes alcohol during her pregnancy runs the risk of her baby's brain being permanently damaged.

- ◆ This permanent brain damage severely inhibits a child's ability to manage impulsivity, succeed academically and develop a full range of appropriate social behaviours.

NOTE: Depending on local custom other terms are FAS (Fetal Alcohol Syndrome), FAE (Fetal Alcohol Effects) or ARND (Alcohol Related Neural Disorder)

- ◆ Fetal Alcohol Spectrum Disorder is an induced form of mental retardation (learning disability, etc.) which is 100% preventable and costs our society several millions of dollars per person per lifetime.

Prenatal exposure to solvents

- ◆ These children are likely to have developmental delays, lower IQ's, poorer language and memory skills, be inattentive and hyperactive. (*Hospital for Sick Children*, Toronto)

Prenatal exposure to cocaine, marijuana

NOTE: The brain alterations found in prenatally exposed animals may provide a biological explanation for subtle impairments in emotional control and behaviour that clinical researchers are uncovering in drug-exposed children.

- ◆ Although they remain cautious, researchers at the National Institute on Drug Abuse (NIDA) revealed a common thread of findings indicating that children who have been prenatally exposed to drugs may have early and persistent difficulties in:

  - ◆ regulating arousal appropriately.

  - ◆ delaying gratification.

- ◆ tolerating frustration.

- ◆ and handling stress.

Pre-natal Stress

NOTE: It is estimated that 8-16% of all pregnant women are physically, emotionally or sexually abused by the father of the still to be born child. The affects of this abuse leads to increased stress, reduced medical care, poorer nutrition, a likelihood of increased use of tobacco and alcohol and lower birth weight of the infant.

- ◆ Mothers who experience stress during pregnancy flood the baby's brain with stress chemicals such as noradrenaline and glucocorticoids. These babies arrive into the external world with higher resting heart rates and have difficulty settling.

- ◆ Stress can significantly influence the synaptic structure affecting neural linkages between the brain's many components, the most critical being the frontal cortex and the limbic areas.

- ◆ In particular, prenatal stress seems to have the ability to impair memory processes. It has been shown that prenatal stress, induced a life-long reduction of the creation of neural cells (neurogenesis) in the hippocampus, which is critical to the brain's ability to store memory.

Prenatal exposure to tobacco and nicotine

- ◆ The negative effects of smoking during pregnancy include depriving the baby's brain of oxygen, increasing the levels of stimulants and perhaps dulling the dopamine receptors in the area of the nucleus accumbens.

- ◆ It has been shown that the fetus of a mother who smokes moderately heavily can have a Blood Nicotine Level 15X that of its mother.

- ◆ Cigarette smoke reduces blood flow through the placenta by as much as 38 percent.

- ◆ New evidence of toxic effects of prenatal exposure to tobacco smoke on newborn's behaviour include later observed effects, including lower IQ and increased risk of developing attention-deficit/hyperactivity.

- ◆ Mothers who smoke during pregnancy are twice as likely as nonsmokers to have an infant with low birth weight. Children born below normal birth weight have increased chances of: (1) mental retardation, (2) learning disabilities, (3) behaviour problems, (4) language/speech impairments, and (5) a combination of all disability categories.
  –Mary E. Tinetti

Nutrition

- A mother's nutrition is critical for the baby's growth. For example if the diet is devoid of nutrients such as folic acid the chances of neurological problems such as spina bifida are significantly increased.

Teenage Pregnancy

Teenage pregnancy increases the chances that the fetus will experience a series of negative effects for the following reasons. The mother is:

- Less likely to receive prenatal medical attention.

- More likely to use alcohol, tobacco and illicit drugs.

- Less likely to follow a diet which will provide the proper nutrients for her fetus.

- Less likely to receive financial and emotional support from the baby's father.

POST-NATAL ENVIRONMENTS

Oxygen deprivation

- Oxygen starvation during the birth process may seriously affect a variety of neurological functions. Cerebral palsy is one of several outcomes of oxygen deprivation.

Traumatic Brain Injury (TBI)

- Head injury or Traumatic Brain Injury can cause a range of neurological problems such as attention deficit, reduced anger management, reduced visual and auditory functioning, impaired speech formation etc. This also applies to brain tumours or cysts which impinge on specific areas of the brain.

- TBI can be caused by physical abuse such as hits to the head, "shaken baby", whiplash or hitting one's head as a result of being violently pushed, or thrown into hard objects or automobile accidents or sports injuries resulting in concussion.

BRAIN FACT # 37

Not all shaken babies die. Many of these babies become children with learning and other disabilities.

BRAIN FACT # 38

Intelligence is not fixed. This has been supported by the research of Gage, Greenough, Diamond and others.

- Although genes determine our natural intelligence or intelligences. Research is showing that a baby's IQ may be changed by +/- 20-25 IQ points depending upon the nature of the child's environment.

- Additional research has shown that the effects of environment is most noticeable in those children who have suffered low stimulation, poor nutrition and emotional distress caused by dysfunctional homes and communities.

- Children in middle class+ families tend to be exposed to an increased level of stimulation, novelty and meaningfulness which automatically create opportunities for neural development.

ADHD

- There are many reasons why children and adults have problems with paying attention. Some of these may be environmentally induced by brain injury, depression and emotional trauma.

- Persons afflicted with ADHD are likely to be teased/taunted and isolated more as well as being subjected to frequent and severe, harsh and inconsistent discipline.

Alcohol and other drugs

- The brains of alcoholics show a reduced blood flow to the frontal lobes (the executive branch of the brain) and an increase in the size of ventricles. This reduces the individual's ability to solve problems, monitor feelings, manage anger and form and recall memory. This also increases the possibility of alcohol induced mood disorders.

- Children raised in homes where one or both parents are alcoholics are at serious risk of being neglected, physically, emotionally and sexually abused and subsequently abusing alcohol themselves.

- Parents who are addicted to one or more drugs are generally less able to provide the physical and emotional stability which children require as they mature. These children often experience inconsistency in care and frequently fear for their own safety causing serious disruption to the brain maturation processes. The damage is shown to last a life time.

BRAIN FACT # 39

Psychological/emotional and sexual abuse puts the brain into intense survival mode.

- Psychological/emotional abuse seriously affects the normal neurological development of the entire brain **most specifically the neural corridors between pre-frontal cortex and the limbic area.**

- Childhood stress may damage the sensitivity of the pleasure reward area and thus set the stage for future drug abuse.

- Sexual abuse is now known to **trigger physical violence among young females and may be a contributor to depression.** It is also thought to cause early onset of puberty.

NOTE: It is not uncommon for abused children to experience two or more types of abuse.

BRAIN FACT # 40

Emotional neglect is ever bit as damaging to the developing brain as are other identified types of abuse.

Babies intuitively expect to be loved and when this doesn't happen they experience stress.

Poverty is a major contributing factor to low levels of physical, cognitive and social skills development.

Poverty increases the chances of:

- Frequent changes in homes, schools and communities.

- Poor nutrition.

- Poor quality of housing.

- Limited access to community services.

- Having unstable and dysfunctional families.

- Developing low sense self esteem.

- Higher stress levels and incidents of depression.

Nutrition

BRAIN FACT # 41

"The brain of the average infant consumes 75% of the calories the baby takes in."– Stephen Cunnane, *Survival of the Fattest*

NOTE: Children who are poorly nourished in their first three years of life are at risk to suffer lower intelligence and increased risk of committing impulsive, aggressive acts in later life.

Oppositional Defiant Disorder

BRAIN FACT #42

Oppositional Defiant Disorder (ODD) is an environmentally induced disorder which is caused by severe stress and emotional trauma.

- The child tends to respond angrily to any person in authority.

- There is evidence that there is a link between strep throat and at least one form of Oppositional Defiant Disorder (ODD).

- Many children with ADHD may also develop ODD.

Conduct Disorder

- Conduct Disorder is a **severe stress-survival disorder.** It is the outcome of extensive physical, psychological and sexual abuse often coupled with one or more genetic contributions.

- Conduct Disorder is often co-morbid with ODD and ADHD.

- Bullying is a behaviour which often has roots in genetics, environment and learning and is one of the criteria for Conduct Disorder.

Young teenage parent(s) all too often provide "horrible" environments for their children. Most teenage parents have:

- Brains which are cognitively and emotionally underdeveloped. See: *Brain Maturation Teen years.*

- Limited capacity to accept responsibility for providing the appropriate stimulation necessary for meeting the child's cognitive and emotional needs.

- Limited concept of the future.

- Limited ability to provide a safe, caring and loving environment for their child. See: *Attachment issues.*

- Limited ability to provide for the physical needs of the child which include nourishment, shelter, clothing and medical attention.

- Increased likelihood to abandon the child for short or long periods of time to pursue normal, self serving teenage activities.

- May tend to see the baby as someone who will love them. Babies are not like that. They come to be looked after and if they experience love they may love back.

- Lack the emotional stability to care for a baby who is unhappy. Babies are highly demanding. This can lead to the child being physically abused.

- There is much more, but from an educational perspective, most babies born to teen mothers are under stimulated and unprepared to enter the school system, as their brains tend to be under developed.

TV and similar media

Far too many children are spending an inordinate amount of time **passively viewing** television and videos of questionable content.

- TV is a non-interactive medium. The child's brain needs activity to foster neural growth, specifically in language areas.

- The child's "mirror neurons" are prone to copying the actions of the actors and/or characters portrayed on TV.

- Most children watch TV in an unsupervised manner. Hence parents or other caregivers provide limited or no censorship and are unable or unwilling to help the child debrief the material.

- TV watching negatively affects physical activity and supports inappropriate dietary practices.

- A review of TV programming for children reveals a great deal of violence which, can in a non conscious manner, shape the child's approach to social behaviour.

- TV watching severely hampers a child's capacity to visualize. This affects a number of learning processes, most specifically reading.

CONSCIOUS AND NON-CONSCIOUS LEARNING

Learned Behaviours/Attitudes

NOTE: Language usage is crucial for all learning including the building of behaviours and shaping of attitudes. However, language is only one medium of instruction and it has its limitations.

BRAIN FACT # 43

A child's ability to use language is dependent upon its age, previous language experiences and ability to combine words and sentences into concepts. This is a two way process.

BRAIN FACT # 44

It is now believed that it is not until late teens or the early twenties that the left and right frontal cortices are mature enough to coordinate all aspects of language.

- Attitudes are consciously and emotionally formed from the formal and informal teachings of parents and other significant adults or peers.

- The emotional component of attitudes are difficult to change.

- Children, to a greater extent, and adults less so, have "mirror neurons" which allow us to mimic the actions of others. For example: An adult's non-verbal reaction to a person of another race can be quickly copied by a child.

- Children learn to love, like or hate other people on the basis of the words and actions of their parents or other significant people.

- Children may learn consciously and non-consciously that they need or need not respect other people. Racism and other forms of bigotry are learned attitudes.

- Many children learn that education is not important. This not only impedes their desire to learn but usually leads these children to developing unproductive behaviours in educational settings.

CHAPTER 11

ENVIRONMENTALLY INDUCED LOW COGNITIVE FUNCTIONING

LOW ACADEMIC AND SOCIAL ABILITY

All too often there is a correlation between low cognitive ability and behavioural problems.

Definition: Cognitive ability is being defined, for the purposes of this book, as one's ability to assess incoming information, review this information in the context of previous experience and be able to act in a skilful and responsible manner.

Examples of good cognitive ability include being:

* Socially conscious.

* Academically proficient.

* Able to build and maintain items.

* Able to plan and project into the future.

* Able to connect the past, present and future.

* Able to drive a vehicle with care and consideration for others.

Academic problems: It is common for a troubled child to be experiencing a range of academic problems. including weak language skills. Additional frustration is a frequent outcome.

*NOTE: However academic success **does not necessarily mean** that the child or adult has mastered all the procedural or processing skills required of a responsible citizen.*

Social consciousness is largely a cognitive skill which is developed through instruction from and social interaction with peers and significant adults.

Language skills: A child's competence in language is often a determinant to acquire a full continuum of other cognitive skills. In fact, the data clearly shows that bullies with low language skills are likely to be more physically aggressive. In addition, children with low language capabilities are destined for school failure unless this situation can be rectified.

NOTE: It is expected that a child with decent to good language skills would be more receptive to counselling and

other discussions related to his or her behaviour. This may be true but there are many cases where linguistically solid individuals effectively use their language skills to advance their antisocial behaviour and "pull the wool over the eyes" of the significant adults in their midst.

Some of these kids develop great "Street Smarts" These survival strategies serve them well in the homes or community environments where staying safe, even staying alive is a constant and paramount concern.

Low cognitive ability can be considered as at least one Standard Deviation (SD) below the mean. This assessment often relates more to **academic performance** than other areas of endeavour. It is important to note that many children who perform below norm in a standard classroom setting may display a **range of talents in other areas.**

If a child had a "**normal**" brain at birth and is raised in a dysfunctional, stressful environment where stimulation is low and need to survive is high their brain's frontal cortex will likely under perform in a number of ways. Nevertheless hidden in every child's brain are strengths to be developed.

NOTE: The school has a choice. It can ignore the child's current skill levels or it can commence the child's education at the child's present stage of development.

Howard Gardner has studied intelligence from the perspective of its multiplicity and plasticity. We now have more hope about the possibilities to develop and optimize a child's intelligence. But these goals are not realized easily or quickly. **The key however, is to work from strength and by doing so not only enhance growth in that one area of the brain but may very well trigger growth in several others.**

BRAIN FACT #45

A child's proficiency in language depends upon a number of factors such as oral vocabulary, meaningful experiences, ability to visualize, the coordination of the left and right hemispheres of the frontal cortex and age related brain maturation.

*NOTE: It is estimated that up to **15% of children psychologically opt out of school** at Grade Three. The primary reason is likely low language skills followed by the children not finding school meaningful.*

Negative environmental factors exist in all socio-economic and cultural groups however childhood poverty remains as one of the most devastating and long lasting contributors to cognitive underdevelopment.

*NOTE: Some rich kids suffer from parental neglect and/or being cared for by untrained, low paid "nannies." These children may perform well below expectations. More over many of these children **have a false sense of entitlement which inhibits them from striving to reach their potential.***

In conclusion cognitive ability is multifaceted, incredibly important and does not develop in a vacuum.

CHAPTER 12

BRAIN MATURATION – MIDDLE YEARS

Once upon a time not too many years ago we generally thought of brain growth, if we thought about it at all, in one of two ways. The first might have been that the brain is like an inverted pyramid and each year of school added another layer slightly larger than the one before.

Another model, and this was supported by some scientific thought was that the brain was finished growing at about age eight and that we as educators were charged with the responsibility of filling it up. Words like sponge, soaking it up and cramming were used to help explain the learning process. The brain was kind of like a race car that was being tweaked a bit and like a cargo van being filled to capacity. As it turned out neither model was right and neither was very useful in explaining middle years and teenage brains.

New research is revealing that the brain has a second **significant synaptic growth spurt** just prior to the onset of puberty. This is similar to the one which children experience in their first 18-24 months of life. This massive number of new synapses becomes the teen's mental launching pad into adulthood.

However, many of these synapses are poorly formed, not well supported by complex neural networks and may have disturbed well established networks that previously existed. There is still a great amount of development work to be done.

Some observable outcomes. The child:

* Seems overwhelmed at times.

* May even appear to be clumsy and poorly coordinated.

* Is rapidly becoming aware of social needs and thought processes.

* Makes unsubstantiated definitive statements.

* Is idealistic or fatalistic depending on mood.

* Makes rapid decisions which are frequently impulsive and inappropriate.

* Desires for independence are poorly thought out and generally self focussed.

* Wants to treated like an adult but accepts little or no responsibility.

* Is increasingly interested in relationships.

* Is increasingly self centred.

* Encounters problems with authentic self esteem.

* **Involvement with relationship bullying takes on a harder edge.**

* Has frequent mood swings.

* Has uneven, unpredictable intellectual growth spurts.

* Believes that he/she is invulnerable.

* The child retreats into his/her self. Listens to the same music or even the same song over and over again. (This may be an attempt to shut out some the world. There is just too much happening.)

BRAIN FACT # 47

It is entirely possible that in the early post puberty years the young adolescent's brain is a little like a run away train. "Lots of speed but few controls." The controls will normally come about as the maturation process which for the most part starts at the back of the brain reaches the frontal cortex.

As the brain becomes more effective it becomes engaged in a new range of learning possibilities, social successes, new behaviours and behavioural management skills and much more.

Nevertheless this brain maturation process is occurring at the same time that the body is experiencing a variety of growth spurts, shape changes as well as sexual maturation. There is a lot happening.

These **"new brains"** will possess new capabilities in or due to:

1. **Myelination:** Beginning at about age eleven, the brain begins an accelerated process of myelinating active axons. This process, in large part, moves from the front to the back of the brain. The brain is becoming faster because it is bio-electrically more efficient.

2. **Brain Maturation:** At about the same time a major pruning of unused synapses, solidification of others and the further integration of neural networks begins at the back of the brain and works forward. The brain is becoming better able to make decisions and process data at ever more complex levels.

3. **Impulse Management:** As the brain matures the frontal lobes become increasingly capable in the management of amygdala's impulsive messages. There is an increase of critical two way neural transmissions between these two vital areas.

4. **New Intellectual Powers:** The child/student begins to interpret the world differently in light of these new-found mental capacities. This may lead to increased questioning, either openly or internally of a number of issues. These issues could include religion, authority, personal responsibility, the local community, the world at large, personal and family values. Teenage defiance is an outward expression of this questioning.

5. **Intellectual and Emotional Insecurity:** The child/student may experience a sense of insecurity simply because the world now seems different. It is bigger, there are more things happening, more possibilities and many mysteries still to be understood. The nature of sex, sexual orientation and how the child's culture handles these issues can complicate the child's thought processes.* Those things which were formerly safe, secure, known or constant may no longer appear to be as they were.

   This combination of intellectual uncertainty and emotional unease may leave the adolescent vulnerable to peer and media pressures.

   NOTE: The computer used by the twelve year old son of a church minister was found, by accident, to contain some pornographic material. Was this a perversion or was it an inappropriate way for the child to gain an understanding of sex?

6. **Abstract Reasoning:** The frontal lobes gradually develop increased capacity and skills to process knowledge in a conceptual, abstract manner. It seems that this begins, in earnest, at about **age sixteen**. This new power allows the individual increased capacity to shift from concrete "rote like" performance to abstract problem solving.

   The child should be gaining a better sense of the concept of "future."

7. **Increased Propensity to Make Judgements:** The adolescent is prone to making judgements which within his/her mind are perfectly sensible but may or may not be accurate, appropriate or in the individual's best interest. These may include, likes and dislikes about subjects, people, health issues, personal safety, drugs, entertainment, sex, value of education and prospects for the future.

8. **Increased Decision Making Capacity and a still Developing Knowledge Base:** The child's decision making capability increases due to an expanded knowledge base and increased mental capacity. The decision process is not yet fully operational and may not be until around age 29.

   Good decision making requires combining:

   - **New information.**

   - **Prior knowledge.**

   - **Capacity to reason.**

   All of the above is happening, as it were, bathed in a sea of emotional memories which include fears, likes, hates, preferences and similar affective memories. **This is not an easy process.**

9. **Each adolescent is on a erratic brain-body growth continuum:** Unfortunately the brain/body maturation does not start for all children at, for example, age 11. For some it starts earlier and for others later. The various growth patterns do not follow a template as the child's genes and environment play major roles in the rate and intensity of physical and neural development.

   *NOTE: The child's **sexual maturation** and a great deal of its **physical maturation** will be achieved long before his/her **brain maturation** reaches a normal adult maturation level.*

10. **Good News:** This rapid brain maturation activity continues until age 29-30 and myelination continues until about age 45. Although you can't wait that long, it is important to note that growth is happening everyday in your classroom and sometimes magical things happen some of which meet even exceed your expectations. **And everyday, a new class!!!**

MIDDLE YEARS BRAIN GROWTH AND BEHAVIOURAL ISSUES

1. **Self Esteem:** The child's self esteem is constantly under stress during this time of uneven cognitive, emotional and physical growth. Many early adolescents are struggling with their self identity and are unable to withstand many of the pressures which are directed at them.

   These pressures include:

   ◆ Invitations to use drugs.

   ◆ Invitations to become sexually active.

   ◆ Difficulty in finding personal contentment.

   ◆ Increased possibility of depression.

   ◆ Intense desire to be socially accepted.

   ◆ Worries about sexual orientation.

   ◆ Concerns about body size and shape.

   ◆ Concerns about appearance.

   ◆ Concerns about meeting group norms.

   ◆ Confusion over dependence-independence issues.

   ◆ Ability to have fun without the use of drugs or other inappropriate behaviours.

2. **Troubled Teens** (At school): Adolescents whose brains are underdeveloped in the areas of language, social skills or appropriate behaviours are likely to be further disenchanted with their academic achievements. Their concerns are in the following areas:

   ◆ Having major difficulties in the classroom

   ◆ Likely on the administration's "watch list" as students who are problematic.

   ◆ Isolated, to some degree, to groups of like minded, skill deficient individuals.

3. **Troubled Teens** (In home and community): Their somewhat underdeveloped brains plus their

   ◆ Age, size, level of sexual maturity.

   ◆ Desire for independence.

   ◆ Use of alcohol and other drugs to mask their emotional pain.

   ◆ Absence of caring, (low levels of social consciousness and social conscience).

   ◆ Shallow self esteem.

   ◆ Parents who are minimally supportive increases their potential to get into a great deal of serious trouble.

In total this is a tough, confusing and challenging time for parents, teachers and, of course, the teens. Stress an be quite high for all parties.

It is no wonder that many teachers are confused, frustrated and often at their "wits end" when dealing with middle years students.

On the other hand there are, thankfully, many teachers who wouldn't want to be anywhere else. These high energy teachers have a plan for these children but also have the flexibility to meet the changing needs of a child or the class almost at a moment's notice. I think of Irene who used music to challenge and otherwise motivate her students and Dave the science teacher who engaged his Grade 7 & 8 science classes with innovation and caring.

CHAPTER 13

EMOTIONAL MEMORIES

Until fairly recently we have believed that behaviours are learned, impulses can be controlled and that the frontal cortex is the only part of the brain which really matters. All of the above are partially correct but all of the above are wrong. **They ignore the influence of emotional memories and the critical role played by the amygdala in virtually all aspects of our lives.**

All behaviour and behavioural change is influenced by one's emotional memories or emotional intelligence.

Although, there is no one single part of the brain which manages emotions. However, for this discussion the key player is the amygdala. (Some of the other components of the limbic area include, the hypothamus, hippocampus, nucleus accumbens and the basal ganglia.)

BRAIN FACT # 47

The amygdala is, gram for gram, the most powerful region of the brain. Within the amygdala there exists specialized zones which appraise virtually all incoming "messages" checking for uncertainty as well as being the storehouse for vast amounts of emotional memory.

BRAIN FACT #48

The nature of the incoming stimulation whether it be one of threat, anger, provocation, love, care and concern, is quickly assessed by the amygdala. This assessment triggers the transmission of a number of internal messages sent to the orbital frontal cortex (and subsequently to other regions of the cerebral cortex) or to areas of brain which initiate the "fight or flight response."

The kind of action that is taken is highly dependant upon the emotional memories existing within the amygdala.

The response time of the amygdala is approximately 5X **less** than that of the frontal cortex.

POWERFUL NEGATIVE EMOTIONAL MEMORIES

1. Phobias

BRAIN FACT #49

Phobias are fears driven by trauma induced emotional memories and are a sub group of emotional memories. The reaction to one's phobias may range from mild caution to complete paralysis.

Examples of phobias include:

Monophobia – the fear of being alone.

Claustrophobia – the fear of confined spaces

Acrophobia – the fear of heights.

The list is extremely long. It is likely that each one of us has at least one phobia.

Example: In 2004 an attempt was made to rehabilitate a number of British youth each of whom **"was known to the police and judicial system."** The youth volunteered to participate in the equivalent of a six week "boot camp." All of the young men chosen were tough "street kids." A number of the youth left the camp because they couldn't handle the discipline or rigour. That was expected. However, a small number, left because they couldn't handle "tenting out" over night. They were terrified of the dark.

BRAIN FACT #50

An overactive underperforming cingulate gyrus may cause the brain to obsess on a given fear.

2. Post Traumatic Stress Disorder (PTSD)

PTSD has been finally and formally recognized as an emotional memory response induced by the trauma of war. In WWI it was called "battle fatigue," in WWII the ailment was called "shell shock" but PTSD came to the forefront after the Vietnam War. Thousands of Vietnam veterans plus veterans of the Gulf War and other recent conflicts have now been identified as suffering from PTSD.

Example: In the early 1990's a Vietnam veteran, 20 years out of service, but still carrying a sidearm, was quietly sitting at his desk. Another student accidentally dropped his books on the floor. The loud crash sent the Veteran into an instant crouch with his gun drawn, fortunately he didn't pull the trigger.

NOTE: A new term OSI, Operational Stress Injuries, has emerged to identify this condition.

3. PTSD in the classroom

Everyday in virtually every school there are students suffering from PTSD. These are children who have been physically, sexually or severely psychologically abused. They have been traumatized in a local "war zone" which often is their home. When they experience the right trigger they will respond in the most "personally appropriate survival focussed" fashion.

NOTE: The appraisal areas of their amygdala and reaction areas of their cingulate gyrus are set on "a high level survival mode". They will act long before their frontal cortex can intervene with controlling messages. The triggers may include a loud noise or a certain specific sound, the tone of a persons voice, a perfume or other smell, a physical presence of someone who reminds the child of the abuser etc.

4. Anxiety attacks

In some ways anxiety attacks are similar to PTSD but in these cases the amygdala is receiving intense inner brain messages of concern about a certain place or event. Often these messages are about helplessness, about impending abuse, torment or failure. The anxiety attack becomes full fledged when the brain and body are pumped full of noradrenaline and adrenaline respectfully, hearts race, faces become flushed, the person perspires, breathing becomes laboured and the person may even faint.

Example: Should the child be a victim of schoolyard bullying, the anxiety attack is likely to be in full force by the time the child walks through the door of the school. The child wants to flee but can't.

Your observations could include, the child:

*   Passing out.
*   Breaking into tears.
*   Having stomach aches.
*   Presenting with low energy.
*   Becoming unnaturally aggressive.
*   Beginning to shake all over.

*   Not being able to concentrate.
*   Being unwilling to answer questions or blurting out wrong answers.
*   Being generally miserable.
*   Wetting or soiling him/herself.

There can also be a linkage between anxiety attacks and depression.

NOTE: It is often difficult for the child and any adult working with the child to initially know what is wrong. Unless anxiety and anxiety attacks are understood and discussed in health and wellness classes the child will be very confused about his/her physical symptoms. The school personnel might have to try several approaches to see if they can come up with an understanding and solution.

5. Unworthiness may lead to abusing others

Children who have been mistreated and abused often develop emotional memories which focus on their unworthiness. In order to give themselves a sense of worth they may emulate the very behaviour that has caused them so much pain.

Example: One young English boy who had been beaten by his brother and other older boys at his boarding school became a bully. He bullied others for about three years, until one Summer he tried to impress a pretty young girl by tormenting a younger boy. She told him that he "Looked like a stupid loser." He thought, "Hey I don't want to be a loser" and gradually began to develop a more socially acceptable way of interacting with people.

FORMATION OF EMOTIONAL MEMORIES

BRAIN FACT #51

Every memory is composed of a multitude of mini neural networks scattered throughout the brain. A recalled memory is in fact a reconstructed memory.

The intensity and longevity of that memory is largely dependent upon the nature of emotions surrounding the event being remembered.

BRAIN FACT #52

Emotional memories are largely stored in the amygdala without language and hence are extremely difficult to reshape by normal counselling techniques.

Example: If a small child was bitten by a dog, she might in later life might start crying or become otherwise anxious when ever she hears a dog barking or sees or meets a dog on the street. Only when that child is able to experience safety in the presence of a dog will her phobia start to subside.

BRAIN FACT #53

Emotional memories may be partially formed by genetics.

NOTE: It is now believed that we have a genetically induced fear of snakes.

BRAIN FACT #54

Emotional memories are often highly influenced by post natal environmental inputs.

The role of emotions as an appraisal system.

1. Certain smells foretell of impending danger or joy.

    Example: The smell of roast turkey may evoke happy memories of family gatherings or may stimulate memories of families who fight a great deal at "festive" occasions.

2. Certain sounds have hidden messages.

    Example: A door slamming shut may speak of an angry person entering the house or it may mean that a child who is happy to be home.

    Example: A young woman would experience an uncomfortable feeling whenever in a car that was driving over a bridge with a long stretch of metal grating. One day she mentioned this to her mother. Her mother immediately replied "Oh that sounds like the noise of the "Buzz Bombers" which used to bomb London in WWII." As a young child this young woman had lived through these bombing

    raids. In fact, the apartment block, next but one, had suffered a direct hit while she and her parents huddled in the stairwell of their apartment block.

3. The sight of a certain street, house or other building may trigger a range of memories which are totally dependent upon one's previous emotional experiences in that location.

    NOTE: Nostalgia is the outgrowth of emotional memories.

4. The feel of a particular piece of furniture or garment may lead one to memories of terror or considerable joy.

    Example: If a child was abused or tenderly loved on piece of furniture, similar furniture may cause the appropriate feelings to arise.

5. The taste of a particular type of food may remind you of comfort food cooked for you by a loving parent or grandparent or something you ate because there was nothing else to eat.

    Example: In the period of the depression through to post WWII many rural families were extremely poor. One such family had a dairy farmer as a neighbour who would give them newborn calves to augment their meagre food supply. The family was grateful and survived but even after 50+ years my friend cannot bear the sight or smell of cooked veal.

6. Few emotional memories are learned by direct command, most are learned through modelling, performing an activity or otherwise experiencing some event. The vocal tone of the command usually has greater impact than the words themselves.

    Example: Racism is a cognitive memory enhanced by emotional messages received from others through their modelling and the way they used language. A sneer which accompanies a statement gives the statement increased emotional currency. See: *The Learned Bigoted Bully.*

7. Emotional memories may stay with you for a life time.

    Example: PTSD or phobias are such examples.

8. Emotional memories will not be destroyed by being told to "forget it."

    Example: For the next one minute "Do not think about someone you love."

BRAIN FACT # 55

The brain is designed to forget and will easily forget a cognitive memory when the synapses are not very well formed or have been weakened by disuse. However, emotional memories formed by trauma or positively exciting events are generally fixed for life.

BRAIN FACT # 56

The strength of any memory is essentially dependent upon four things.

- The intensity of the stimulation.

- Amount of rehearsal or drill.

- Frequency of recall.

- Relevant emotions.

BRAIN FACT # 57

In order to replace an old memory, a new memory must be well rehearsed and the motivation to retain this new memory must be strong.

Example: It is difficult to like someone who you have once despised.

9. Emotional memories are difficult to "over write."

   Example: In a marriage if one partner cheats, it is almost impossible for the other partner to forget. "Forgiveness maybe, but forgetting never."

   NOTE: Some success has been achieved with cognitive behaviour therapy coupled with physical, artistic, musical or dramatic activities skilfully conducted in an environment appropriate to the end result. The activities tend to engage the emotional sectors of the brain.

   NOTE: Passive, low involvement, rehabilitation activities are almost always doomed to failure.

10. Emotional memories are far more difficult to "reach" than cognitive memory or cognitive thoughts.

    Example: Even after a quarter of a century, whenever I see a picture of an African market I can still recall the smells, the noises and human interaction.

11. Emotional memories may influence your behaviour in unusual ways.

    Example: My friend mentioned above was, and I suspect still is, truly bothered when food is left on a plate. He would ask if he could "finish up the french fries" left on your plate. His amygdala keeps, as it were, saying, "Don't waste food."

12. The nature of an emotional memory depends significantly upon the "state" that was in existence at the time the memory was being formed.

    Example: People who have lived through depressions or wars or who were poor have emotional reactions to food, money and property which are not easily understood by others who have not had that "state " experience. Many of these people have difficulty throwing stuff away.

    NOTE: The behaviour of most bullies has a significant emotional memory component. This coupled with the emotional rewards the bully receives when he or she is abusing someone makes the initial attempts to have the bully reform difficult. The bullies residual emotional memories must be over ridden, new means of providing emotional hits must be provided and new cognitive understanding must be achieved.

CHAPTER 14
ATTACHMENT ISSUES

Major reference: Daniel Siegel *The Developing Mind* Pages 67-120

Attachment or bonding may be thought of as the **emotional umbilical cord** which binds a child with an adult usually one or both of its parents.

BRAIN FACT # 58

A baby's brain is hardwired to form an attachment with a significant adult.

For a variety of reasons such as familiarity with the mother's heart beat, immersion in the mother's smell, familiarity with the mother's voice, the emotional soothing during breast feeding, it is highly likely that babies will bond quicker with the mother than other adults. However, bonding does also occur with other adults as well.

NOTE: The oxytocin released within the mother's brain while she is holding or breast feeding the child generally solidifies her desire to bond with her child. Oxytocin increases the dopamine levels in the brain's reward centre.

BRAIN FACT # 59

The critical period for forming the attachment is preferably in the first few months to first year of life.

This does not preclude bonding taking place outside of this time period. Bonding at a later date is dependant upon a number of factors such as early trauma the child might have experienced, the emotional plasticity of the brains of both the child and the new caregiver, the level of stimulation the child experiences and the child's innate ability to sense safety and security.

BRAIN FACT:# 60

The key to bonding is the synchronous emotional alignment between the adult and the infant. There are times when the baby needs the Tender Love and Care (TLC) of the parent, right then, right now. And there are other times when the baby is quite content to ponder the universe by itself and is comfortable being left alone. The essence to building strong attachment is the availability of emotional communication.

1. SECURE CHILDREN

These children have parents who are emotionally "in synch" with them by responding easily, timely and empathetically. There is consistent positive emotional interplay.

Example: A mother was observed taking her toddler for a walk, every few steps the child stopped to examine a bug, a flower, a crack in the paving stone or anything else that took his interest. As a result their progress was very slow. A neighbour commiserated with the mother on how her child was delaying the walk. With a smile the mother replied "I gave him the world, the least I can do is let him show it to me."

Here was a mother who knew instinctively what her child needed and how to provide it. As a result of her understanding the toddler was satisfying his brain's insatiable need for information and was doing so in a safe and secure environment. The child and mother were emotionally in synch with each other. The parent and the child are like two ball room dancers.

The secure child is:

- Comfortable with self and relationship with other children and adults.

- Willing to risk and to try new things.

- Is confident that parents will be there for him/her.

- Likely to grow up with a highly developed sense of emotional security.

- Able to integrate and cooperate with other children.

Approximately 55 to 60% of all children.

2. RESISTANT AMBIVALENT (INSECURE)

These children's parents have a history of "**managing**" their interactions with their children, almost to the point of scheduling an "**appointment**" to spend "**quality**" time with their child. The parents tend to "**pounce,**" as it were, into the emotional world of the child. In these "quality time" periods the parent often makes the decisions as to the nature and location of the activity. The children feel they have limited control over these interactions and a sense of personal helplessness sets in. They feel ambivalent about their relationship with their parent or parents. The sad part is that the parents think they are meeting the child's needs by providing "quality time" but "quality time" only counts when it meets the child's needs. Since emotional time is being allocated, it is common for a child to feel abandoned by a parent especially when he or she wants to be emotionally close to the parent and the parent is not willing to make him/herself available. In addition, if something more "important" (to the parent) {i.e. a phone call, a visitor} happens, the session with the child will be interrupted or ended. This teaches the child he or she is, at best, of limited interest to the parent and so the child may engage in various levels of disruptive behaviour in an attempt to regain the parent/caregiver's attention. It is also common for the child to honestly desire time with a parent when the parent is "scheduled" with a sibling. The child may then begin to feel that the parent likes the other child better.

Parents may also be tempted to "dish" out their love to the child or children who respond to their wishes. This may result in the child defining him or herself in light of the parent(s) aspirations. The "jock" father who drives his son to become a winning athlete. The mother who wants her daughter to be the most beautiful and talented little girl in the whole community. These children might try to oblige but lose themselves in the process.

NOTE: The child feels pressured to match his/her emotional needs to those of one or both parents.

Child intuitively senses that:

- Parents are inconsistently available and intrusive.

- Parents are or appear to be preoccupied with other matters.

- There may be inconsistency from parent to parent.

- An inconsistency between attention given to itself and siblings.

Child becomes:

- Either indifferent or overattentive when spending time with parents.

- Overly competitive for parent's attention. Hence the potential for excessive sibling rivalry.

- Overly competitive to reach their goals.

- Very manipulative in seeking and gaining the attention of parents or other adults.

- A potential learned aggressive bully.

Approximately 5 to 10% of all children.

3. AVOIDANT (INSECURE)

Parents have a history of consistent negative, neglectful or indifferent emotional interaction with their children.

There is an air of controlled emotional indifference. The parents and the child develop a "cold" relationship. The parents may argue that they are helping the child become independent, and seem to regard the child's emotional needs as insignificant, bothersome or too frivolous to be addressed.

The parent and the child are not connected emotionally. Whatever the cause, whether it be a mental dysfunction or simply being afraid of connecting emotionally with their children, these parents seem to regard their children more as objects requiring physical care and material goods rather than developing human beings with feelings.

Example: The father, of a 14 year girl who is involved in relationship bullying, was recently heard saying to his daughter and her two friends, "Well it looks the three **ho's** (whores) are back, just in time for supper."

Example: Often when I give workshops on bullying I use as props two plush toys which represent a mother bear and her baby. I keep the baby bear and have the mother bear passed around the room and I ask each person to say something mean to the baby bear. This is difficult for most people but I am trying to make the point that children hear many negative emotional messages from people who are supposed to love them and that these messages are often retained as hurtful emotional memories. The most devastating comment was made by a lady who held the mother bear for a good ten seconds, her eyes went cold and then she said, "**You – were – a – mistake.**"

Obviously this had been said to her and the hurt was still very much alive in her adult brain.

The Avoidantly Attached Child:

- Develops a survival plan. Tends to internally bury their disappointment.

- Learns to live with the emotional indifference of the parent.

- (After some time) avoids any serious further attempt to emotionally link with the parent.

- Is very self focussed and consequently tends to be unaware of the emotional needs of others.

- May become a very controlling individual such as "Social Power" bully.

- Will, likely as a parent, be unable to emotionally connect with own children.

- Is difficult to reach with traditional counselling due to their inability to be in touch with their emotions.

- Very likely to have low levels of social conscience.

Approximately 20+% of all children.

4. DISORGANIZED/DISORIENTATED (INSECURE)

This is an extremely serious category. Parents have a history of inconsistent but mostly intense negative emotional interaction with their children. The child does not know what to expect from the parents except that it will likely be unpleasant. The parent(s) may have problems with alcohol, anger management, personality disorders or a mental illness.

Some parents try to buy their children's affection with gifts one day and then next day deal out indiscriminate physical or verbal abuse or punishment. The children are often left wondering what the next parental interaction will be. They are unable to invest either mental or physical energy in trying to develop a relationship.

Example: A parent was preparing to take his two children to school, but just before they left the house he realized that one of the children had turned off the TV. He then spent the next ten minutes hurling verbal abuse, liberally laced with profanity, at his children, only then did he drive them to school. The son is a bully and the daughter has a horrific speech impediment.

NOTE: Children feel cheated because intuitively they know that their parents are supposed love, nourish and protect them but know they live in a home which is often an extremely dangerous place.

Children are:

- Operating in a survival mode most of the time.

- Dealing with a number of conditions induced by stress or threat.

- Very tentative when engaging parents or other adults into their lives.

- Are likely to have difficulty establishing social relationships.

- Likely to form allegiances with parent who is less volatile. (This may not be fruitful, as this parent may side with the violent parent for reasons of personal safety.)

- Very likely to have difficulty trusting teachers.

- May be a candidate for ODD, Conduct Disorder, Impulsive Aggressive Bully, the Personal Power Bully and "Sociopath" Bully.

  Note: Extremely likely to develop complex and serious behavioural disorders. Many are superb liars.

- These children have a propensity to bully in a physical manner.

- Very likely to have low levels of social conscience.

Approximately 20+ % of all children.

(It is further estimated that **80+% of these children** have been emotionally, physically or sexually abused.)

*NOTE: **Earned Secure:** Although never having had a secure relationship with the parent, a person may establish a secure relationship with a therapist, friend, lover, teacher or another adult. This relationship substitutes, to a point, for the secure relationship they intuitively wanted with the parent but were not able to attain. In some cases the child **can then** develop a more satisfying relationship with the parent.*

NOTE: Emotionally insecure teenaged girls are often found in dysfunctional relationships with older controlling males and are unable to leave the relationship.

NOTE: Research shows that childhood bonding patterns resurface in adulthood and parents tend to bond with their children in the same manner that they bonded with their own mother and father. This is a case of non genetic inter-generational transmission.

CHAPTER 15

THE NATURE OF OUR SOCIETY AND THE STATE OF SOCIAL BRAINS

THE CHALLENGE IS TO CREATE A SOCIABLE BRAIN

BRAIN FACT # 61

The reason for our relatively gigantic brain is allow us to interact successfully with other humans. The human is intended to be a social being. Establishing and maintaining social relationships is a complex brain activity.

A social brain is best developed within a "village." "Where everybody knows your name."

Villages provide a level of consistency, security and a sense of mutual responsibility.

Many of today's children do not emotionally relate to the geographical region of their home but rather to a collection of mini communities, for example, teens have mini communities at the Mall, at school and on the INTERNET.

Villages were populated by citizens of all ages including members of immediate and extended family.

Many of today's children do not meaningfully connect with adults of various ages hence are less able to relate to the wisdom, the stability and care which the elderly can provide or model. Children do not learn to respect or to be of assistance to adults within the "village".

In the village the child learned a sense of place and later a sense of responsible citizenship.

All to often today's children live in world of movement. Their home is a place to eat and sleep but not a place to "live." Other children, especially those living in poverty, move from one house or one apartment to another with great frequency not only changing geographical location but also schools, playgrounds, community centres, churches and other human contacts.

In the traditional village people were often of the same ethnic heritage or have lived in proximity with their neighbours for so long that ethnic differences were of minimal importance.

In today's schools children come without the security of the village and mix with people of a vast array of ethnic and cultural diversity. Far too many older children are unprepared and unwilling to handle the stress of this new social milieu. Younger children tend to be "more colour blind."

Counter Example: It is known that students from small semi isolated communities often experience the stress of culture shock when they enter a large multicultural university.

NOTE: We seem to be entering a new age in our society. We have ever increasing numbers of children who have not developed useful, integrative social skills. More seriously they have not developed a sense of community nor a sense of social consciousness.

They have, essentially, lived alone with TV, Video Games, highly competitive, structured play, travel in the family vehicle to disparate mini community activities or have lived in fear within dysfunctional homes or "isolated" urban locations.

They have spent **limited** time developing a range of integrative skills which could be translated into **Authentic Self Esteem.** They therefore rely on purchases to define their personality or to create their happiness. It is little wonder that a number of these individuals will resort to bullying, use of addictive substances or other anti social acts to help define themselves.

CRITICAL CHARACTER QUESTIONS

- Why is it easier to hate than to love?

BRAIN FACT # 62

The amygdala is the brain's early warning system and will initially take a defensive stance whenever threatening or potentially threatening messages are received.

Unless the frontal cortex can intervene and some positive emotional memories can be created the impulsive negative messages will prevail.

◆ Why is it easier to argue against something than to argue for something?

BRAIN FACT # 63

The brain finds it easier to say no than to cognitively create an alternate solution or be supportive of an idea.

◆ Why is it easier to align yourself to a person of the same race, creed or colour, than to befriend a person who differs in any one of the three categories?

BRAIN FACT # 64

The brain most often is less threatened in the presence of elements which are known.

To befriend a person who is different requires one to connect to a new culture which may be at some variance with one's dominant cultural thinking and practices.

◆ Have you noticed, in multi racial schools that kids of same ethnic origins tend to group together? Are they moving to something or away from something?

NOTE: Both actions may be in play.

BRAIN FACT # 65

Since survival is always a key brain objective people may group together for protection.

BRAIN FACT # 66

The brain is lazy and will tend to repeat actions and thoughts which fall within its current realms of meaningfulness.

THE CHANGING SET OF ROLES FOR SCHOOLS

◆ Schools are caught in an array of conflicting social and economic pressures. These include, global migration, multiplicity of students from radically different racial and religious traditions PLUS a constant cry from certain pressure groups about the costs of education.

◆ Some urban and nearly all rural schools are dealing with children who travel great distances from many "pseudo villages." The belief that there are efficiencies to be found in large schools amplifies the problems identified above PLUS bussing students is expensive, very time consuming and inhibits student interaction in "out of class" time activities

◆ Other than attending school these children have limited reasons to socially connect with each other. There is limited opportunities to build new social relations or break down barriers that have existed for many generations.

◆ Many of the students still participate on local community sports teams where there exist long standing rivalries which further support non integration. In addition, less affluent parents of students who live great distances from the school may not be able to support their children's participation in after class activities with either money or their presence at these after school activities.

COMPETITIVE, ADVERSARIAL NATURE OF OUR SOCIETY

NOTE: Our society has evolved into being highly competitive, adversarial, individually focussed even to the point of being openly combative. We have focussed more on simple means of assessing our own values than learning new ways to value group strengths and success.

This results in:

1. Society demanding that our schools should be safe without exploring the reasons for the lack of safety and investing in solutions that deal with the issues as well as the results.

   Zero tolerance programs frequently punished the wrong people, are unevenly administered, released troubled and troublesome students onto the streets to interact with others of the same mind set without programs of remediation and re-integration to the school environment. They placed great pressure on school administrators to appear to be delivering a sound action plan. In fact it was often a "Catch and Release" program that was full of action but devoid of resolution.

2. Schools are experiencing an increase in the number of dysfunctional children whose behaviours are environmentally created. These children are suffering from social and other developmental deficits.

   NOTE: The word deficit is used deliberately to convey the concept that their brains are under developed to meet the challenges expected of their age group. In order to have success these children must have the opportunity to "catch up" on that they have missed.

   Reading programs are a good start but if the child's ability to read is limited to word recognition and not thought formation the program will have limited value.

In addition, the child's fears, angers and anxieties must be addressed. A stressed, angry and overly fearful child will not be able to develop the necessary social skills so essential to becoming a responsible citizen.

3. Schools are performing functions which were previously the realm of the family, the extended family, the church and community at large.

    The faculties of education within our universities must add significant course work for aspiring teachers, counsellors and administrators on the necessity and means to develop working relationships with all the external stakeholders.

    The school is not a factory producing widgets but it is part of the biomass which is the community at large. In order for this biomass to reach its potential there is no room for any of its parts to be mouthing declarative statements such as "It is not my problem," "It is not in my jurisdiction." There is a need for a new level of community and school leadership. There are no simple answers.

4. A great many parents live beyond an easy commute to the school. This, they will tell you, makes it difficult to connect with the school. This may be true because many parents are financially limited in what they can or can not do.

    But there is also an emotional distance factor. Emotional distance speaks to the issue of intrinsic motivation. **If one is intrinsically motivated to be somewhere, geographical distance is usually not the problem.**

    *NOTE: A teacher reported another scenario. She worked in an **alternative school** which serviced a small city and some surrounding communities. The parents are unconnected to this school. In many ways there was less connection to this school than the parents have to a neighbourhood big box store.*

There are a number of challenges here:

*   For most of the children and parents this is not their school of choice.

*   These children are attending this alternative school because they had either or both academic and social problems at their previous school or schools.

*   These parents may be quite frustrated with their child's performance and may have given up.

*   Other parents may intuitively realize but will not externally admit that they have contributed to their child's lack of success.

*   School staff and parents have not found a way to communicate with each other so that they can jointly work towards the child's success.

*   Parents experienced similar problems, as students, as their children are now having and now relive their angst every time they make contact with a school official.

*   Physical and economic distance may be significant factors for non participation.

RELATIONSHIP BUILDING, CONNECTING WITH PARENTS

Suggestions and solutions

*   Analyse your school, home and community relationships.

*   Restructure the schools administrative responsibilities so that each principal and vice principal devote a certain amount of time to relationship building and school-community development.

*   In the case of the alternative school mentioned above, it is necessary to visit the homes. Usually the teacher or a special educational consultant who works closely with the teacher are best suited. Determine what other services need to be provided?

CHAPTER 16

THE BULLY AND THE CROWD
ie. BYSTANDERS

Frequently when a suicide occurs as a result of bullying the press become activated on the issue for a short period of time. If it becomes clear that the bullying activity was very public the question is asked, "Why did other children, other students not intervene?" The answer, that often comes from some expert, is that bystanders must be encouraged to be socially responsible and take the necessary action to prevent such the bullying from occurring. Oh, if it was so easy.

A key goal is to increase the child's sense of:

- Social responsibility through an increase of **social consciousness and an increased level of social conscience.**

- The **harm being done** in an act of bullying.

- **Empowerment.**

- External support from other children and adults.

- Being **skilled in problem solving** at some level.

  NOTE: It is not easy for students to leap into the fray when they are under skilled in so many ways. In addition, groups have an synergy which often over rides the contributions of individual members.

In this chapter I want to deal with some of the basics about group dynamics specifically as they apply to children-students and then look at how these affect bystanders when ever they encounter bullying.

NOTE: Many bullies are very public when they harm and humiliate their victims. In fact many thrive on their exploits being recognized with applause, or at least, the implied consent of their peers. The victims, in addition to being hurt or publicly humiliated, are further hurt by being seemingly ignored by friends and acquaintances.

GENERAL GROUP DYNAMICS

A group's physical and mental reactions generally fall into one of the following categories of:

- active support of the dominant person.

- tentative intervention.

- uncertainty.

- indifference.

- and on occasion, active intervention.

"State" is also important when considering this topic. What is the group's "state" in terms of:

- social development?

- mental maturity?

- one's personal security (within the group)?

- community standards and values?

- intellectual awareness?

Group dynamic topics

These topics will include group think, inclusive-exclusive groups, administratively or socially established groups, mental maturity, and sub-diffusing personal values.

1. Group Think

   Group think occurs when ever people are assembled for some purpose. It could be the kindergarten class on the play ground, teens in their various clusters in the school or mall or adults in the corporate boardroom. The essence is that the individual gets "swallowed up" by the thought processes of a dominant few or the corporate or community philosophy. Individuals feel that they must support the majority train of thought, even though they have information or values which strongly opposes the "group think," they feel **powerless to contribute.**

Example: Group think was at the core of flawed last minute decision making of the ill fated space shuttle Columbia.

In the case of bullying **group think:**

- Prohibits many individuals from making thoughtful and helpful attempts to intervene.

- May also inhibit students from becoming actively involved in a school program which could make the school a safer place to attend for all.

- May also limit the willingness of responsible adults in both the community and the schools from becoming active in an anti bullying program.

*NOTE: Mob violence is a case of **Group Think** being completely out of control.*

*NOTE: Classroom management techniques can and should teach and continually promote **Positive Group Think** principles. This then **shares** some of the responsibility between the school's adults and the students for productive and safe learning environments.*

Positive "Group Think"

There are six basic thought processes which should be addressed when working with students on this topic.

- The rights of all must be honoured. Everyone should feel empowered to express their opinion or exercise their values.

- The minority cannot be ostracized, shunned or victimized.

- **The minority position must be listened to and acknowledged.**

- Personality differences and personality conflicts must be overridden in the decision process.

- The group decision should be made based upon acceptable social practices and the best possible input available at the moment.

- **Fear and intimidation** can not be tolerated.

2. **The inclusive-exclusive groups.**

   Humans are by nature social beings. Most of us are energized by being in the presence of others and we actively seek out companionship. The level of companionship varies between those who are quite content to have close friendships with a select few and others who feel the need to be interacting with large numbers of people.

- Groups whether large or small can help us form our identity, status, achieve our goals and of course be a great source of personal enjoyment.

- Groups tend to take on their own characteristics. Some are highly exclusionary for reasons of status, entertainment, protection, power and, in the cases where social bullying is involved sheer *bloodymindedness.* These groups seem to have no other purpose but to exclude, taunt, humiliate, exercise control of and, by doing so, provide a power base for one or two individuals. See: *Relationship Bullying.*

  Example: In a middle school a "**group hug**" phenomena emerged. At first it started out with a handful of students but soon grew to some size although only a small percentage of the student body was involved. The principal had to move to break up this activity on grounds that it was blocking traffic flows and was becoming a general nuisance. Some parents got upset and the media became involved by asking "What could be so wrong about hugging?" In reality the group hug was not about universal love and sharing but rather about the public exclusion of certain students.

- When this type of activity occurs in schools many children are forced to the perimeter of the group or even the school's culture. They are in the "out group." It was not a willful decision on their part and the rejection can be emotionally painful and, **now recently discovered, academically crippling**.

NOTE: Students who are shunned, ignored and otherwise ostracized are shown to do less well on standards testing.

- Another subset of the "Outgroup" classification are whose members who feel **driven away** from the central crowd and who join together for mutual support and/or protection. This may lead to gangs or small groups united for the purpose of vengeance.

- Still other students are not **interested** in belonging to a popular group or have given up trying to belong. They may form small subgroups focussed around common interests, personal friendships or they may emotionally drop out of the social scene.

Strategies:

♦ Assess the nature of the community at large with reference to inclusiveness.

♦ In your school try to assess who are the members of the various groups. You can use surveys, socio-grams, focus groups and/or staff brain storming sessions.

♦ Young children need to be engaged in as many group and group building exercises as possible. While these activities are essential for building social consciousness they are absolutely critical for building the affective domains of social conscience.

♦ The use of literature, music, dance, art and sport enables children to gain the cognitive and emotional skills of inclusion.

♦ Employ responsibility activities which will enhance the building of social conscience.

♦ Generate programs and projects whereby students FEEL ownership of the school and an emotional connection to other students.

3. **Administratively or socially established groups.**

It is not uncommon for a school or community to unintentionally establish conditions whereby groups are formed for all the right reasons but over time take on lives of their own which are negative and disruptive.

Example: In many schools cheerleaders were chosen, decade after decade, for their physical appearance, skin colour that matched that of the majority of the students and "femininity." As cheerleading became increasingly athletic new selection criteria emerged and this has caused considerable consternation among those who thought they should be the chosen few and even their mothers who had been cheerleaders in the past.

NOTE: Determine if there are features of your school culture which foster such groupings. Consider student subcultures which may coalesce around race, academics, age, sports, music, creed, economics or some other factor.

Example: One school decided that it was going to be a "hockey school." Their program involved enrolling middle school age boys from a wide catchment area and providing them with top quality coaching. The problem in the school was that the "hockey clique" had little common with most of the local students and felt they were special. They removed themselves from the general student body and became a problem from both academic and behavioural perspectives.

4. **Lack of mental maturity**

Much has been written about the popularity of the school bully. For a number of reasons many a school bully does seem to have a higher profile amongst students than is healthy for the bully or the other students.

Some of the reasons include an ever present element of fear. In addition adolescent children are struggling to determine their own self identity, their social skills and values. They are often unlikely or unwilling to assess the bully beyond some superficial attributes.

It is not until these children progress in their social maturation that they will be able to better analyse the behaviour of the school bully for what it is and distance themselves physically and emotionally from him or her. This not easy for them. In fact many adults can get caught up in the **smoothness of a politically astute, gladhanding bully.**

NOTE: A school in Chicago made a deliberate effort to counter this by including abstract thinking activities in all aspects of the curriculum. The levels of complexity of the thought processes were appropriate to the ages of the children. The outcome was a greater skill level in academic problem solving and far fewer student confrontations on the playgrounds and in the classrooms.

5. **Inability to establish and stay with socially acceptable values.**

Groups can submerge or overwhelm an individual's value systems. Teens can get caught up with the group attitude of "Ah come on, every one else is doing it". The "it" could be teen sex, drugs, driving while impaired and more.

As children become more comfortable with their self identity including authentic self esteem they become more willing to risk being rejected by others over issues of values. This is a true test of courage. **However, they need your support which includes the behaviours you model.**

THE PRESENT BUT SEEMINGLY UNINVOLVED POPULATION

Barbara Coloroso has referred to these students as Bystanders and some of Rosalind Wiseman's "Wannabees" could also be included in that group of people who are standing on the periphery of the bullying action oscillating between becoming involved in a negative manner, wondering if they should do something positive, being afraid of doing anything and ignoring the entire event.

In reality they are involved in the bullying activity because they are doing nothing to help the victim.

Much has been made about the need for bystanders to jump into the fray by taking direct or indirect action.

Indeed it could be a powerful force but, let us try a get a better understanding of the position of the bystander from the perspective of personal safety, social responsibility, social consciousness, cognitive awareness, "group think", peer pressure and feeling secure about the school's policies and the actions of pertinent officials.

Types of Bystanders

There are at least four general types of bystanders.

1. **Bully Support Group:** This group is cheering the bully on. In fact they may even take an occasional swipe at the victim, form a tight circle to prevent the victim from escaping or act as sentinels to warn the bully of approaching authorities. The rationale for their actions may range from being friends of the bully, becoming emotionally engaged in this "blood sport", feeling that is safer to support the bully than to be seen as being in opposition or not having sufficient social consciousness or awareness to recognize the seriousness of the incident.

   These individuals may also become the unofficial enforcers for the bully and may intimidate other children from reporting incidents or assisting the victim. If the bullying incident has racial overtones it is likely that members of this group will be of the same racial background as the bully.

2. **The Want to Support the Victim Group:** This group stands by and observes the bullying activity and within their "hearts and minds" know that they should do something to help the victim. But they are caught in a quandary. What should they do? What can they do? What might the consequences to themselves if they do take action?

   Example: A vice principal came upon a situation where a student was being severely beaten by a bully. As soon as the bully was made aware that the VP was approaching he ran but at least one of his friends stayed at the scene. The VP asked some friends of the victim what had happened and when they began to report the incident they were taunted (with the intent to intimidate) by the friend of the bully who called them "rats."

   The VP's first action was to very forcibly inform the victim's friends that what they were doing was socially responsible, necessary and courageous. He got their story and then began a **series of sessions** with the bully and his "friend."

   Example: When I am doing workshops on this topic I often ask the participants to think back to a time when they were in their early teens and what it was like to be caught in this situation. They report that it was a tough time and most are embarrassed to report that they often did nothing.

3. **Those who take positive, supportive action:** (We would like all bystanders to belong to this group.)

   These individuals are often blessed with certain skills, size or status within the student body. The essential ingredient is that these individuals possess a high levels of social consciousness and social conscience. They not only see it as their duty to interact, they also feel a great deal of empathy for the victim and they have certain assets.

   - Physical size can also be an asset. The bigger the person the more likely the bully and his/her supporters will take heed.

     *NOTE: I have also witnessed persons of smaller stature be equally effective by use of their voice. They speak clearly with force and authority. They command attention by not wavering or giving the appearance of uncertainty. **They are assertive, not aggressive.***

   - Programs of awareness and responsibility can be delivered to students and by students. We cannot ever assume that students are fully cognizant of the harm and damage caused by acts of bullying.

   - Conflict resolution and mediation skills can be of value as the person knows the right questions to ask and the manner to re-direct responses.

   - They know the process for reporting incidents and know that their actions will be treated quickly and professionally.

   - Lastly student leaders may be able and willing to use their status to intervene and promote "in school" programs.

NOTE: A school district has recently made it a policy that bystanders "MUST REPORT INCIDENTS OF BULLYING OR RISK BEING DISCIPLINED FOR NOT DOING SO."

The questions that must be addressed are as follows. What training has been provided to students so that they know what bullying is but also know that they have a responsibility to act and the means to do so? What **immediate** actions will be taken by school officials? Are the school officials developing and delivering student growth programs so that students understand the nature of bullying, are better able to assess their own interactions with others and are less likely to provide moral support to the bully? Are the staff within the school sufficiently trained to appropriately and quickly respond to incidents of bullying?

NOTE: Without the proper structure being in place the bystander is uncomfortably caught between two bullies.

NOTE: The school must have a program in place which will minimize bullies retaliating against people who report on their behaviours.

4. **The Uninvolved Group:** These individuals are cognitively and emotionally detached from any incidents of bullying. "Its none of my business". "As long as no one bothers me, I am not concerned."

NOTE: "Hey, It is Not My Problem."

This is all too often the reason for turning one's head and walking away. Its not my:

- Neighbourhood
- School
- Friend(s)
- Responsibility
- Neck

The bully is likely to see this lack of concern as support for his or her actions and the victim feels further abandoned.

General mitigating factors which inhibit bystanders from taking action.

- Victims are often seen as "losers" and to intervene on behalf of a victim can be detrimental to ones social standing. Somewhat analogous to the irrational fear of lepers.

- Peer pressure can be far more influential than the edicts of school officials and other adults. This is especially true for adolescent students.

- Many students do not feel that adults will act appropriately should they report an incident of bullying.

- The still growing child-adolescent brain is much more concerned with personal safety and well being and self identity than the welfare of others.

- Many students have limited ability to empathize with another's suffering.

- Some children have difficulty distinguishing between telling and reporting.

- Children may not recognize the harm being caused to the victim.

- **"Mob rule," "group think," popularity of the aggressor** are difficult matters for students to deal with when an incident of aggression or bullying is taking place.

Strategies for creating a bystander response program successful.

- Train all staff so that they can take quick and decisive action when a bystander reports an incident.

- Train all students, with age relevant programs, on the nature of bullying, the effects of bullying and means by which they can increase the safety of the school through a variety of interventions. The repeated use of drama, informed guests, stories within the literature, physical education are very useful. **Remember, once is not enough!**

- Create a "STATE" within the school which emphasizes mutual respect. This means that all adults and students within the school speak about and model respect for each other.

  *NOTE: Respect, in the long run, is more than good manners, acceptance of others, being willing to help others succeed etc. These can be taught, enforced and even committed to rote memory. But unless the individuals are able to **accept the rules of living in a civil society at a positive emotional level** they may only comply to the rules when an adult is watching or when it is otherwise advantageous to do so.*

NOTE: Even a sociopath is capable and skillful at blending into social groups, families or an individual's life when it is to his/her advantage to do so. Most con men are incredibly "smooth" and will use this smoothness as a major tool when committing a scam.

- Cooperative learning environments not only increase children's potential to learn subject material effectively it also gives children additional social skills including the ability to value the worth of others.

- Group activities such as peace circles, communication circles are valuable means to help adults and students safely share their thoughts and feelings.

- Programs such as peer mediation, conflict resolution, restorative justice and peace making are essential parts of a school community program. But these are not the only programs that should be followed.

SPECIFIC COUNTER OR REMEDIATION STRATEGIES

*NOTE: It is important to remember that all too frequently children who are bullying or who are supporting the bullies are not able to either **recognize their behaviour** for what it truly is or the harm it is causing others. One cannot operate on the **assumption that even a well designed and implemented proactive program will reach all the students**. Therefore, it is necessary that direct intervention be taken. See also: Confronting the bully. See: Chapter 29.*

1. Bully Support Group:

- Determine the critical factors which are linking the bully and the bystanders.

    NOTE: Some of the common ones are, race, academic performance or lack there of, team or gang affiliation, homophobia or gender discrimination. In some cases the bystanders are being rewarded with material gifts.

    Example: A school bully is the son of a prominent person in a mid sized city. Aside from his own improper behaviour he often has his friends carry out bullying activity at his behest. His friends are rewarded with passes to games, time and related privileges at the family lakeside cottage and the opportunity to ride in a really cool vehicle.

- Since these bystanders are every bit as culpable as the bully they must be dealt with as if they were bullies themselves. Meet repeatedly with the bystanders and address your concerns. Focus on those aspects which are seen as positive attributes and use these to try to over ride their negative behaviour.

    NOTE: Use reflective discipline techniques.

- If gangs are involved, outside assistance from the police or other local agencies should also be utilized. Furthermore, students need to understand that they could be charged with being accessaries to a crime.

- If the members of this group are adolescents it may be helpful to work at having them project themselves into the future. The focus here is have them think beyond their immediate wants to what they may want five or more years down the road. See: Appendix V.

    NOTE: Mentors and role models from the community can be enlisted. Supported and monitored work placement can be beneficial. The later has less clout if the students are from wealthy families.

- Work with them in the area of assuming personal responsibility and determining socially responsible ways to be cool. See: Appendix IV.

2. Want to Support the Victim Group:

- These children are caught in a conundrum based on fear, inability to access one or more responsible adults, peer pressure, an inability to fully appreciate the seriousness of the situation but still have instinctive desire to help.

- Make sure that every student knows how to report an incident.

- Ensure the students that action will be taken. **Students will feel betrayed if nothing happens.**

- Include the concepts of responsible citizenship in as many aspects of the curriculum as possible. This includes building social consciousness within the classroom and trying to develop a high level of social conscience.

- These children need to know that their courageous action is appreciated both by the victim, the victim's parents, the school and the community at large.

3. Those who take positive, supportive action:

The support these children need is fourfold. They need:

- Continuous assurance that the school officials are acting responsibly and skillfully when incidents of bullying are reported or when these children intervene.

- To feel that they are essential members of the school team and that the school officials are not off loading responsibilities onto them.

- They need to feel appreciated and not used.

- The opportunity to continue to increase their skill base in leadership, conflict resolution and mediation.

4. The Uninvolved Group:

Our society is overpopulated with children and adults who choose to remain blind to the needs of others. Examples include, people who grieve alone without the support of their neighbours. People who will step over drunks on the sidewalk. The politician who ignores the plight of the homeless or the needs of single parents on social assistance.

In contrast, there is the "Lady Bird" girl in Winnipeg, Canada who has raised thousands of dollars and considerable awareness for the homeless in the city. She was moved to action when she saw a homeless man climbing into a dumpster in search of food. Her actions are so outstanding that she has been featured in the press, radio and TV. She has spoken to influential bodies and before the Prime Minister. Why is she so newsworthy? The answer is because she is different and she is concerned. And that is scary, only because her social consciousness far exceeds many of the leaders of our governments.

The themes of children and adults having increased social awareness, increased social consciousness and increased social conscience run throughout this book because a mutually involved society is a healthy society.

Possible solutions for students include:

- Increased opportunities to become engaged in the school beyond academic pursuits. This could include taking care of the classroom plants, animals and fish.

- Opportunities to work with children who are in need of extra attention.

- These children might be encouraged to participate in fund raising activities for social causes, becoming involved in one of the various clubs within the school, volunteering in personal care homes, day care centres or soup kitchens etc.

NOTE: There are schools which give credits for volunteer activities which are overseen by school authorities.

BUILDING RESPECT: SOME TEACHING STRATEGIES

- **Talking Sticks** are a wonderful aboriginal custom, which are used as a means of insuring just and impartial council meetings. Holding the Talking Stick, allows each speaker, in turn, to speak uninterrupted. According to Aboriginal tradition, he who holds the Talking Stick has the power of words. Only he/she can speak, while holding the stick; other members of the circle must remain silent.

NOTE: The speaker should not forget that the Talking Stick was sacred. If he cannot honour the Talking Stick with his words, he should refrain from speaking, so he will not dishonour himself.

- **Respecting Group Interaction:** The rules of procedure such as Robert's "Rules of Order" should be used at all student meetings to help students learn how to incorporate fairness and procedure into their deliberations.

- **Respecting the Game.** "Respect the Game" is not telling you to behave in a "sporting" manner, whatever that might be. It's not about telling you what to do at all. **"Respect the Game"** is just a reminder of what you already know, school athletics are important and valuable. But it is the game that is always worthy of respect. And when people involved in a game treat each other badly, disrupt play, or generally behave in a manner unworthy of the game itself, they are devaluing the game. Perfecting one's skills and observing the rules are critical to respecting the game.

- **Respect Yourself.** When you remember this, you don't need anyone else to tell you how to behave. You'll know. You'll act with courtesy, dignity and pride.

NOTE: It is not easy for the children adolescents and even a few adults to accept their role as responsible citizens and always do the right thing. They need training and they need your continuous support.

CHAPTER 17
ATTENTION ISSUES

A child's ability to focus and stay focussed can play a significant role in their **social and academic lives.**

NOTE. Children who have attention problems may feel "out of the loop", may be ostracized, ridiculed, shunned and disciplined more frequently and indiscriminately. They can become targets for bullying.

Children present a variety of attention issues in the classroom, playground and general social interaction.

These may be either inattentive or inattentive and hyperactive and these may or **may not be classic Attention Deficit Disorder or Attention Deficit Hyperactive Disorder.**

Again the causes of these may be genetic, environmental, learned or may be a combination of all three.

WHY IS THIS IMPORTANT?

Children who live with attention deficit problems often have difficulty learning, making and **keeping friends,** "staying out of trouble" or inadvertently drawing **negative** attention to themselves.

Attention problems seriously affect the child's ability to **learn good social skills, feel in control of themselves, be able to act "normally" and also hinder their development of authentic self esteem.**

It is extremely easy for a parent or teacher to assess the inattentive child as lazy, unmotivated or to comment that the child could do better if he/she tried harder. In many jurisdictions, it is very easy for parents, perhaps at the suggestion of a teacher, to have the child placed on medication. **In some cases this is warranted but in others the inattention may require other forms of remediation.**

NOTE: Regardless of the type of remediation used psychotherapy must always be an key component.

WHAT ARE THE POSSIBLE CAUSES OF POOR ATTENTION?

In this section I want to help you to ascertain with a reasonable level of accuracy, the true nature of inattentive behaviour and its source(s).

The following is list of possible reasons why Johnny or Jenny cannot stay "on task" or stay in "one place" for any length of time.

Low blood sugar: Low blood sugar is largely due to two dietary problems misnourishment and malnourishment and perhaps dietary additives.

◆ **Misnourishment** Many, far too many, children have diets which are super saturated with simple sugars and other simple carbohydrates.

For example: Take a walk down the children's breakfast cereal aisle of your local food store and read the labels on the packages. These cereals are sugar saturated.

A surplus of sugar leads to an increase of insulin which in due course depletes the sugar levels leaving the brain "sugar starved." The amygdala is able to capture most of the remaining sugar while the executive management region (frontal cortex) is sugar starved and is unable to do its job of managing the impulsive messages being generated by the amygdala.

NOTE: It is also important to note the amount of sugar in other foodstuffs such a soft drinks, processed foods, food dressings such as tomato sauce, hamburgers, fries, snack foods etc. These are foods of misnourishment.

◆ **Malnourishment.** The second possibility is that children are being **malnourished.** The brain is sugar starved and goes into a panic mode thus increasing the levels of adrenaline and inturn asks the body to extract sugar from body tissue. This child is not only unable to stay focussed but in all likelihood may be edgy or hyper vigilant. In this condition the brain is in survival mode, unable to learn and **prone to unpredictable or aggressive behaviour.**

Diet additives. There are conflicting opinions and research results about the role food colourings and preservatives may play in attention deficit matters. Are these chemicals, getting into the brain? If so what are they doing? How are they interacting with the 70+ neurochemicals already in the brain? With the new technologies available, hopefully there will be further research on this topic. It is unlikely, however, that the food companies will want to pay for this research.

Example: A dried soup mix contains aside from vegetables and vegetable products the following: Monosodium Glutamate, Sodium Caseinate, Titanium Dioxide Colour, Maltodextrin, Disodium Inosinate and Disodium Guanylate, Dipotassium Phosphate, Silicon Dioxide, Mono and Diglycerides, Yellow #5 and Annato Colour. How much of this stuff enters the blood stream and how much passes through the brain-blood barrier. If it does get into the brain how does it interact with the myriad of neural transmitters and proteins which are naturally there. **I don't know! I just hope these things are AOK!**

Allergies: Allergic reactions to certain kinds of foods, chemicals and pollutants may also cause the child to feel ill, tired, uncomfortable, irritable, physically drained and less able to become engaged. Allergic reactions may also cause the person to feel edgy, hypersensitive and depressed.

Low Blood Iron Count: Blood Iron is critical to the movement of oxygen to all parts of the body. Since the brain utilizes 20% of the bloods oxygen supply in order to function at an optimum level it is essential that the Blood Iron Count be within an acceptable range.

NOTE: Studies have shown that teenage girls may be at additional risk to experience learning and behavioural problems due to low Blood Iron levels.

Sleep deprivation: Too many of our students are appearing in school with moderate to severe cases of sleep deprivation. This plays itself out in at least three ways.

1. The person is lethargic and may even fall asleep in class.

2. The person cannot recall information because sleep deprivation impairs memory building and memory recall.

3. Lack of sleep causes increased levels of adrenaline and noradrenaline resulting in the person to be **hyper vigilant, restless and over sensitive to any stimulation perceived as threatening.**

Dehydration: Brains which are running low on water operate at a slower pace. This may lead people to believe that the student is inattentive. Coffee and many soft drinks are diuretics and although the student believes he/she is consuming adequate amounts of fluids the body is expelling fluids at a greater rate than is acceptable for good brain function.

Stress: Children who are stressed are less able to focus or be able to stay calm. Stress raises the adrenaline and noradrenaline levels in the body and brain. **PTSD is a severe form of stress and anxiety.**

Depression: Although stress may lead to depression not all persons experiencing stress will become depressed. The brains of persons suffering depression are over stimulated, usually from excessive internal messaging. There is so much happening in their brains that they have difficulty focussing on external stimulation or on matters that are not highly personal. **Persons suffering depression especially children, are prone to outbursts of anger and physical aggression.**

Caution: Psycho stimulants are normally not be prescribed to persons suffering from depression.

Brain injury: Children who have suffered head injuries to the front and/or temporal lobes have less capacity to manage emotional impulses, mood changes and anger. They are also less likely to be able to anticipate consequences. **Remember not all "Shaken Babies" die.**

Fetal Alcohol Syndrome(FAS), Fetal Alcohol Spectrum Disorder (FASD), Fetal Alcohol Effects (FAE): Virtually all Fetal Alcohol Spectrum Disordered children will have considerable difficulty paying attention, staying on task, creating and recalling memories and living beyond the moment.

NOTE: One category who are frequently mis-diagnosed are those who have FAE. They do not present physical clues, even though their brains can be as severely underdeveloped as other fetal alcohol affected children.

NOTE: The damage covers a broad spectrum of severity, is non reversible and is totally preventable.

Prenatal exposure to Nicotine and other Tobacco Chemicals: The blood within the fetus's brain has been found to have nicotine concentrations up to 15X the nicotine concentration in the mothers blood. This increases the level of hyper vigilance within the baby's brain, reduces the child's ability to experience pleasure and lessons child's ability to become intrinsically motivated. Because of neural adaptation many of these brains are vulnerable to future addiction problems.

Postnatal exposure to Second Hand Smoke. *(See above):* Note: New research reveals that men who smoke as few as 20 cigarettes a day increased their chances of erectile dysfunction by 24%. This has nothing to do with the child except that if more men realized this and more men stopped smoking this would enhance the cleanliness of their children's environment and their overall brain performance.

Mother's Heightened Pre-natal Stress: An elevated level of adrenaline within the mother's blood stream may cause the fetus cum child to be over vigilant or super sensitive to external messages. These babies tend to have greater problems settling.

The Child is Naturally Kinesthetic: These children, especially young boys, are often mis-diagnosed as being ADHD. It is important to check the child's history and document the nature of his activities including hobbies, kinesthetic skills and periods whereby the child remained focussed for long periods of time.

NOTE: It is also important to try to capture the child's learning style by the use of kinesthetic learning activities.

CHILD MAY BE ADD OR ADHD

Classic ADD – Attention Deficit Disorder, (Inattentive behaviour)

More and more evidence is pointing toward a genetically induced condition where dopamine is quickly transported away from the synapses in the striatum. The striatum is responsible for, among other things, the screening incoming sensory messages and activating the frontal cortex. **An under performing striatum may leave the frontal cortex under stimulated and unable to focus.**

Classic ADHD – Attention Deficit Hyperactive Disorder: Again the brains of persons afflicted with this condition are showing underactivity on brain SPECT scans. The diagnosis is essentially the same as for ADD except there appears to be a greater amount of transporter gene activity with these individuals.

NOTE: See: www.amenclinic.com

Basic facts about ADD/ADHD students.

NOTE: Many ADD students could be described as having EDD. (Easily Distracted Disorder is not a defined disorder but is stated here to help the reader understand a major problem many of the children experience.)

♦   Most have difficulty establishing short term memory due to an inability to stay with the material long enough for the brain to process it to another level.

   *NOTE: These brains tend to respond to far more input messages than normal with "**many many**" things assigned equal values of "importance."*

♦   Most have great difficulty with organization because they have great problems with priority and sequence.

♦   Most have difficulty starting an assignment. Essay assignments and essay exam questions are especially frustrating.

♦   Stress magnifies the attention problems an ADD student has in the classroom.

♦   Sleep deprivation, lack of nourishment and other factors mentioned above generally affects the ADD/ADHD child more than others.

   NOTE: See: Attention Strategies Chapter 24

CHAPTER 18

OPPOSITIONAL DEFIANT DISORDER (ODD)

A NON-CONSCIOUSLY DEVELOPED SURVIVAL RESPONSE

ODD is a serious and chronic personality disorder which is characterized by **explosive anger, verbal aggressiveness, a tendency to bother others, a confrontational attitude** particularly to adults and a disregard for the feelings of others.

Conditions: ODD

- May be non-consciously used by the child as a defensive response.

- Is largely seen as an environmentally induced disorder. Contributing factors include abuse, stress, ADHD, PTSD and an overactive cingulate gyrus.

- ODD is equally distributed between the genders.

- Often co-morbid with ADHD and a precursor to Conduct Disorder (CD).

Symptoms

- Frequent losing of one's temper. Easily annoyed and/or angered by others. **"They tend to have a very short fuse."**

- Aggressively arguing with adults, defying or refusing adult's requests or defying rules.

- Often **appears** to deliberately annoy people.

- Blames others for own mistakes.

- Often angry, resentful, spiteful or vindictive for no apparent reason.

- Swearing and using obscene gestures.

- Generally displays evidence of low authentic self esteem.

- These children are more likely to be noncompliant, defiant, and aggressive.

Environmental Contributing Factors

- Single teenage parents.

- The stress that single parents and parents living in poverty experience may cause them to use harsh, inconsistent parenting practices.

- Dysfunctional or under functional homes include those with alcoholism, violence, depression, teenage parents and frequent changes in family constellation. (Often due to transient males.)

- Parents at all economic levels who emotionally neglect, abuse or excessively control their child's development.

- Fathers who hold their spouse in distain and/or are highly punitive towards their children.

- Persistent high adrenaline levels which may be caused by:

  - Excessive viewing of violent TV.

  - Physical, sexual and emotional abuse.

  - PTSD or anxiety disorders.

  - ADHD and an overactive cingulate gyrus.

  - Inconsistent discipline.

  - Poor school performance.

- Some children who have suffered strep throat may develop ODD (See: *PANDAS on the INTERNET*).

- Approximately 50% of ADHD sufferers also have ODD. It is estimated that approximately 12% of all children have ODD or ADHD or both.

- That girls who have been sexually abused are also candidates for ODD.

- Disorganized bonding with parents.

*NOTE: Most ODD children have been beaten by their parent(s) or surrogate parent and are confused when teachers don't use the same level of punishment. They may see **teachers as soft targets** for their misbehaviour.*

NOTE: A version of ODD was brought to my attention, the student is oppositional only with female teachers. (The boy's father treats the boy's mother with derision. A learned form of ODD?)

NOTE: Inflexible teachers will likely clash with ODD students on a regular basis.

CHAPTER 19

CONDUCT DISORDER: KIDS WAITIING FOR JAIL

Conduct Disorder (CD) is a serious, persistent, chronic, socially disruptive behaviour pattern exhibiting a lack of social conscience resulting from a combination of: specific genetics, brain damage and/or environmentally induced brain trauma and learned behaviours.

NOTE: Untreated CD may lead to adult Anti Social Personality Disorder, aka Socio-Path or Psycho-Path.

*NOTE: Low social conscience refers to the person being **unable or less able to emotionally connect** to other people.*

CONTRIBUTING FACTORS

- Severe underdevelopment of and/or damage to the frontal and temporal lobes.

- Genetic predisposition towards violence, depression, alcoholism and low pleasure zone activity.

- Neural transmitter imbalance and overactive amygdala.

- Childhood abuse, environmentally induced genetic damage.

- ADHD, ODD, prenatal exposure to nicotine and stress.

- Traumatic life experiences generating deep implicit and explicit memories.

CO-EXISTING CONDITIONS

The most common co-existing factors are ADHD and Oppositional Defiant Disorder(ODD).

Other coexisting conditions include mood and thought disorders, PTSD, substance abuse, learning problems, depression, narcissism, low adrenaline levels, weak language skills, anxieties and phobias and in some situations even schizophrenia.

*NOTE: Conduct Disordered persons tend to have a very "positive" sense of self. This may due to narcissism or a psychotic sense of self. They operate without guilt or shame and feel justified in their actions. **Their extreme sense of self should not be considered as Authentic Self Esteem.***

EXAMPLES OF THE BEHAVIOURS

The Diagnostic and Statistical Manual of Mental Disorders (DSM) categorizes conduct disorder behaviours into four main groupings:

Aggression to people and animals

- Bullies, threatens, or intimidates others. *

- Initiates physical fights. *

- Uses a weapon to cause serious harm to others.

- Physically cruel to animals.

- Steals while confronting a victim. *

- Forces someone into sexual activity. *

Deliberate Acts of Destruction

◆ This includes fire setting, vandalism to school or other property, stealing and trashing cars, destroying another student's school work* etc.

Deceitfulness or theft

◆ This includes, forgery, shoplifting, "conning another", break and entry, fraud* and lying.*

Serious violations of rules

◆ This includes repeated "stealing away" from home, running away from home or care provider, truancy from school, failure to obey conditions of probation etc.

Denotes CD behaviours which are the behaviours of many bullies.

NOTE: Individuals with CD are highly inclined to engage in self destructive activities such as, unsafe sex, alcohol abuse, smoking, use of street drugs, joyriding at high speeds, petty to serious criminal activity and more.

EARLY AND ADOLESCENT ONSET – CONDUCT DISORDER

Childhood-Onset Type

This is deemed the most serious because the behaviours and mental processes have been emotionally acquired, "set in place" at a time when the child had a low level of cognitive ability.

Adolescent-Onset Type

Is deemed to be less serious not because of the nature of the transgressions but because there exists greater likelihood the child will respond to cognitive psychotherapy.

Readers may wish to refer to a DSM manual.

Frequent Educational problems include:

◆ Has limited attention spans, low levels of communications skills.

◆ Has poor reading skills.

◆ Unwilling to risk or commit to learning.

◆ Limited ability to work in groups.

◆ Finds school to be irrelevant.

◆ Limited parental support for treatment and homework issues.

◆ Thinks in the immediate.

◆ Over focussed on self.

◆ Distrusts adults in the school environment.

◆ Is supersensitive to suggestions that personal behaviour "needs work."

◆ Increases level of tension in the classroom by hitting, taunting and swearing.

◆ Makes vulgar comments to teachers.

◆ May physically attack a teacher.

◆ Insensitive to feelings of classmates.

◆ Often experiences low grades, suspension or expulsion. Very high dropout rate.

◆ Is an extremely dangerous school yard bully.

NOTE: It is important to recognize those problems which are symptomatic of ADHD or ODD.

CHAPTER 20

INSTANT AND DELAYED GRATIFICATION

INSTANT GRATIFICATION (IG)

We live in a world of "the present." As a population we want all our needs met right here and right now. The advertising media promotes instant happiness and instant gratification. We also have instant potatoes.

Parents give their children toys and games, often of poor quality and questionable value just to stop them from whining.

NOTE: Without showing disrespect to teachers and other administrators who attend my workshops, many come hoping that I will have a quick solution to their problems with bullies. I know why they want this because they are at their wits end dealing with this problem. I would love to be able to do that but reality is reality.

Examples of IG from the adult world.

Feeling edgy – take a pill, have a drink.

Want to feel happy – take several pills, drink more.

Want a nice car – get a loan.

Having some problems in a relationship – split.

Want instant salvation – find the right church.

Boss gets on your case – quit.

Examples of IG from the child's world.

Want some candy – demand it, create a fuss or **steal it.**

Don't like another kid – hit him.

Can't play a game to your satisfaction – quit.

Can't play a musical instrument – give up.

A subject in school is hard – don't try.

Feeling down – find some drugs.

Want friends – buy them.

The research on instant and delayed gratification flows from a study of 4 year old children. Each was stationed at a small table with a marshmallow placed just at the outer limits of the child's "easy reach." Each child was told that the adult would leave the room and when the adult returned to the room all those who had not eaten their marshmallow would get a second one. **Approximately 35% could not wait.**

What might have been the background of those children who could not wait? Some might have:

- Had ADD or ADHD.

- Been otherwise impulsive.

- Been hungry.

- Limited trust in adults as a result of poor emotional bonding with one or more parents.

- Limited sense of time or the future.

- Been conditioned to believe that they would get the second marshmallow by other means.

NOTE: It is interesting that the mental processes which had been genetically and environmentally positioned and learned in the first few years of life had long term affects on future behaviour.

*NOTE: The longitudinal studies revealed that most of these persons who **couldn't wait** lead unfulfilling, unhealthy and unsuccessful lives including increased problems with drug addictions. See: Addictions.*

DELAYED GRATIFICATION (DG)

There is an old story about a perky young man with a guitar slung over his shoulder. He stops in Greenwich Village to ask a hippie the following question. "Hey, how can I get to Carnegie Hall?" The hippie looks up at the young man and says **"Practice man, practice."**

One of the greatest challenges we face in life regardless of vocations or other responsibilities is to accept the value of delayed gratification. It is so natural for us to want instant success, a problem to get solved right now, our golf game to improve and home life to be like the model family on TV. (Simpsons not included). The reality is that brain change is slow and incremental.

The results of the longitudinal study revealed that about two thirds of the children exhibited delayed gratification. As adults they were more positive in their approach to the world and others, they were able to self motivate, persevere in times of adversity and pursue their goals. They had more successful marriages, higher average incomes, greater career satisfaction and healthier and more fulfilling lives.

NOTE: The approximate 66% relates somewhat to the 55-60% of children who formed emotionally secure relationships with one or more parents. My guess is that these are essentially the same people but the studies have not, to my knowledge, been cross referenced.

Building delayed gratification. It is important to:

♦ Work at building trust.

♦ Stress skill development and provide constant feedback. (As the child matures they will be able to self motivate with greater frequency and effect.)

♦ Teach the child how to learn.

♦ Provide increased coaching and mentoring.

♦ Help the child develop a useful concept of time particularly, the concept of the future.

♦ Teach the child how to budget and save money for items of significant importance.

♦ Take the child to workplaces, colleges and universities or similar places of skill development to help them start the process of career planning.

♦ Teach the child impulse management skills.

♦ Ensure the child has had opportunity to learn the skills of social consciousness.

CHAPTER 21

ANGER AND ANGER MANAGEMENT

SOME ANGER FACTS

1. A neurological explanation of extreme anger would be that the **Amygdala** becomes so overstimulated that it completely overpowers the Frontal Lobes.

2. The degree of anger rests with the delicate balance that exists between the controlling frontal lobes and the impulsive amygdala.

3. Even though the frontal lobes are being overpowered, it appears that the right frontal lobe is functioning slightly better than the left frontal lobe. This is observed as angry statements are often much more general or global. "She/he **always** does.....," "I can **never** count on him/her...." We seldom hear statements such as **seven out of eleven** times he/she does the following.

4. It is difficult holding a conversation with angry people because the cognitive portions of the brain are less dominant at the moment since the reactionary areas are taking charge. So when you tell some one to "Cool down" their verbal response may be "Make Me" or "Stick it your Ear."

5. When a person is angry their body is overstimulated with adrenaline and cortisols, their heart is racing, their muscles are full of glycogen, their hippocampus is shutting down and basically the brain-body is a fight or flight machine.

   NOTE: It is quite possible that anger is damaging your heart which is serious enough, however an extreme bout of anger may result in you seriously hurting or even killing another person. Road rage is an example of anger taking hold of a person and absolutely refusing to let go. Very, very dangerous stuff.

ANGER MANAGEMENT STRATEGIES

1. You have to get the **adrenaline and noradrenaline out of the system** and get the brain, heart and muscles back to normal. A physical or a relaxation exercise is usually a good first step.

*NOTE: Hitting a punching bag is **not recommended** as many angry people are also violent people. An angry person is usually unable to distinguish between a punching bag and another person's head.*

2. **Taking Stock** When the person has "cooled down" it may be a wise thing to start doing some analysis of the situation.

   a. Getting angry is a human emotion. Everything doesn't go right all the time. How often does the person "Fly off the Handle? Once in "Blue Moon," no big deal, two or three times a day "Looks like a problem."

   b. Help the person develop a "First Aid" anger management plan so that when he/she feels anger creeping up they do something to keep things in perspective. For example they might: do deep breathing, take a fast walk, have a long drink of cold water, count to ten, walk away etc.

c. Determine the issues or triggers which are causing the person to feel anger?

Diet. Too much sugar, coffee, fatty food, too many "nerve settling" drinks, too few glasses of water? Are steroids involved?

Physical health. Is the person getting enough exercise? What is their blood pressure? Are they over weight?

Mental Health. Is the person stressed or suffering from depression?

Daily events. Meetings? Traffic? Certain people? Finances? Relationships? Work?

Miscellaneous. Personal or family illness? Death of a family member or friend? Children's behaviour? And more!

NOTE: The intensity and frequency of these anger messages can, if a system is not in place, leave the brain in a constant state of agitation.

3. Anger management is more than just taking long fast walks, it is rather the ability to be proactive.

a. Determine what is causing the pain.

b. Do something. Seek out that help.

   NOTE: If the triggers are found in #2, above, then become proactive and find ways which will reduce the impact of those triggers.

c. Many teachers work with children who are prone to anger. A number have developed a level of trust with the children and the children use a coloured card system to let the teacher know how they are feeling. See: *Oppositional Defiant Disorder.*

d. Some teens seem to be angry all the time because their life seems to be happening beyond their control. The anger may be arising from hormonal changes, relationship problems, dependence – independence and general maturation issues.

e. The state of being hyper vigilant may be an inherited quality. For some reason either the genes process too much adrenaline or the level of MAO is too low and hence adrenaline does not become metabolized as rapidly as we would like.

4. **Classroom Strategies.**

   ◆ Monitor your own anger. Monitor your language.

   ◆ Role play anger scenarios in class.

   ◆ Teach children some anger release strategies.

   ◆ Use age appropriate interventions to try to deal with the cause(s) of anger.

   ◆ Help people determine those things that trigger anger.

   ◆ Whenever anger is part of a piece of the curriculum take time to discuss it.

   ◆ Teach children how to handle the anger of losing a game, getting a bad mark etc.

   ◆ Teach some elements of bio-feedback, ie. just by taking your pulse and doing some meditative activity can reduce the heart rate.

   ◆ Think about how you are going to handle the situation the next time you are angry in the classroom.

CHAPTER 22

SETTING THE STAGE FOR CHANGE

In the following chapters we will examine the nature of "brain change," building of social, cognitive and related personal skills which are critical to acceptable functioning within our society.

*NOTE: Specific chapters will be devoted to strategies to help you deal with the issues of ADHD, ODD, Conduct Disorder and of course **bullying**.*

BRAIN FACT # 66

It is estimated that the average adult's brain operates with 500 Trillion synapses +/- 20-25%. The average teenage brain may have 600 Trillion synapses +/- 20-25% of varying degrees of sophistication.

NOTE: A goodly number of teenage synapses are still in the maturation process, new neural networks are being refined and integrated with others to increase the brain's effectiveness to deal with life's daily issues.

BRAIN FACT # 67

The number of synapses in the brain of a child aged 18-24 months is estimated to be 1000 Trillion.

NOTE: It has been suggested by a mathematician that the brain could theoretically possess 10 to the power 800 synapses (or 1 followed by 800 zeros.) But the number we have seems to get us through most of life's challenges.

BRAIN FACT # 68

The brain is incredibly plastic and the potential for growth is virtually unlimited. The power of the brain rests with both the number and maturation of its synapses.

*NOTE: Change will cause the creation of new synapses or enhance the effectiveness of existing synapses or both and further extend the complex integration of neural networks. **Change is real!***

BRAIN CHANGE 101

Very few of us welcome, easily accept or quickly adapt to change because the brain tends to like the status quo. Why not?

From a brain perspective this is not easy, because once the brain has become "wired" to naturally proceed in a particular manner, it wants to stay the course. This is the established or default program. Since it is not possible to delve into the brain and remove/replace or tweak the portion of the brain that is to be changed as one might with a faulty car part. The brain has to **be restructured so that it can act or think differently.**

An oversimplified real life example: Let us say that you have a three bedroom house and you need five bedrooms but you can't afford to buy a five bedroom house you would have to make changes to you existing dwelling. **You can't get a new brain you have to change the one you have.**

In the emotional realm change can be threatening or exhilarating. Change can cause us to worry ourselves into a psychological stalemate or it can challenge us to succeed beyond our wildest expectations.

From a **cognitive perspective** change requires that we act or think differently about things. In order for this to happen we must "rewire" certain sections of the brain.

Education is change

For too long we, as educators, have failed to fully understand that the 3R's, dates in history or the binominal theorem, as important as they are, are the medium for brain growth not the end result. The ultimate goal is to have children cum adults develop brains which will allow them to function effectively in what ever roles they will play within society.

While it is important that each brain has acquired certain academic, technical and social skills, it is perhaps even more important that these brains develop the complex skills of information processing and decision making.

We are not simply accountants, doctors, maintenance personnel, teachers, etc. but we are people who have social responsibilities as parents, friends, spouses, neighbours, sons/daughters, lovers, care givers, income earners, leaders, role models and much more each day of our lives. All of this can become reality only because our brains have changed to meet a multitude of expectations and demands.

Change is a neurobiological process

Whenever change takes place new synapses and new neuro integration links are formed **and/or** old synapses and neuro links become more efficient. However, at the outset, **new neural structures tend to be fragile and easily "lost"** in the vast complexities of the brain unless special attention is paid to their development.

Six Essential Brain Requirements for Change

1. **Repetition:** Since it is not possible to physically remove old habits, it is necessary that you build new habits, and use these over and over until these new neural pathways become the "default" patterns of behaviour or thought.

2. **Coaching:** It is necessary to provide the child with the skills to perform the task or learn something new. Coaching involves establishing challenges, providing incremental technical refinement and giving feedback.

   NOTE: Coaching the techniques of learning can be of inestimable value to almost all students.

3. **Motivation:** Motivation is the positive emotional support to learning something new and the support to overcome fears and other emotional impediments to change.

   Extrinsic motivation is provided by an external source and may include immediate feed back, privileges and rewards including non-monetary rewards to help the child to become excited about their accomplishments.

   NOTE: However, extrinsic rewards especially those which are material in nature can divert the child's focus from learning to paying excessive attention to the reward.

   Intrinsic motivation is the ultimate motivator as this allows the child/cum adult to become emotionally engaged in and be in greater control of the project or process. These internal forces become the drivers that propel a person to success.

   NOTE: Feed back should always be used but as the child becomes increasingly capable of being intrinsically motivated, your feed back may take a less frequent

and different format including a more challenging approach.

NOTE: When giving feedback always avoid using the word BUT.

4. **Replacement:** When deleting one behaviour, another behaviour must be taught.

   It is simply not good enough to say to a child, "I want you to "behave." Many of these children do not have an "automatic default **behave** neuro network." They may not know how to behave, have the cognitive ability to maintain a state of behaving, know what **you mean** by "behave" or have an appreciation of the value of behaving.

   NOTE: Once again it is critical to be conscious of the need to generate an emotional memory which will reinforce and sustain the cognitive growth.

5. **Competitiveness:** Unless the child feels completely defeated, which may include experiencing Learned Helplessness, feeling extremely unworthy or suffering from depression, the child will want to succeed at something. Use brain's natural competitive tendencies, to help the child strive for "Personal Bests." This allows the child to compete with him/herself and record their own growth.

6. **Other Features include:**

   - **Safety** – a brain under stress has limited ability to engage its frontal cortex.

   - **Willingness to Risk** – children or adults who are prepared to take calculated risks will respond to change with confidence.

   - **Small Steps** – incremental change reflects synaptic growth and restructuring of complex neuro pathways. People need time and the opportunity to experience success.

   - **Supporting Emotional States** – the emotional environment must be consistent with the behaviour you wish to have achieved.

   - **Clear and Congruent Input** – acknowledge that the child's language skills may be less well developed than might be expected.

MODEL BEHAVIOUR – USE ROLE MODELS WHERE POSSIBLE

Effectiveness of two training approaches

A: **Effectiveness #1. Telling and Coercing** Keeping the above in mind, consider the effectiveness of the following behavioural change statements.

1. "I told you to **never** do that again."

2. "I want you to change your behaviour."

3. "I want you to conduct yourselves properly in the future."

4. "Behave yourself."

5. "Why **can't** you behave like your brother or sister?"

B: **Effectiveness #2 "High Performance Coaching."** The coach is responsible for:

1. Developing a multifaceted training program which involves repetition, monitoring detail including both improvements in performance and any regression to previous default actions.

2. Directing the person to make incremental improvements which are just beyond the upper edge of the child's current performance level and personal strengths.

3. Providing regular feed back recognizing growth and skill level.

   NOTE: Children with attention issues need immediate feedback.

4. Stressing Personal Bests – competition like evaluation is part of the learning process not the ultimate goal.

5. Assisting the child to gain a sense of being **honestly worthy** by recognizing skill growth and willingness to take calculated risks.

6. Increasingly shift the responsibility for development to the child so that the child becomes the owner of his/her progress.

C: **Focussing on the difference in principles and practices** in Effective practices #1 and #2 above it is easy to see why #2 will get better results than #1.

Bad Behaviour and Remediation Strategies

D: **Why do kids and some adults exhibit bad behaviour. Some of the reasons are:**

1. They don't know any better.

2. They have been rewarded for bad behaviour in the past.

3. They possess poorly developed skills in the areas of social monitoring, social consciousness and social conscience.

4. They are bullies.

5. They have been neglected, abused, are suffering from some mental dysfunction, are intellectually challenged or a combination of the above.

6. They are under performing and have neither the skills or incentive to perform at a higher level.

7. They are gifted and bored.

E: **Elements of basic programs which can be of benefit to a significant proportion of the above individuals.**

1. Identify student strengths. Repeatedly build on these strengths.

2. Modify curriculum, if necessary, to ensure that the student can be competitive with themselves.

3. Stress incremental growth within curriculum.

4. Effectively use challenge and feedback.

5. Coach students on the learning process. **Teach them how to learn.**

6. Teach reading at every level. Most learning disabled students are deficient in reading skills.

   NOTE: Correlations have been found between weak language skills and poor behaviour in school.

7. Use motivational strategies appropriate to the cognitive and emotional development of child.

8. Wherever possible, engage child in a non 3R program eg. athletics, music, drama, art, industrial arts, citizenship, leadership etc. where success may be possible.

9. If necessary, place student in a behaviour modification program which provides the necessary repetition, cognitive and emotional stimulation and clearly identified objectives **and the opportunity to succeed**

10. Spend time and effort on human development activities such as conflict resolution, restorative justice, assertiveness training, playing for enjoyment and inclusion style activities

11. **Build cause and effect, abstract thinking into the teaching process.** Neuro research is showing that children are not able to master abstract thought in a significant manner until about age 15-16. Nevertheless, while it may be too much to expect young children to process complex abstract notions, it is AOK to routinely ask elementary and middle school children Why, Where, When, What and How questions to help them grow beyond their basic concrete thought patterns. You may not get the level of thinking you are aiming for at the outset but perseverance will yield results both in classroom work and in general student behaviour.

    Remember success brings about success. The brain is highly integrative and learning one set of skills may transfer to learning other skills. Furthermore, the emotional impact of having success can be sufficiently motivational to lead the child to take calculated risks which will lead to new growth.

Key Individuals, Structures and Practices

F: Who are the key individuals in this change process. In essence this is a 24/7 series of activities.

NOTE: Training may be necessary for many included in the following list.

1. Teachers and Parents.

2. Educational assistants and resource teachers.

3. Learning specialists and all appropriate consultants.

4. All support staff.

5. Fellow students as in Marvin Marshall's "Discipline without Stress." peer mediators and student mentors.

6. Mentors such as Big Brothers and Big Sisters.

7. Other family members.

8. Coaches and other persons providing training for the child.

    NOTE: We need all of these individuals modelling positive behaviours.

G: Changing school structures or frailties which might be contributing to the behaviour.

1. Ensure the subject material is meaningful to the student.

2. Utilize reading programs.

3. Acknowledge student strengths.

4. Walk the talk.

5. Honour the role of emotions within the school's learning environment.

6. Focus competitiveness less on winning and more on knowledge and skill building.

H. In conclusion, practices to be considered.

1. School staff seeing themselves as student change agents.

2. Accept change as a slow process that is usually resisted at the outset.

3. Change may not happen unless initiated by an outside force.

4. Recognize that the change process is paramount to establishing new behaviours.

5. Strive for a safe learning environment.

6. Strive to make the learning process personally rewarding and an enjoyable experience.

    NOTE: Too few problematic children really know how to enjoy life and how to create pleasurable experiences through their own endeavours.

Positive emotions will build positive memories.

CHAPTER 23

CREATING SOCIAL BRAINS IN A LESS THAN SOCIABLE SOCIETY

BRAIN FACT # 69

Our social brains are shaped by a complex integration of cognitive, emotional and genetic inputs garnered from the environments that support them.

Socially responsible brains simply do not just happen as there are many elements in our society that mitigate against children growing such brains. It would be nice if all children, adolescents and adults could interact with **social competence, confidence, compassion and courtesy**.

Unfortunately stress, individualism (largely focussed on survival) and formal and informal structures which are ingrained in our society preclude many opportunities for the social intercourse so necessary for this aspect of a child's development.

The attainment of the following skills leads to the development of a socially responsible brain.

- Social Monitoring.

- Social Consciousness.

- Social Conscience.

BRAIN FACT # 70

The brains of virtually all bullies are underdeveloped in one or all of the above critical social skill areas.

The essential question: How big is this child's (I) in his/her social skill set? Or in other words how much emotionally energy does the child direct towards him or herself. **"I" stands for Individual.**

NOTE: When working with a problematic child you may wish to consider the size of the child's (I).

Small (I) **people.** There are many individuals who put the needs and presence of others ahead of their own needs. **These are the** S O C (I) A L **people.** They may see themselves to be unworthy and insignificant.

Mid Sized (I) people. Most of us establish some level of balance between ourselves and others. These are the mid sized S O C (I) A L people.

Lastly the large ([) people, This percentage of the population are those **who are not connected either cognitively or emotionally** to others. **These are the** S O C ([) A L **people.** The large ([), means that these persons are over focussed on self and oblivious to others.

They may have lived a life or are living a life where survival is a paramount concern. The trauma of neglect or abuse has left them unable to emotionally empathize with or be cognitively aware of the presence of others. In other cases the adults of their lives have modelled behaviour which showed themselves to be over concerned with themselves and to be **minimally concerned** with others even their own children.

Example: Parents who are bullies frequently fall into the small (I) or large ([) camp. Although on the surface it might appear that they are extremely concerned about the welfare of their children, closer examination will show that they are trying to control situations for their own benefit and not necessarily for the benefit of their children. Their children are prone to modelling this external behaviour.

NOTE: These are difficult people to work with or help change for what is cognitively and emotionally meaningful to you in a social sense, is simply not meaningful to them. It is simply not on there radar screen. These are the people who are the most troubled and troublesome within our society.

SOCIAL MONITORING

Few of us have not experienced the following question from either one of own young children or one of our students. Mum, Dad, Teacher are you angry at me? Your answer, most times, is "No," but because you were self absorbed in a thought, your serious expression was interpreted by the immature brain as anger, dislike or complete lack of concern.

There are at least **three competing mental** processes at play. The reason for the question is that:

- Accurately reading facial expressions, body language and vocal tone is not an easy task for young brains and until these brains mature they will seldom be able to analyse, with any degree of certainty, the array of facial expressions, body language and vocal tones presented to them.

- Young children are extremely ego centred, hence they perceive your actions to be exclusively connected to them.

- Children who have been exposed to neglect and abuse are very often **cognitively delayed** in this critical social function. Routinely you have and will continue to experience social misbehaviour in classrooms and hallways that is directly related to this dysfunction. These children are far more sensitive to serious expressions because these can be easily related to previous hurtful or dangerous situations with adults. They tend to be more hyper vigilant than normal and their failure to read body language correctly only serves to increase their feelings of anxiety.

Examples of this anxiety and (I) centredness occur in the hallways when you hear.

- "What are you looking at?"

- "Why are you looking at me like that?"

- "Who are you laughing at?"

- "You had better not be laughing at me."

Remediation

NOTE: The initial focus for this and most other remediation programs is to further develop the frontal cortex which is the child's executive management committee and control centre. Until this region develops sufficiently to "read" the various nuances that are presented in non verbal communication it is highly likely the child will assume the most negative or most dangerous of messages and their overactive amygdalae will continue to dominate this aspect of their decision making process.

Strategies:

1. Cut out pictures from news papers and magazines and invite the students to guess what the persons might have been thinking.

2. Role play serious faces, smiling faces, laughter.

3. Role play situations when clenched fists and raised hands are not intended as threatening.

   NOTE: The simple gesture of raising your hand to emphasize a point can be misread by an anxious child.

4. Help students understand that loud voices are not necessarily threatening but rather may be a speakers attempt to reach the back of the room or get people's attention for emergency reasons.

5. Create role play exercises where children have the opportunity to "look another person in the eye." A pre-exercise might include studying the eyes of the people in exercise #1.

   NOTE: Be aware! In some cultures this is a sign of disrespect or a sign of aggression.

6. Use art classes and have students draw a variety of faces and have them discuss their drawings and come up with several thought processes for each drawing.

7. Have the children work in pairs and practice making serious and happy faces plus laughing together.

SOCIAL CONSCIOUSNESS

Social consciousness consists of:

- **A cognitive awareness** of the presence and needs of others.

- **A learned set of behaviours** which enable the person to effectively and responsibly interact with others and within the norms of the community.

- The **cognitive ability** to balance one's personal needs with the needs of the community at large.

Social Consciousness is usually a precursor to being able to emotionally connect with others.

Examples of low social consciousness:

- Use of vulgar language specifically in public places.

   Example: A close relative of mine was "caught" on a plane with a group of "foul mouthed" males who repeatedly used the F word in all possible grammatical configurations. To make matters worse the plane couldn't land at the designated airport due to heavy ground fog. They were diverted to another airport and were required to sit on the tarmac for two hours. All the while the torrent of bad language continued. The saddest thing about this experience is that my relative learned that a number of these men were fathers.

   Example: Tom Utley of the London Telegraph wrote about the abuse his wife endures from passengers and motorists alike as she endeavours to do her job as a driver of a double decker bus through the congested streets of London, England.

- A range of inappropriate driving habits such as speeding, driving while impaired, street racing, driving dangerously on bad road surfaces, etc.

Example: On a snowy blustery day a male driver in a 4X4 truck is tailgating a vehicle who is driving at a speed which was safe considering the road conditions, suddenly the 4X4 driver swings out to pass and drives head first into an oncoming car killing the driver.

◆ Queue jumping, cheating, lying, stealing.

◆ Showing disrespect, unwilling to cooperate or share, not "holding the door" for another.

NOTE: To receive respect may be one of the driving forces behind relationship bullying.

Example: Dissing or showing "no respect" is a particularly serious offense among some groups of teenage males.

Example: In an inner city a fourteen year old male walked up and shot an eighteen year old male. When questioned why he did it, he replied, **"He didn't show me no respect"**. The rule on double negatives does not apply in this situation.

◆ Verbally or physically assaulting a sports official.

◆ Teaching your child to cheat or denigrate others.

◆ Seldom saying "please," "thank you" or "you're welcome."

*NOTE: I am starting to have a problem with the phrase "Not a Problem." which is used as a substitute for **"You Are Welcome."** To me **Not a Problem** says, I was going your way anyway, I wouldn't have done it if it had been an inconvenience, I didn't put myself out for you. On the other hand You Are Welcome implies it was my pleasure to help and I would do it again. The two phrases don't carry the same meaning. **Wouldn't it be better if both the sender and the receiver were to feel valued by the activity and the statement?** Just a thought!*

The list is endless.

NOTE: Increasing the level of social consciousness within the student population is a critical element in reducing the level of bullying and other forms of violence.

NOTE: A curriculum which gives credence to inclusion, character education and student responsibility can be one of the pieces of the puzzle.

Question: At your school are all staff ie clerical, custodian, teacher assistants, teachers, administrators, nurse, social worker etc. included, where possible, and made welcome at assemblies, staff meetings, professional development days and social gatherings? If we want students to practice inclusion then we, as educators, have to find ways to model inclusion.

NOTE: Social consciousness is a behaviour, a character trait or a set of social skills that are cognitively learned. Social courtesies can be taught. School and classroom expectations can be met. There must be action not just words.

Example: In elementary schools in Winnipeg and Moose Jaw the head custodians were retiring. Several grade six students went to see the principals and asked if the schools were going to have retirement parties for these gentleman. The answer was in the negative. So the students organized their own parties for these persons who had been key parts of their school lives for seven years.

NOTE: Social conscious behaviour can become a habit with emotional overtones and will provide the individual with intrinsic rewards. Therefore to help a child learn a new social skill it is very important that the emotional dimension be recognized and re-enforced.

*NOTE: The socially competent brain is capable of balancing and managing cognitive and **emotional messaging** of the frontal cortex and the amygdala.*

INCLUSIONARY, CHARACTER, AND RESPONSIBILITY FORMING PROGRAMS

Inclusion

1. **Value of Mutual Respect.** Early years education is the optimal time to commence this type of training. It is important that children learn how to say each other's name, have communal play, reading and work time so they can learn to interact. One school uses variation on Gardner's Multiple Intelligences to form groups so that each child has the opportunity to make a significant contribution from their position of strength.

2. **Engage the Community to Promote Cultural and Racial Diversity.** For far too long schools have been isolated from segments of the community.

   *NOTE: This may have been satisfactory when communities were essentially unicultural, when there was a vigorous, often singular church presence and when family units were strong and often multi generational. Such is no longer the case, and the school has, by default, become the **only central institution within the community.** The school is being asked to "connect all the dots" as it were.*

3. **Multicultural committees.** In principle these have great strengths but it is **not uncommon** for people to join such committees to vent on single issues or to use the committee for a specific power base. Use, but approach with care.

4. **"Unteach Racism"**. Since racism has to be taught, develop curriculum and school activities to help people to cognitively and emotionally come to grips with their racist feelings and to learn new ways of interacting with people of different colour, race creed, gender and gender orientation.
See: *Emotional memories.*

5. **Respecting the unique talents of others.** Helping students understand it is perfectly acceptable to recognize another's talents without feeling deficient or insecure in anyway. Teach children to celebrate each other's talents and successes.

Character Building

An essential element of character building exercises is to combine cognitive learning with positive social interactions. This means that social consciousness which has already being acquired is being augmented by new social skills and emotional memories surrounding these skills.

1. **Cooperative Learning:** CL helps students form long term, **process oriented** memories and ultimately helps students **achieve higher scores.** Research shows that children working in a cooperative learning environment have scores that are 0.5 SD above those involved in other forms of learning. Furthermore, children can build **positive social skills** by interacting with others on mutual learning exercises. This is a triple win.

2. **Engage High Profile Individuals from Sports, Music, Drama, Fine Arts communities* to serve as role models and school mentors:** Many children, boys in particular, suffer from not being able to interact with male role models. It is important to recall the power of "mirror neurons." * Please continually expand the list so that it reflects the community talent base and the needs of the students.

3. **Teach "Fair Play":** This includes, teaching skills, teaching rules, expecting students to adhere to the rules, teaching teamwork and play making, teach team building and focus on growth not just winning. It is important for children to respect the game or activity they are involved in.

4. **Teach and model moral values** of honesty, caring and consideration of others and striving for excellence in a multiplicity of ways. Children who achieve excellence through their own endeavours have an increased sense of personal pride and a greater chance of being intrinsically motivated to succeed.

*NOTE: **Word of Caution.** Some more conservative religious groups may have certain moral positions which are exclusionary or at considerable odds with the views of most of the community or parents of the majority of the children. Furthermore, these views may inhibit a school from meeting the needs of the children.*

*NOTE: Studies have shown that students who work at **achieving excellence** at some skill area such as music, an art form or a sport have a greater potential to achieve in other areas. It may be that the discipline of practice plus the recognition of earned success are critical maturation factors.*

NOTE: Administration and teachers of schools which are multicultural in nature should familiarize themselves with some of the customs and beliefs of the cultures. This is beneficial from the aspects of knowing what sensitive issues may arise, why certain problems are occurring and developing skills to address these matters.

Example: My wife was an elected school trustee for sixteen years in two quite different school systems. She recalls the time she was sitting on a committee reviewing the special needs of some of the incoming kindergarten children. One little chap identified as a behaviour problem had been removed from three day care centres. While everyone was considering psychological assessment for this errant young lad, my wife asked if they considered that the problem may be cultural and that it was entirely possible that he was from a culture where women did not discipline boys.

5. **Emphasize Teamwork:** In "Punished by Rewards," Alfie Kahn writes of the negative aspects which evolve when individuals are encouraged to be competitive at the expense of others. Teamwork implies, sharing, trusting and relying on others and jointly working to enhance each other's skills. Team work, of course, falls apart when people seek out ways to get the best of their associates little alone their opponents. In other words associates become adversaries. In addition, rewards can shift the attention from the process of learning to some "bonus."

6. **Good Deeds:** Years ago there was a national radio show called the Good Deed Club. Five lines of the show's theme song were "Do a good every day, obey the Golden Rule, never say an angry word, or be unkind and cruel, in work or play or school."

Neelin High School in Brandon has an annual goal of a 1000 Good Deeds.

7. **Acknowledging Random Acts of Kindness.** Teachers, support staff and students can "turn in" students who have "committed a RAK". See: *Appendix IV "Being Cool."*

8. **Strive to inculcate Self Discipline.** The more self discipline children can incorporate into their daily behaviours the greater joy they can take of their accomplishments and there is less need for you to monitor them.

9. Establish dress codes for teachers, support staff and students. A recent newspaper article wrote about teachers coming to school with curlers in their hair, wearing tops and jeans/shorts or skirts that were incredibly short, male teachers wearing torn jeans and tee-shirts of questionable taste. All of the above distract from the image of leadership which teachers should be modelling. Furthermore, students who see teachers dressed in such a fashion are inclined to go them one better in inappropriateness.

   NOTE: A school in Toronto which is dealing with adolescents who, as the principal has described, have made one or more bad decisions along the way, has a dress code for these students. The code is simply no hats or other head gear and clothes that you would wear if you were going to work.

   NOTE: To some this may be considered an old fashioned idea. However, my years as a teacher, counsellor and administrator has lead me to believe that one's dress generally reflects attitude and dictates behaviour.

Building Responsible Attitudes

1. **Promote Mutual Responsibility:** Promote the idea that each student is a partner in making the school a better place to attend and learn.

   It is important to create projects and other school improvement activities where students have a major voice and role in implementation.

   Seek out ways to engage the usually **"unengageables."**

   NOTE: Do only the nice, bright and seemingly promising students get to care for the plants, the fish or the animals? Many other kids are dying for the opportunity.

2. **Responsible Citizen Program** This is an Australian term for a **year long, school wide "anti bullying" program which brings bullying to the forefront.**

3. **Volunteerism.** Children need the opportunity to feel useful. In all too many homes and communities children are not given tasks, or if given tasks, are not given the time or assistance to complete these tasks.

Hold a or a series of brain storming session(s) in your school to identify all the volunteer possibilities which can be created within the school and also all those which may exist outside the school in personal care homes, daycare facilities, hospitals, community centres etc. In some jurisdictions school credit can be given based on number of volunteer hours served.

4. **Focus on Responsibility for Self.** This means more than looking out for **Number One.** It means learning to be **intelligently responsible** for one's **body, brain and future.** Children who have a healthy vision of who they want to become are more likely to connect present day activities to future goals.

NOTE: The concept of the future is tied to brain maturation. It is not until early to mid teens that most students start to become fully aware of a concept of the future. This fact may help to explain teenagers sense of invulnerability. Children whose brains have been damaged by neglect or severe stress will have greater problems in this area.

SOCIAL CONSCIENCE

Social Conscience is one's **emotionally charged** and internally driven response to the needs and presence of others. This is embedded within one's emotional memories and is the product of genetic input, the learning of social consciousness but is heavily **influenced by the emotional forces within one's environment.**

Children who have been neglected or suffered sexual, physical or psychological abuse are prone to being less able to **feel empathy** for others or harbour **positive feelings** to property and animals.

They are likely to possess negative **feelings of indifference, hate, anger, contempt, spite, a motivation to cause pain or destruction, unjustified superiority** and **blatant disregard** for anyone but themselves.

On the other hand children who are **emotionally secure** are more likely to possess a range of feelings which allow them to **feel** connected to people, animals and property.

There is some overlap between the more cognitive social consciousness and the highly emotional social conscience. For example, a person who has learned an array of positive social behaviours will be more likely to perform these behaviours if their social conscience is in congruence.

On the other hand if one is not motivated by one's social conscience to do "good things" it is unlikely that one will act in a socially acceptable way regardless of previous training unless there is a tremendous cost to not acting responsibly.

NOTE: In fact, persons with anti social personality disorder are likely to be more dangerous if they are fully versed in rules of good social conduct. They will often use these skills to disguise their lack of social conscience.

Examples: Fraud artists such as men who prey upon lonely widows or divorcees for their money, or persons who sell seniors unneeded home repairs and perform shoddy work. The list is long.

Building Social Conscience

Acquiring social conscience is a better term because you can't teach emotions in the same sense as you can teach arithmetic. Social conscience is acquired through living within an environment which is safe, caring, loving and allows the person to feel respected and emotionally secure. But building the social structure is of paramount importance. See: *www.search-institute.org*

1. The child needs to feel valued and accepted. See: *Secure attachment.*

2. The child thrives best in an environment which supplies consistent, positive emotional reinforcement.

3. The child's brain has not been traumatized and hence does not feel the need to operate in "survival mode."

   NOTE: Traumatized children must be provided with the necessary therapy to help them into a "state" of feeling safe and valued.

4. The child needs to feel trust and safety in the presence of adults.

5. The child experiences success and becomes motivated to seek further success.

6. The child can definitely benefit from caring for others, caring for pets and plants, doing chores within the home and community including volunteer work.

7. The moderately afflicted child may respond positively to counselling which incorporates role play and similar activity. Other children may require more long term intense therapy.

8. When dealing with children who are exhibiting low social conscience, it is important to know why this condition exists. Possibilities include insecure attachment to parent or parents, living in a variety of foster homes, neglect and abuse, feelings that adults have failed them repeatedly in the past and cannot be trusted. The depth of their pain is usually proportional to their age.

In simplistic terms "holes" within their social conscience can only be filled with hope, love, success and trust and participating in activities where they see themselves as valued.

CONCLUDING STATEMENT

Social Skills Development has previously been the domain of the home, the community and the church/ synagogue/mosque/temple. However, we no longer have homogeneous, unicultural communities with strong well supported families. Instead we often have the exact opposite. **Once again, the school has, by default, become the central, unifying, institution within a diverse community.**

While it seems unfair to ask or even suggest that schools need to become more proactive in going well beyond the 3 R's and deal effectively with Social Skills Development. Nevertheless, schools which divorce themselves from the issue are less productive, experience less academic success and more student dysfunction.

But schools cannot do this alone. Social Skills Development is a 24/7 job. While the school must take leadership all other components of the community must be brought on board. These components are:

- Parents. *
- Coaches.
- Political Leaders. **
- Informal Community Leaders.
- Informed Religious Leaders.
- Leaders in the Arts and Culture Community.
- Members of the Law Enforcement and Judicial System.
- Social Services System.

*See: *Appendix II which is devoted to programs which are designed to increase parental participation in their children's education.*

I have, all too frequently, attended public meetings when elected officials have made platitudinal statements about education and student behaviour without knowing the dynamics of the issues or being committed to supporting resolutions. **Education of these individuals is also essential.

CHAPTER 24

SHALLOW SELF ESTEEM VS AUTHENTIC SELF ESTEEM

This chapter will focus on the over used and much abused psychological term "Self Esteem" AND the need to understand the **continuum** which exists between:

◆ extremely superficial, "quick fix," shallow, skinny, phoney, pseudo "Self Esteem"

and

◆ fully substantiated, inner directed, "**Authentic Self Esteem.**"

NOTE: "Authentic self esteem" is frequently a missing element in the social development of many children and adults but definitely most bullies.

*NOTE: Attempts to **superficially** enhance the self esteem of bullies and also their victims may very well lead to disastrous results.*

Description: "We need to help foster the development of people who have healthy or authentic self esteem because (these people) trust their own being to be life affirming, constructive, responsible and trustworthy." *– R. Reasoner*

Definition: "Self esteem is the disposition to experience oneself as being competent to cope with the basic challenges of life and of being worthy of happiness." *–N. Branden*

Description: "Authentic self esteem" results when people reach an emotional – cognitive balance which allows them to feel honestly good about themselves and be quietly confident in taking these "selves" to the outer world. They enjoy who they are, are willing to take calculated risks, able to acknowledge their large and small successes and/or frailties, willing to accept responsibility, are able to give themselves to others without fear of loss and while they appreciate honest feedback they are not dependent upon the applause of others." *– D Halstead*

When I am giving workshops on bullying the question always arises. "Why does a child who has high self esteem still bully?" Or phrased another way "Why do kids who seem to be popular, seem to have most things going for them and are doing well need to bully? Its particularly troublesome because I state that practically every bully is controlling or trying to control others for his/her personal reasons, is operating from some level of personal insecurity and has a low a sense of self.

But many **appear** to have high self esteem. Again, the operative word is **appear**.

Is there a relationship between bullying and self esteem? It is my contention that most bullies have some serious inner issues with their own self esteem. The major exceptions are the pathological stalkers, the sociopath killers and others who are severely conduct disordered and narcissistic. (In these cases the individuals are so disconnected from their own emotions and the emotions of others that they possess an inflated psychotic sense of self.)

Most other bullies are using their actions to "bulk up," as it were, they own self image or a self image they wish to create for the benefit of others. Why are they not willing or able to achieve their goals through other means?

A Canadian Criminologist recently stated on CBC Radio "that a good deal of juvenile criminal behaviour is due to our society's preoccupation with **phoney** "**self esteem.**" The reason that "phoney self esteem" is so attractive is because it is marketed well and it promises a **quick fix** for complex self identity problems. This superficial or phoney self esteem tends to absolve individuals from serious development of their inner being or to take the risk of attempting to develop beyond where they are currently.

TODAY'S SELF ESTEEM MODEL

The line from Saturday Night Live on self esteem goes like this. *"I am good enough; I am smart enough, and doggone it people like me."* In the worst case scenario, self esteem can be equated to a "new paint job on an old, rusty car". It looks good for the moment, but don't look too close and don't rub the surface.

Phoney self esteem is the created image which people buy into to bolster their personal identity. While it may temporally support their personal belief system, it is really only a quick fix and is subject to rapid break down. This leaves the person experiencing failure, feeling vulnerable and prone to being defensive.

People attempt to gain self esteem from a variety of sources including reading and absorbing countless pages of countless popular self help books.

NOTE: Want to make a quick million dollars? Then write a short, flashy book entitled. "How to develop incredible Self Esteem in Ten Minutes."

SELF ESTEEM – MATERIAL CRITERIA

How many people do you know who base their self identity on the kind of car they drive, the clothes they, wear, the holidays they take, the type and amount of alcohol they drink, the status of their work, the size of their office, the location of their parking spot, their physical size or shape, their power over people, the kind of hockey stick, skate or snow board they own, the status of their family, the accomplishments of their children etc. **None of these items necessarily speak to the issue of inner strength, inner character or authentic self esteem.**

BULLIES AND SELF ESTEEM

Do certain bullies **seem to display** high self esteem? The answer is, **YES.** Are these same bullies comfortable with their **internal** sense of personal security, personal integrity, acceptance of responsibility for their actions, acceptance of others as valued human beings and be willing to risk? The answer in practically every case is **NO.** The pseudo or phoney self esteem of many bullies does not **equate to true authentic self esteem.**

In fact pseudo, phoney, shallow or skinny self esteem leaves the bully prone to acts of violence, disrespect of authority and other anti social behaviours. The reason lies in a basic function of the brain. Since the brain's number one purpose is to keep us alive. Individuals with skinny self esteem tend to be hyper vigilant, extremely sensitive to criticism or perceived attacks. They do not possess the necessary inner stability or confidence which would allow them to function in a socially acceptable manner. **They bully, in an attempt, to bolster their own self esteem.**

AGE AND SELF ESTEEM – A STORY

Young children are less likely to be hooked on pseudo self esteem. I am encouraged by a story related to me by a good friend of ours.

"Their family was engaged in educational development work in East Africa and their children were attending a multicultural school where the children were those of European, North American and Asian expatriates, Afro-European marriages, and local African officials. On one occasion Maxine's daughter, Beth, was invited to Mirissha's birthday party. After driving to an unfamiliar part of the city they finally came to the house and were greeted by a flood of little girls of varying ethnic backgrounds. Maxine asked Beth which one was Mirissha. Beth replied "Oh, she is the one in the blue dress."

In this case, status, skin colour, ethnicity or creed were cognitively and emotionally invisible. The only thing that mattered was the mutual friendship of a group of little girls. **They all had great self esteem.**

It is interesting to note that racial, religious and social bigots all share the common factor of fear. They use their bigotry to prop up their **shallow self esteem** to shield themselves when ever someone or group from another race, creed or social group are perceived to be threatening their "status." Rather than evaluating the community as a whole or working at making themselves more competitive, more knowledgeable or relevant they embark on an attack of denigration. Their self esteem needs constant boosting.

SUPERFICIAL SELF ESTEEM AND GAINING FRIENDS

Skinny self esteem and authentic self esteem separate when individuals begin to want to be what they inwardly feel they **are not.** I think of Jack, the over weight outsider who suddenly gained a group of friends when his Dad let him drive the family car to school. His "new buddies" found that Jack was more than willing to drive them all over town. Jack told me, "I didn't used to have any friends and now I have lot's of friends." His shallow self esteem took a real bump upward but did he truly **feel** better about himself. I don't know. Perhaps not!

SELF ESTEEM – ECONOMIC AND SOCIAL STATUS

Disparity within a school usually leads to informal clusters of students. Economic differences start to divide the school into those that have and those who have not. In addition, subtle differences occur within each of the subgroups as individuals vie for status. In actual fact many of these students are attempting to buy their self esteem. If $150.00 running shoes are the base line for a certain subgroup, then the $175.00 XXXTriTEC gives the owner of these shoes new status, new skinny self esteem.

Students who have less money to spend on running shoes may adopt the "look" and while to the outsider the "look" is unidentifiable, the insiders know who has it and who doesn't

Think about the Grade XII student who drives a huge military style SUV to high school every day. Without knowing this individual we can't jump to conclusions. But it is always possible that the vehicle is an essential ingredient of his self esteem and/or the parent who bought it for him.

BEHAVIOUR – SELF ESTEEM

Behaviour can be a self esteem item. Some students take a perverse pride in being an "active slacker." These students usually have low self esteem. They are reluctant to put forth an effort just in case they fail to meet their expectations or the expectation of others. Their skinny "self esteem" arises from being successfully unsuccessful.

Other students perceive that their status will rise if they act outside of the rules and will do so to get applause. The feedback feels good and re-enforces their behaviour. Do they ever reflect on their behaviour? Sometimes, but for the most part, these troubled children live for themselves and in the moment.

THE VULNERABILITY OF TEENAGE "SELF ESTEEM"

Teenage self esteem is often derived from personal appearance, style of clothes, the car they drive, access to drugs and alcohol, parental income, participation in team sports even though they may hardly ever get to play, belonging to the right crowd, having friends, having the "sexiest" mobile phone and under achieving.

NOTE: When we consider the many rapid and sometimes conflicting neurological, physical and social developmental issues teenagers encounter from puberty to age twenty it become increasingly understandable why teenage self esteem is so fragile.

Most of the above speaks very little to personal achievement or personal development. Most are of a material nature bought either by the teenager or the teen's parents. Almost every thing is external. As mentioned earlier this code of self esteem is marketed, fostered and supported by teen magazines, electronic media advertisements, TV sitcoms, teen music and peer pressure. These are the norms to be met and maintained.

This superficial approach to personal identification definitely leaves these teens vulnerable to making decisions which can have serious short and long term effects upon themselves and others. Again, one of the undesirable outcomes is their obsession with self and limited concern for others. Teenage female anorexia and teenage male use of steroids **may in part** be attempts to deal with their self esteem issues by controlling their body shape.

People with **authentic self esteem** are comfortable with themselves within society. They are also likely to be seen as people having a considerable level of social consciousness and social conscience.

NOTE: One should be clear that self esteem may or may not be a component of an individual's affliction with anorexia and bulimia. These are complex disorders.

SOCIALLY UNACCEPTABLE BEHAVIOUR AND SELF ESTEEM

Some people have suggested that children who are successful "car thieves" or "drug dealers" are held in high regard in their "communities" and may have good self esteem. While these individuals may feel a sense of pride by mastering the skills of their craft, they, like terrorists, constantly need to have "criminal hits" in order to feel good. Their sense of self is transitory. Nevertheless, these are difficult children to rehabilitate since shallow self esteem is complicated by limited sense of self and the future.

PSEUDO SELF ESTEEM AND DEPRESSION

Research is also suggesting that the self esteem "movement" is a significant contributor to teenage depression. It is nearly impossible for teens to meet all the expectations that the media and other external environments are placing upon them. Under normal conditions when teens "don't feel good enough" or "smart enough" over a sustained period of time they may begin to sense that they have failed. They fail yet again when they are not able to meet the **artificial expectations** of today's pressure ridden teenage world.

SELF ESTEEM – MOTIVATION

External motivation is promoted to be a key factor in developing self esteem so that the person establishes the inner strength to move to the next level of human achievement. But a severely overweight male or female is not going to become a highly competitive figure skater and by the same token a 98 lb weakling is not going to hit many home runs. Most of the time these accomplishment are not possible or at least not immediately possible. There is no quick fix.

In addition, a child's longing to be something which is clearly beyond their immediate attainment speaks to two issues. First, the child's inability to accept the current reality of the situation and secondly the child's unwillingness and perhaps inability to purposefully strive to reach the goal. Therefore attempting to quickly affect change usually leads to failure and may even lead to lower self esteem.

NOTE: The benefits of most motivational presentations are lost within 24-48 hours after the presentation.

POSITIVE THINKING – SELF ESTEEM

Positive Thinking is essentially language which is created and stored in the left frontal cortex. Unless the person actually establishes a substantive thought and action plan and takes the necessary action the positive thoughts will simply remain as words and soon fade away.

INSTANT GRATIFICATION – SELF ESTEEM

Persons with shallow self esteem tend to live in the present with little concern for the future or the results of their current activities. Instant gratification is upper most in their minds. Persons with **authentic self esteem live consciously in the present BUT act with a keen awareness of and focus to the future.**

CONCLUDING STATEMENTS

Authentic self esteem

- Is knowing and being comfortable with your inner and outer self.

- Is developed over time.

- Is measurable in the sense one can account for personal talents, skills and accomplishments.

- Helps build resiliency.

- Gives the individual courage to take calculated risks and meet new challenges.

- Provides a level of "immunization" against depression.

- Provides a level of "immunization" against chemical abuse.

- Allows the individual to make independent decisions.

- Allows the individual to seek help and guidance on life's big issues.

- Allows the development of an inner sense of integrity and an increased sense of personal acceptance.

- Forms within the person an increased willingness to accept responsibility and be accountable.

- Encourages an increased sense of purpose.

- Grows an increased sense of self within the community.

- Allows people to laugh at themselves.

- Allows people not to be unduly defensive when they make a mistake.

- Reduces their chances of becoming overcome by "road rage" or similar acts of aggression

- Reduces the need to denigrate people for personal gain.

- Places material possessions in perspective.

- Allows the person to be an accepting parent, teacher, supervisor or leader.

Growing Self Esteem

1. Persons who have formed a secure attachment with one or more adults have a greater likelihood of developing authentic self esteem.

2. Individuals who are able to accept themselves as they are, are less likely to need the approval of others.

   NOTE: Programs which encourage individual development such as track and field, swimming, archery, music, art or dance allow the individual to advance on their own initiative.

   NOTE: From my perspective I prefer activities where quantitative measurement is the assessment tool. It is easier in these activities to measure growth and establish Personal Bests (PBs).

3. Freedom from guilt. This means that the person honestly lives without the burden of either external or internal guilt. The person takes responsibility, makes amends and strives to not make the same mistake again. **Caution:** Persons without a social conscience may also operate without a sense of guilt.

   NOTE: Guilt is a complex topic. In some segments of our society, to think well of yourself is a sin. In other cases to seek or find pleasure is also a sin. In still another sector one can be quickly absolved of sin and hence there is no need to feel guilt or take personal responsibility for one's actions.

From the perspective of most children, adolescents and adults guilt evolves around doing harm to another person or committing an act which has brought shame upon yourself. In the first case resolution involves showing sincere remorse and making appropriate restitution, if possible. In the second case it is essential to accept responsibility for your act and set in place a plan which ensure this will not happen again.

4. Enjoy the excitement of being responsible. Children should be taught by word and deed to be responsible for their actions. For example, when they experience success, they can say "Yes, I played a major role in this success." They can also acknowledge the role played by others. However, the real test comes when they must admit to wrong doing or mistakes. They then must accept the consequences and move on.

    Children who are encouraged to lie about events or who are punished excessively or inconsistently are unlikely to take ownership of their mistakes or take calculated risks to succeed.

5. As implied above, **honesty is the best policy** in order to live a life with integrity.

BRAIN FACT # 71

The brain uses less energy and fewer neural networks when telling the truth than it does when telling a lie.

Persons who live a life of honesty and integrity find it easy to make socially responsible,value based decisions. They have congruency.

6. Some children have old **emotional memories** which are hindering their ability to feel comfortable with their mind and body. These memories could have come from living in dysfunctional homes, being told repeatedly that they are worthless, ugly a perpetual failures, always making mistakes and/or having parent who was suffering from depression or an addiction.

It is critical that such children be helped to gain a more positive view of themselves. A counselling/ therapy program such as described in Martin Seligman's book *Learned Optimism* can prove to be invaluable.

7. The final element of building authentic self esteem is to be able to **help others succeed.** This could mean helping a competitor improve his her performance.

    Example: I can recall a young man who was part of a group of exceptional students who were all vying for a number of prestigious university entrance scholarships. There was an interview process and after his interview he shared information about the interview with all his competitors. He was one of the winners but he sure made the interview panel work hard to select the other winners.

IN CONCLUSION

Authentic self esteem is not about:

◆   unbridled self obsession.

◆   displaying unfounded superiority.

◆   suddenly discovering a new persona.

Authentic self esteem is about being:

◆   comfortable with yourself.

◆   willing to take calculated risks.

◆   congruent to your positive values.

◆   able to integrate with the larger world.

◆   able to balance cognition and emotions.

◆   internally motivated.

◆   able to say "Thank You" and "You're Welcome."

See: *Appendix III.*

CHAPTER 25
ATTENTION STRATEGIES

When Johnny or Jenny cannot stay "on task" or stay in "one place" for any length of time. First try to determine the reason, perhaps through a process of elimination and then choose one or more strategies. See: *Chapter 17.*

STRATEGIES

Low blood sugar

1. Try to educate students about the affects of diet on their brains.

2. If a school lunch program is in place, hopefully it is largely comprised of complex carbohydrates.

3. Encourage your school to get rid of soft drink dispensing machines.

4. Breakfast programs should include oatmeal, bread, milk, fresh fruit, eggs and bacon or at least not be solely dependent on sugar rich muffins etc.

5. Teach children how to cook and prepare inexpensive but nutritious meals.

6. Create within the school or elsewhere in the community, a community kitchen where mothers can learn and work together to prepare lowcost but nutritious meals for their families.

Allergies

The elimination or reduction of foodstuffs or avoidance of irritants is desirable but not always easy to accomplish. It is helpful if the child knows that allergies might be the cause of his/her irritability. Some antihistamines can cause the user to become drowsy

Oxygen to the Brain – Low Blood Iron and Blood Flow

1. LBI is often a problem with teenage girls. A blood test is often called for; medication, supplements or diet changes may be in order.

2. Exercise will facilitate increased blood flow to the brain which enhances brain function

3. Stretch breaks with deep breathing activity can increase oxygen flow to the brain.

Sleep deprivation

1. Emphasize to parents the value of sleep to the learning process and behaviour

2. The rule of thumb for children and adolescents is:

   ♦ 10-12 hours for ages of 5-10 years.

   ♦ 9-10 hours for ages of 11-14 years.

   ♦ At least 9 hours for ages of 15-18 years.

Dehydration

1. Ensure the availability of water either at the desk or within easy access.

2. Educate children on the value of water and the counter productiveness of most other drinks which are often diuretic.

Stress

1. Welcome children to your school or classroom.

2. Play quiet music in classroom and hallways.

3. Have rooms painted in a calming colour.

4. Follow a routine (Stressed children can benefit from structure.)

5. Work at managing your personal stress.

6. Have the children take stretching and deep breathing breaks.

7. Use movement as a learning medium whenever possible and practical.

8. Teach children to monitor their own stress by checking their own pulse.

   To start the process have the students take their pulse every two hours and make a line graph. They can also note how they were feeling at each measurement. Once this has been done for a couple of days the children will have a ready reference for future checks.

9. Help children develop their own stress management programs.

Depression

1. Employ the services of the school nurse, counsellor or psychologist, if available.

2. Try to find "windows of opportunity" to engage the student.

3. Try to involve the child in some form of distracting or anger release exercise when appropriate.

4. Attempt to have the student participate in physical activity. Exercise increases the brain's serotonin levels plus lowers the noradrenaline levels.

5. Medication **may be** a necessary part of the management program.

Brain injury

Parents and/or children may recall a time or times when the child was unconscious for even a short period of time. Parents may also recall changes in behaviour subsequent to these events.

1. Some medical practitioners are recommending low to moderate doses of psycho stimulants to stimulate damaged frontal cortex areas. If this decision is made, it should be based on the specific situation and should be monitored very closely.

2. If anger and violent behaviour is an issue an anti convulsive may be in order to calm damaged frontal and temporal lobe areas.

3. Determine subject areas, skills or interests which might engage the student.

4. Physical and Occupational Therapy may be effective in helping students build new mental processes and thus gain confidence and new management skills.

5. Anger management programs may also be considered.

Fetal Alcohol Syndrome(FAS), Fetal Alcohol Spectrum Disorder (FASD), Fetal Alcohol Effects (FAE)

Diagnosing the level of pre-natal brain damage and trying to capitalize on the child's capacities is never easy. It is important to be prepared for both positive and negative surprises. For example, one teacher found that although this student seemed to be functioning at a very low level, he always knew within minutes when recess would occur.

1. Follow a rigid routine.

2. Focus on rote learning.

3. Be prepared to repeat instructions.

4. Use concrete learning strategies well beyond the normal age for such strategies.

5. Have the student follow certain behaviour patterns. Praise when you can even for the smallest of successes.

Prenatal exposure to Nicotine and other Tobacco Chemicals

1. Certain of these children may benefit from anger management training to help counter feelings of hostility.

2. Because of neural adaptation it is important that these children can gain **feelings of success** through sport, academics or some other area.

Postnatal exposure to Second Hand Smoke

(See above)

Mother's Heightened Stress Level during Pregnancy

1. Use stress management exercises such as deep breathing, calming visualizations, stretching exercises, yoga and calming music.

2. Teach children to measure their stress levels using simple biofeedback techniques.

The Child is Naturally Kinesthetic

1. Assess the child's physical behaviour and determine if this behaviour excessive for child of this age.

2. Involve the child in learning activities which have a significant opportunity for kinesthetic input.

3. The use of role play may help these children gain understanding of reading assignments which otherwise they might find boring in a more passive setting.

4. Take activity breaks.

    NOTE: I recently saw a model classroom on TV. One of the students was sitting on a large stabilizer ball. Those of you who use one of these in your exercise programs will note that you are always in motion. I am wondering if children who are hyperactive or simply kinesthetic might benefit by sitting on one of these balls instead of a chair.

    Perhaps you could try this in the corner of the room designated as the child's quiet place.

THE CHILD MAY BE ADD OR ADHD

Teaching and Classroom Management Strategies for ADD, ADHD and other students with Frontal Lobe Dysfunctions

Caution use only the items with which you have the most comfort.

Establishing the Proper Learning Environment

NOTE: Many ADD students tend to focus on too many things.

- Seat students with ADD near the teacher's desk, but include them as part of the regular class seating.

- Place these students up front with their backs to the rest of the class to keep other students out of view.

- Allow the child to keep a nerf or similar type ball at his/her desk. Just repeatedly squeezing the ball can prove to be soothing.

- Surround ADD students with good role models.

  NOTE: If however, the ADD or ADHD student is causing these students to be distracted from their learning on a regular basis then a student rotation or abandoning this suggestion may be in order.

- Encourage peer tutoring and cooperative-collaborative learning.

- Avoid distracting stimuli. Try not to place students with ADD near air conditioners, high traffic areas, heaters, doors or windows.

- Children with ADD do not handle change well, so avoid unnecessary transitions, physical relocation (monitor them closely on field trips), changes in schedule, and disruptions.

- Be creative! Establish a stimuli-reduced study area. Let all students have access to this area so the student with ADD will not feel different. There must be rules established for this zone.

- Encourage parents to set up appropriate study space at home, with set times and routines established for study. Parental review of completed homework and periodic notebook and book bag organization is essential.

NOTE: One father, with the necessary monetary resources hired an organizational expert to work with his child on a regular basis.

NOTE: I know of a teacher who herself has ADHD who has very few problems working with ADD or ADHD students.

NOTE: A teacher who is also the mother of an ADHD child commented in one of my workshops, that she feels that the stress the child experiences trying to conform to a school's structure actually makes the child's behaviour worse than normal. Daniel Amen would concur with this as he has SPECT scans of ADD brains relaxed and under stress. Their stressed brains have far less capacity to exercise executive control.

Giving Instructions to Students with ADD/ADHD

- Maintain eye contact during verbal instruction.

- Make directions clear and concise.

- Avoid implied instructions. Set reasonable time limits. Break assignments up into short manageable chunks.

- Be consistent with daily instructions.

- Simplify complex directions. Avoid multiple commands. (Actually this applies to all students.)

- Make sure students comprehend the instructions before beginning the task.

- Be prepared to repeat instructions in a calm, positive manner.

- Help the students feel comfortable with seeking assistance. (Most children with ADD will not ask for help or they may state "I don't know what I am supposed to do."). ADHD children will likely become restless and bothersome if they can't get started on a task.

- Gradually reduce the amount of assistance, but keep in mind that these children will need more organizational help for a longer period of time than other children.

- Require a daily assignment notebook logbook or agenda.

- Make sure each student correctly writes down all assignments each day. If a student is not capable of this, the teacher should help him or her.

- Sign the notebook daily to signify completion of homework assignments. (Parents should also sign.)

- Use the notebook for daily communication with parents.

Giving Assignments

- Explain one task at a time.

- Monitor frequently.

- Maintain a supportive attitude.

- Modify assignments as needed. Consult with special education personnel to determine specific strengths and weaknesses of each student.

- Develop an individualized education program, if necessary.

- Make sure you are testing knowledge and not attention span. Give extra time for exams etc.

- Give extra time for certain tasks. Students with ADD usually work slowly, largely due to organizational problems. Do not penalize them for needing extra time.

- Teach the children to use graphic organizers as tools for the writing of essays or doing other tasks.

NOTE: Keep in mind that children with ADD are easily frustrated. Stress, pressure, and fatigue can further break down their self-control and lead to poor behaviour.

*NOTE: It is absolutely essential that **feedback** be supplied to ADD/ADHD students **immediately,** if at all possible, upon completion of a piece of work.*

Modifying Behaviour By Providing Supervision and Discipline

- Remain calm, state the infraction of the rule, and avoid debating or arguing with the student

- Have pre-established consequences for misbehaviour and set up desired behaviour. Model behaviour that you want to have happen.

- Administer consequences immediately and monitor proper behaviour frequently.

- Enforce classroom rules consistently.

- Make sure the consequences fit the "crime."

- Avoid ridicule and sarcasm criticism. Remember, children with ADHD children are often the butt of many jokes and or comments about their behaviour and usually become irritated being made fun when it is not their fault.

- Avoid publicly reminding students on medication to "take their medicine." This can be very embarrassing plus makes the child a target for petty drug dealers.

By Providing Encouragement

- Reward more than you punish.

- Discipline by teaching behaviours they can master.

- Model the behaviour and where possible have a mentor also model the behaviour.

- Immediately praise good behaviour and performance.

- Change rewards if they not motivating behavioural change.

- Determine what will motivate the child?

- Teach the child to reward himself or herself. Encourage positive self-talk (e.g., "You did very well remaining in your seat today. How do you feel about that?"). This encourages the child to think positively about himself or herself.

Other Educational Recommendations

- A private tutor and/or peer tutoring at school.

- A class that has a low student-teacher ratio.

- Social skills training and organizational skills training.

- Training in cognitive restructuring (positive "self-talk," e.g., "I did that well").

- Use of a word processor or computer for schoolwork. Helps maintain attention and allows the student to produce work that is readable and at least from an appearance perspective acceptable .

  *NOTE: Many ADD or ADHD children have **poor handwriting**. This is largely due to an underperforming basal ganglia, which normally is responsible for fine motor movement.*

- Individualized activities that are mildly competitive or noncompetitive such as bowling, walking, swimming, jogging, biking, karate. (Note: Children with ADD/ADHD may do less well than their peers in team sports unless there is a great deal of activity.) Playing outfield in baseball is "murder" for ADD kids.

- Involvement in social activities such as scouting, church groups, or other youth organizations that help develop social skills and self-esteem.

- Allowing children with ADD to play with younger children if that is where they fit in. Many children with ADD have more in common with younger children than with their age-peers. They can still develop valuable social skills from interaction with younger children.

Medication

NOTE: It is extremely important to provide counselling and other supportive therapies to children who are being medicated for ADD. While the brain may be performing in a more efficient manner, the child will becoming a "different person". They have, in effect, a new brain. This can be very confusing for the child and they can use help in making the adjustment.

NOTE: In addition, it is uncommon that the first prescription will completely meet the child's needs. The dosage may be too strong, too weak or it may be the wrong medication for that child's personal chemical mix. In the best case scenario the medication should not leave the child "feeling drugged". The medication is not a sedative and if taken in prescribed dosages is not addictive. It is most imperative for the teacher, counsellor, parents and doctor communicate openly and often on the child's progress or lack of it.

NOTE: In addition to the above, ADHD children may have several other issues. In some cases the child has defined himself or is being defined as the class clown, as the kid who creates situations which throws the teacher off base or as the child who is inconsistently disciplined. Should this child go on medication special care must be taken to help the child become comfortable with their new behaviours and social standing.

NOTE: ADHD children may also be afflicted with Oppositional Defiant Disorder (ODD) and in smaller numbers Conduct Disorder.

References

1. *Beyond Ritalin* – Stephen Garber, Marianne Garber

2. *Healing ADD* – Daniel Amen

3. www.amenclinic.com

4. *Answers to Distraction* – Edward Hallowell, John Ratey

5. *Why Johnny Can't Concentrate – Coping with Attention Deficit Problems* – Robert A. Ross

CHAPTER 26

WORKING WITH OPPOSITIONAL CHILDREN

There is a strong possibility that the ODD child under your care also has ADHD.

NOTE: Most ODD children have been beaten or otherwise abused by their parent(s) or surrogate parent(s) and are confused when teachers don't use the same level of punishment.

ODD behaviour can quickly escalate into a full blown emotional outburst.

TEACHERS AND ODD STUDENTS

- The challenge for the teacher is to avoid contributing to the emotional scene.

- Since the cingulate gyrus in the child's brain is under performing it is necessary for the teacher to provide alternatives.

- The teacher and all others working with the student must develop a plan on how the child should be managed. The essential ingredients of the plan are consistency, firmness, not rigidity, stated objectives, avenues for anger release and frequent communication between all parties.

  Example: A workshop participant related this story. It was a middle school situation, the teachers, the counsellor and the principal had a plan but for some reason a teacher who had the student for only two hours a week hadn't been included. **You guessed it!** There was a two person meltdown that perhaps could have been avoided.

- ODD students are often weaker students and become quickly frustrated with school **work.**

STRATEGIES

- **Change focus.** Give options, "You can do it this way or this way." With older students you can give them the option of doing it their own way after getting your approval.

- Be clear with your instructions. ODD students have limited ability to make sense of inferences. In addition, emotionally loaded directions may further activate their limbic areas.

- Again, develop, follow and update the plan. Work with parents, psychotherapist, case workers to devise a coordinated plan of action. **ODD students can effectively play one adult against another.**

- Use extrinsic motivation, however, do not use monetary items, use privileges instead.

- Choose your goals carefully. Be consistent, different goals on different days or too many goals are confusing to this troubled student.

- Be prepared for a long term remedial, developmental process.

- Have a plan for each ODD student. There are always some similarities but there are unique differences.

- Seek out their strengths and use these to your advantage.

- Teach the child anger management techniques.

- Teach biofeedback techniques.

- Work at gaining child's trust. Let the child know that you are firm, fair, consistent and want the child to succeed.

- Involve the child in a appropriate developmental behaviour management program.

- Establish a "cooling off" place for the student.

- Use a colour card system to help the student communicate stress levels is helpful for some ODD sufferers.

  RED – Very Tense
  ORANGE – *Somewhat stressed*
  BLUE – Fairly Calm
  GREEN – AOK/ Cool

TAKE CARE OF YOURSELF

- Take care of your own anxiety level. Pick your "fights" carefully. Don't become obsessed with this behaviour. You are the inadvertent target of a child's dysfunctional brain in "survival mode."

- Use relaxation exercises, soft music and quiet space to relieve some of the tension.

NEAT STORY

A special education teacher was assigned an ODD student. She also had a developmentally delayed child in her room who attempted to befriend everyone. Initially the ODD student was resistant to the other child, however he was won over by the low level of expectations and gentleness of his new classmate.

- Avoid power struggles. **Please avoid getting your cingulate gyrus "stuck" and becoming ODD yourself.** (Teachers who tend to be confrontational with students will, almost to a person, be in constant conflict with ODD students.)

- Encourage the use of art (probably large art), writing or "Journaling" as means of self communications. This gives the student time to reflect on the material.

- Consider treating the ADHD with medication and/or other therapies.

- Exercise, diet changes and therapy which are intended to increase serotonin levels and/or reduce anger may help.(Diets high in sugar, caffeine and simple carbohydrates will likely exacerbate the situation.)

- Encourage parents to use parent support groups. A single parent can easily become overwhelmed.

CHAPTER 27

THE CONDUCT DISORDERED – TEACHING AND CLASSROOM MANAGEMENT STRATEGIES

WORD OF CAUTION

Treatment of children with conduct disorder can be lengthy, complex and challenging. Adding to the challenge is often the child's uncooperative attitude, lack of needed mental processing skills*, **lack of emotional response**, distrust of adults and limited family support.

*A person's IQ score provides a very limited assessment of a person's **overall cognitive ability** and no assessment of the person's emotional functioning.

Word of Warning: These will, in all probability, be the most difficult and problematic children you will ever deal with. Their behaviours and attitudes may demand skills beyond your expertise. Don't be offended by the previous statement and certainly don't be embarrassed to seek expertise either within or outside of the school system.

MAJOR INTERVENTION

In developing a comprehensive treatment plan, access and use the services of a child/adolescent psychiatrist, and every other powerful and capable resource available to you.

Even counsellors and psychotherapists who specialize in this area are often frustrated by the slow progress made with CD clients. As sad as it is to say, a small percentage of these damaged children verge on being "unfixable."

Possible Interventions may include addressing:

- ADHD, ODD
- Intense, long term anger management training.
- Strategies supported by MI, learning styles.
- Trust building and capitalizing on interests.
- Remediation on reading and learning disabilities.

  NOTE: Children with Conduct Disorder are often found to be 28 months behind normal peers in reading.

- Skill training and behavioural training using rote learning.

- Medication may be necessary.

Once again **early** remediation offers the child the best chance for growth and hopefully a non criminal life. Therefore, early training in conflict resolution, social relations and mutual acceptance building hold possibilities but should not be relied upon to resolve all CD problems.

*NOTE: It is usually necessary to deliver remediation programs in a rote learning fashion. Their weak language skills, **low ability to emotionally connect** with others, strong survival needs and limited sense of right or wrong provide major challenges for routine therapy being successful.*

NOTE: CD children are likely to have an exaggerated even narcissistic sense of self.

School-Related Factors

A bidirectional relationship exists between academic performance and conduct disorder.

A: Frequently children with conduct disorder exhibit low intellectual functioning and low academic achievement from the outset of their school years.

- Try to enhance their external world of knowledge, with field trips, visitors to the classroom, nature videos, manipulative play and learning situations, one on one discussions, use of volunteers. **They need real stuff.**

- The use of art, music and play are critical for these children.

- An extended time in Pre-Kindergarten, Kindergarten, Grade One, perhaps four years instead of three, may be required and prove to be beneficial.

- Work at ways to reduce the student's stress levels as evidenced by aggressive acts.

- These students generally think younger than norm, **again teach behaviour i**n a very concrete manner.

NOTE: Their street smarts may cause you to rate their cognitive capacities higher than they actually are.

- Try to get parental support for homework and other school issues.

- Seek ways to engage and support the parents.

- There is a need to address their extremely limited, socially unacceptable vocabularies.

- Model acceptable behaviour. Many do not cognitively or non-consciously know what acceptable behaviour is.

- Build trust. (They tend to distrust any adult.)

- Be consistent, warm, fair and firm. Again be aware some of these individuals can be very manipulative.

- Encourage a highly visible presence for the Principal/Vice Principals in the hallways and in the classrooms.

- Seek out the assistance of respected individuals within the community.

- Know the names of all students, if possible.

- Assign responsibilities as frequently and appropriately as possible.

- Encourage them to treat the school with respect and pride.

- Use challenge and feedback carefully, appropriately and frequently. These students are supersensitive to criticism or suggestions for work or behaviour improvement.

- Provide a quiet place for students to go when they are emotionally over taxed.

- Recognize all aspects of student success consistently.

Examples of other interventions

- Give students an exciting new outlet for emotional release. A Winnipeg inner city school established a Blue Grass group for its most severely behaviourally challenged students. The detention room is now being used for storage.

- Help students build critical thinking skills. A school in rural NW Ontario has an extremely active chess club for children who normally would not have taken any interest in chess. They now travel to local chess tournaments.

- Again, a school in Chicago is having excellent results by focusing increasing the amount of critical and integrated thinking in all aspects of the curriculum.

*NOTE: In CD students the prefrontal cortex is the area of the brain which is **least well developed** largely due to ADHD, a lack of appropriate stimulation and/ or continued high levels of stress.*

- Give students productive skills A Jesuit priest in Milwaukee's South Side is training drug addicts and gang members to become computer programmers. He believes that nothing stops a bullet better than a job. See: *www.economist.com/business/PrinterFriendly.cfm?Story_ID=825468*

- Give kids respect. A grandmother who manages the detention room in a Northern Alberta school, tries her very best to treat every student with **respect** resulting in a quieter and more productive detention room.

- Teach reading and language skills. A group of teenage boys were removed from a regular high school for discipline reasons. They were sent to an alternative school where the major focus was on reading. As their reading skills improved so did their behavior and a number were eventually able to return to and graduate from their former school.

Some essential elements of a successful treatment-remedial program.

- Wherever possible build a mentor sstem. Many CD children do not have adult role models, which they can emulate. Many do not see a future for themselves. These mentors need not always be within the school system.

- Establish behavioral guidelines and expectations for each child. Teach and re-teach them how these guidelines can be achieved.

  NOTE: Remember that behavior is "state dependent." What is the state of your school?

- The brains of these "at risk," young children and teenagers are extremely susceptible to addiction. Studies indicate that the stress they have endured may have "dulled," as it were, their ability to feel pleasure from normal activities.

- Their immature, concrete thinking brains do not handle humor very well. To them hurting some one, pushing someone down a flight of stairs or seeing one get hurt in another way is often funny. They are also very suspicious of people who laugh in their presence. Humor therapy has value, but it would take a skilled practitioner to pull this off.

- Very few of these individuals have ever mastered a skill requiring complete control and co-ordination of mind and body. Activities such as learning a musical instrument, learning how to paint, mastering a craft, learning a non-combative activity such as Tai Chi, holding down a job, being responsible for another person or a specific function would also give them a greater sense of self and self worth.

- Acknowledge success with care. Excessive rewards may be seen as manipulative, on the other hand some students will be "hungry" for recognition. Grant privileges not items of monetary value.

Create an environment of hope, concern and optimism

- Create and maintain exciting learning environments for all children. Realize that **you may be** one of only a few people who are seriously attempting to provide **a safe, energizing environment for these children.**

CHAPTER 28

ADDICTIONS, ADDICTIVE SUBSTANCES AND BEHAVIOURS

THE NATURE OF ADDICTIONS

We become addicted to a substance or a behaviour when embarking upon this activity we repeatedly achieve a "high", not all addictions are bad. Many people are addicted to caring for their families and rejoicing in the joy of a happy home.

SAFE AND HARMLESS ADDICTIONS

There are many things we do on a repeated basis which give us pleasure, that do us no harm and do not harm others. For example, someone who paints landscapes or still life will become so absorbed in their activity that they lose all sense of time and gain a great sense of accomplishment from their endeavours. Others spend time building and maintaining friendships which are mutually beneficial. Sports provide many opportunities for highs. An example might be even the most amateur of golfers will get off an occasional great drive, a fine approach shot or an amazing putt. This momentary and often fleeting success is enough to bring the person back to the course.

The key determinant of harmless addictions is self control and safety. If we are in control of what we do and if it is safe from the perspectives of one's brain, body and community then it is likely to be a **harmless or healthy addiction.**

Additional Safe and Helpful Addictions

It is important to become addicted to the brain's natural substances. Dopamine and/or serotonin boosts can naturally come from activities listed below.

- Exercise which raises levels of serotonin and helps to lower depression.

- Exercise lowers levels of noradrenaline and adrenaline thus leaving the brain-body more receptive to "hits" from playing games, listening to music and playing musical instruments, enjoying a walk through a park etc.

- Long distance running creates a "runner's high" which results from a flood of endorphins.

- Success in academics, sports, music, arts, drama, work etc. Achieving "Personal Bests."

- Receiving honest positive feedback.

- Helping someone.

- Regularly using relaxation techniques to reduce the levels of stress chemicals adrenaline and cortisol and leave the brain open to low level hits.

- **Being able to delay gratification.**

- Learning and practising a hobby.

Unsafe and harmful addictions

By way of argument harmful addictions are those over which one has no or limited control and which will or are causing harm to one's mental and physical self. Few people ever set out to deliberately become addicted.

Persons more likely to become harmfully addicted are those who:

- Need instant gratification.

- Are ADD or ADHD.

- Have suffered childhood neglect and trauma induced by neglect or sexual, physical and emotional abuse.

- Have been bullied in school, home and community.

- Have not been securely attached to one or more parents.

- Suffer from depression.

- **Bully others.**

There are generally two entry points on the road to harmful addictions. The first is rather innocuous. The person takes their first smoke, drink or drug hit because it looks "cool" and/or because everyone else is doing it. The second often has a bit more substance. This is when the person deliberately takes a drug to feel better or to manage some emotional pain. They are now using a substance to self medicate. Research is showing that pre-teens, teenagers and adults may attempt to **self-medicate** when:

♦ The brain is feeling emotional pain caused by loneliness, low self esteem, rejection, depression and failure.

♦ Natural brain excitatory chemicals are being produced in lower than normal quantities.

♦ There are reduced number of dopamine receptors or an increased number of dopamine transporter genes in the pleasure reward area.

NOTE: "There is some suggestion that when you look at people across addictions, people who are obese, alcoholics, cocaine addicts, methamphetamine abusers, etc., they all have low levels of D2 (dopamine) receptors. Vocci points out that D2 receptor density is influenced by environment and genetics."
– The Scientist, March 2003

♦ Dopamine receptors which have been **dulled** by intense and prolonged exposure to stress and trauma tend not to respond easily to natural increases of dopamine.

♦ The brain hasn't learned to feel joy and contentment through low level "hits" of skill attainment, family connections, playing games for fun, modest competition and positive social interaction.

NOTE: Some brains will be genetically inclined to self medicate, others will be altered in this direction due to pre and post natal environments and still others will be drawn to self mediation through their interactions with peers or media advertising.

NOTE: Most addictive substances "trick" brain into believing that these foreign molecular structures which are intruding into the neuron are natural brain substances. In actual fact they may cause the synapse to "fire" with greater intensity than normal or cause the synapse to "fire" in a manner totally opposite to what it was intended to do.

ADDICTIVE SUBSTANCES

Most of the following substances will cause the brain to experience short term hits most often by increasing the amount of dopamine delivered to the synapse or by "holding" the dopamine at the synapse for longer than normal periods of time.

Sugar

♦ Provides a "quick hit" of **energy** which enables the body and brain to perform well in the short term.

Caffeine

♦ Tricks the brain, because of its chemical structure, resembles adenosine, a natural neurochemical which serves as a relaxant.

♦ By binding to adenosine receptor sites caffeine blocks the normal relaxing affects of adenosine and leaves the brain in a state of high arousal.

Nicotine

♦ The nicotine molecule mimics the molecule of the common neurotransmitter acetylcholine.

♦ Releases a flood of beta-endorphins resulting in an increase of dopamine which enhances mood.

♦ Teenage smokers develop twice as many neural receptors for nicotine than do people who begin smoking in their twenties or beyond. This results in higher highs, lower lows and increased difficulty in smoking cessation.

♦ Teenage girls may become addicted after having smoked a single cigarette.

- Nicotine is a gateway drug. There are very few children or adults who are addicted to other drugs who are not smokers of tobacco.

Alcohol

- Alcohol is an analgesic which reduces the neural activity in the prefrontal cortex thus reduces inhibitions.

- Causes an increase of GABA, a neuro inhibitor, which lowers activity at the synapse. This eases the symptoms of depression which return once the alcohol is metabolized. Therefore, more alcohol must be consumed. Depression related alcoholism follows the onset of depression by 3-5 years.

- Approximately 50% of population has the "fast acting enzyme" a genetic quality, which metabolizes alcohol rapidly thus allowing the people to drink large quantities of alcohol without passing out or being sick. Possessing this gene and enzyme is the best predictor of adolescent males becoming alcoholics.

- People with a low pain threshold are more likely to become alcoholics.

NOTE: Sugar, caffeine, nicotine and alcohol are all "socially acceptable", legal substances cum drugs which are addictive to many or at the very least short circuit the brains of others into moments of "pleasure."

Marijuana

- THC – the active ingredient in marijuana has a chemical structure equivalent to anandamide.

- **THERE IS NOT A MARIJUANA RECEPTOR SITE ON THE NEURON.**

- Marijuana impairs cognitive processing and mood management. See: *www.amenclinic.com*

- Repeated use results in lethargic, self defeating behaviour resulting in loss of interest in work, school, long term plans and pleasure found in normal activity.

- The current strength of marijuana is many (perhaps 10) times more potent than the marijuana that was on the market a generation ago.

- SPECT scans show that the brains of marijuana users have much lower activity in the frontal and temporal lobes.

- New research is showing a relationship between marijuana use and the onset of depression and schizophrenia.

Cocaine

- Cocaine molecules block the reuptake of dopamine leaving the dopamine in the sympatric gap longer than normal.

- Cocaine highs may exceed the those of nature's biggest hit which is the orgasm.

- Cocaine restricts blood vessels to the brain which results in, at least, a minimum of brain dysfunction and, at worst, permanent brain damage.

- Children exposed to cocaine "in uteri" have IQ's which are 3-5 points lower than normal, experience a variety of brain malfunctions, have less ability to understand language and are more likely to need special education assistance.

Opiates such as morphine and heroin

- Mimic the natural endorphins and cause an increase of dopamine at the synapse.

Ecstacy

- Causes an abnormal increase of serotonin at the synapse leaving the person with an enhanced sense of well being.

- Animal studies are showing that as little as one significant hit of ecstasy so impacts on serotonin producing neurons so that they become severely under productive. From these studies it is projected that in 10-15 years there will be an epidemic like increase in depression among the 25-30 year old North American population.

Crystal Meth

Crystal meth is an amphetamine that is mostly produced in clandestine labs where quality control is virtually non existent. Crystal meth:

* Super charges the pleasure zone with large influxes of dopamine.

* The intense pleasure lasts only a few minutes.

* Another hit is required to repeat the rush.

* Addiction can happen very quickly even with low doses.

Aside from the rush users of crystal meth may also experience irritability, anxiety, paranoia, increased aggression and after more intense usage hypothermia, convulsions and death.

Steroids

Anabolic steroids or versions thereof are primarily used by:

* Athletes who are attempting to enhance their performance where strength and short term endurance are requirements of the sport.

* Body builders who are looking to build "the perfect body."

* Teenage males who want to look good on the beach. Some of these children can be as young as twelve years.

Some of the results of steroid use include, shrunken testes, increased chance of impotence, extraordinary weight gain, heart problems, breakdown at the attachments points between muscles and tendons

AND "ROID" RAGE. Steroid use greatly increases the possibility that the user will experience high levels of **intense anger** both while using the drug and in some cases for the rest of the user's life.

ADDICTIVE BEHAVIOURS

Harmful and Potentially Dangerous Non-Substance Addictions

The following activities increase the dopamine and dopamine like levels through an increase in noradrenaline

* Extreme Sports.

* Playing Violent Video and Computer Games.

* Driving at High Speeds.

* **Committing Violent Acts against People and Animals.**

* **Feeling compelled to commit Abusive Sexual Acts.**

* **Controlling the Activities and Lives of People.**

* Winning by Intimidation.

* An abnormally intense obsession to have sex.

* **Bullying.**

NOTE: One of several reasons why bullying is difficult to stop is because the bully gets a "hit" from his or her activity. It feels good to dominate, control or hurt someone else.

Bullying is addictive and schoolyard bullies have a significant likelihood to become substance addicted at some later point in life.

CHAPTER 29

REMEDIATION AND MANAGEMENT OF THE NINE BULLY TYPES

This section is dedicated to help you, the teacher, counsellor or administrator be either proactive or reactive to a bullying situation. Your action will, however, be dictated by circumstances.

Obviously, well developed proactive programs delivered with skill and conviction will benefit most of the children most of the time in their day to day school, family and community activities.

But some children will not or may not be able to develop the cognitive **and social skills** essential for being a responsible citizen on their own. **They must be managed in a reactive manner.**

MEETING THE "CHANGE NEEDS" OF THE NINE BULLY TYPES

Adherence to some or all of the following guidelines is essential.

Cognitive maturity. You, as the adult, as a result of your age, education and life experiences, possess the cognitive capacity to take the leadership role.

The student because of his/her chronological age, stage of development or current "brain state"is almost certainly to be operating at lower cognitive and social skill levels than you would consider age appropriate in one or more areas. This becomes a serious social consciousness issue.

Emotional maturity. It is important that you manage your emotions – specifically your anger, during these trying events. Failure to do so causes the "action central" of your brain to **down shift** from the pre-frontal cortex to the limbic area and beyond.

The level of **social conscience** the child brings to the situation is critical. If the child has the capacity to express and genuinely feel empathy for the victim then your job becomes easier. If such is not the case then you are dealing with someone who is somewhere on the continuum approaching being considered conduct disordered.

Language gap. There is bound to be a significant language gap between you and the child. You, as the educated adult, will have capacity to convert words into thoughts and thoughts into words. Generally the child is less skilled at this.

Do not, I repeat DO NOT assume that just because you have made a statement about the inappropriateness of an act or the need to change a behaviour that the child will be able to correctly understand the full meaning of what you have said or will have the skills to implement your wishes.

Values. It is important to ascertain the role that the child's value system may be playing in his/her behaviour. In cases, such as bigotry and excessive aggressiveness, values may be the driving force behind the behaviour. Creating opportunities for the child to establish new, more appropriate values will have to be part of the remediation program.

Build a resource base. Who are the individuals within the school, family and community who have the talent, time and inclination to assist you in resolving the bullying situations in your school. Do not overlook anyone. Help can often come from unexpected sources.

Know the family. Some families will rally to the cause and others will want to "fight you to the death" as it were. Some families will come to you for help while others will try to off load their responsibilities onto you and still others will adamantly deny that a problem exists.

Some families are going through a "bad patch" while others are burdened with alcohol or other drugs, depression or other mental illnesses.

STIMULATION, NOVELTY AND MEANINGFULNESS

When you embark upon any reactive program with a child or children it is imperative that you assess both the child(ren) and the programs on the basis of **stimulation, novelty and meaningfulness.**

Stimulation reflects the level of energy the program has or the child needs.

Novelty high lights the intriguing nature of the program or the child's willingness to be captured by something unusual.

Meaningfulness speaks to the cognitive and emotional maturity of the child's brain to manage the material under discussion. While all three are critical for learning, **meaningfulness** will have the greatest impact on future success in all types of learning including behaviour modification.

The child's brain may be configured, as a result of aggressively focussed genes, inconsistent or non-existent discipline or certain learning experiences, to act in a non-social way. It will be hard, at the outset, for the child to understand that the act they have just committed is wrong.

Furthermore, such children will have difficulty understanding why you want a behavioural change or what that change would look like. Meaningfulness determines the point upon which remediation can effectively begin and points to the program which will give the greatest chance for success.

CONFRONTING THE BULLY

It is important to realize that no matter how proactive your school's anti-bullying program is and no matter that it is extremely effective it is for most students there will always exist the possibility that you will have to go one-on-one with a number of bullies and some of their peers. This is to be expected. Not every student will be cognitively or emotionally mature enough to realize that their behaviours are outside of the expected norm. But your work is not in vain. The preparation provides a backdrop and support system for your work with these individuals.

The act of going head to head with a bully is fraught with many pitfalls. It is extremely unlikely that this will be a "one off" event. **Bullies seldom "fix easily."** The essential requirements are patience, flexibility, perseverance and the ability to communicate that you want this kind of activity to stop and that you are prepared to stay the course. Here are some strategies you may employ.

The encounter

- Meet one on one. Many bullies like an audience, Don't give them one. Close the door, sit down and begin in serious organized fashion.

- Start a file and write things down.

- Give the bully the facts as you or your colleague(s) have **observed them.**

- Depending on the age of the person, have them write a reflective response to the situation.

- Discuss this response with them. For example, "What do you mean when you say?"

- Interview as many of the other perpetrators as possible or as deemed appropriate.

- **Never, Never** say "**Don't let me catch you doing this again.**" If you ever say this, 99% of the most devious bullies will mutter under their breath "That's right you'll never catch me again, but I'll keep on doing it."

- You can say. "This has to stop." This is unacceptable, it has to stop and I am going to be part of the team to ensure that you become capable of acting in a responsible manner."

NOTE: Remember that the child may be presenting a mental shortfall which inhibits their ability to immediately recognize the gravity of the situation.

Student's response

Be prepared for:

- Real or faked surprise.

- Denial, anger at being caught.

- Accusations of unfair targeting.

- Willingness to shift the blame to peers.

- Blaming the victim.

Look for evidence of the bully's:

- Limited social conscience.

- Limited social consciousness.

- Limited awareness of the seriousness of their actions.

- "Thinking younger" than you would normally expect.

Be careful that you don't get caught in the bully's survival techniques.

Many bullies have incredibly well developed survival based "Street Smarts" **and** will be quick with:

- Apologies.

- Clever excuses.

- Skilful attempts to get you on his/her side.

- A rapid commitment to "Never do that again."

Explain very carefully what bullying is and why you are disturbed by his/her actions. This part of the session is very much situation dependent to the child's level of development.

- Cognitive and social development will dictate what materials and methods you will use.

- Older children may be able to handle written definitions of bullying.

- Many will have difficulty with **the criminal nature** of bullying.

- You may wish to share with them the **Prognosis for Bullies.** See: *Appendix V.*

Listen very carefully. Take notes! Lots of notes!

Note taking accomplishes at least three things:

- It gets the file underway.

- It is intended to convey to the child that you are taking this very seriously.

- It allows you to keep a record of events including planning a course of action and monitoring growth.

Inform the student that a course of action will be taken. Start something ASAP

This course of action will depend on the nature of the student/situation the school's policies and procedures, the available school and community resources, the support of parents and other agencies and what ever else might either help or hinder the process. See: *Policies, Chapter 35.*

1. BORDERLINE BULLY

The family

Usually in the case of the borderline bully the family is only too willing to assist. In fact, if the incidents are an outcome of some family issue such as illness, death, a relocation etc, the family may seek outside help. These parents:

- Are usually actively involved in child's education.

- Are usually active in helping child develop social, artistic and athletic skills.

- Are usually supportive of child's performance but not "hooked on winning."

- Seem to be providing a stable family environment for child.

Academic performance

The child:

- Generally has strong language and academic skills.

- Likely to have at least one or two dominant academic interests.

- May be operating in the above average to "gifted" level.

Child's response to being called to task.

- "Was I doing that? I didn't realize my teasing was getting out of line."

- "I guess I have stepped over the line."

- "Maybe I was trying to impress some of the other kids."

- "I hope I didn't hurt anyone too much."

- "I guess I had better apologize."

- "What can I do to make things right with the other student(s)?"

- "Can you help me deal with this issue?"

- "Can you help me know when teasing is OK? When does it becomes a problem? What are the guidelines?" (Here a simple counting process can really work. If the score is six for you and zero for the other person, then there is a problem.)

School's responses

Proactive

- It is important that the school be vigilant on all matters relating to bullying and victimization. If the problem can be "nipped in the bud" then weeks, years or even a life time of harm and sorrow can be avoided.

- Always be on guard. Pick off the early signs of bullying before it becomes an ingrained habit and modus operandi. Even **good kids** will bully from time to time.

- Provide a variety of social development activities whereby children can learn how to effectively live together in work and in play.

- If boredom is the issue, create new challenges for the student.

Reactive

- Depending upon the severity of the circumstances, either immediately demand the behaviour be stopped or remove the child from the environment and deal with the issue in another venue.

- Determine what may be the cause of this unusual behaviour.

- Seek parental support.

- Determine what programs and actions can be implemented to help these borderline "bullies" learn new social management skills.

- If the child is gifted it may be wise to modify his/her academic program to provide greater challenges and less boredom.

Why would this work

- Strong parental support.

- Good language skills which allow for meaningful discussion.

- Child-teacher relationship is strong.

- Child sees teacher as someone who is trustworthy and interested in his/her well being.

- The child's cognitive and social maturity is sufficiently developed and the change required is minimal.

- At this stage it is relatively easy to substitute a more acceptable behaviour into the child's repertoire.

- There is limited **emotional commitment** to pursuing a bullying pattern of behaviour.

*NOTE: There is both **good news and bad news** about the resolution of the "Borderline Bully" problem. The Borderline Bully fits into the stereotypical belief that bullying is simply a phase of life. **Just talk to them, ask them to stop** all too often **becomes,** the proposed solution for all bullies. In fact, with the vast majority of bullies, this approach only makes things worse. The old adage of "knowing your enemy" is so applicable in this and many other behavioural situations.*

Case study

Billy was 8 years old and in the top 3-4 children of his class. He got along with all his classmates and participated well in all group activities. In early February 2005 Billy was repeatedly observed verbally abusing his classmate Michael who has a reading problem. The teacher quickly realized that this behaviour was uncharacteristic and showed no signs of relenting. She took Billy aside and quietly challenged him on his actions. He immediately broke into tears and blurted out "That his dog had just died and he missed her so much." Billy was an only child. The dog had always been there and he was deeply grieving the loss of his life long companion.

His parents met with the teacher and a plan was put into place to help Billy deal with his loss but also to help him once again become a positive contributor to class activities. He sincerely apologized to Michael and made an sincere effort to try to help him.

2. THE "LEARNED" BIGOTED BULLY

The Family

Listen to the parents when you are having parent-school conferences or dealing with discipline issues. What are they saying? How do they phrase it? What is the tone of the voice, the eye movement, the curl of the lips? Is this a family who will be able to help in this matter or will they provide active resistance to any attempt the school makes to have the child become less bigoted and more socially responsible? Again it is important to note that **bigotry is supported by intolerance of all kinds.**

- Are the parents actively involved in the child's education? If so, in what manner?

- Do the parents feel that their child or children are treated unfairly and others are given preferential treatment?

- Do the parents see the school as vital to their child's success?

- Are the parent's attitudes and actions compatible with those of other parents in the community?

Child's academic performance

- Generally bigoted individuals only strive in a half hearted fashion to achieve excellence.

- They often fear the embarrassment of failure should they try to compete with "the other" students.

- They are less willing to risk.

- They blame their lack of success on the preferential treatment given to others rather than recognizing the willingness of others to strive.

Child's responses to being called to task

- They are usually very defensive.

- They try to deflect accusations of wrong doing by using common bullying defences of "Just teasing," Can't they take a joke?"

- Very often they let their biases "shine through."

- Most are unable to understand that they are doing anything wrong. It is their right to defend their traditional part of the school and community turf.

◆ Most of these children know that they will be supported by their parents and others in the community.

NOTE: Many teachers are from the "outside" and as a result may not be seen as supporting the values of the community.

School's responses

It is important for the school to understand that it is a microcosm of the world. It is also important to meet the challenges of having children legitimately increase their own sense of self, to feel a sense of comfort in the midst of others and to be willing to strive together for the common good. These are the major tasks in building social consciousness.

Example: A case in point rests with a former captain of a high school football team which had a record of social insensitivity. After one year of sensitivity training he said "That XXX High School was a great school except for the ...." The empty space was filled with, negative references to racial groups, gender and gender orientation and non athletic students.

*NOTE: This response reflects not only the deep seated nature of bigotry but also that the **emotional feelings** surrounding bigotry are **very resistant to cognitive messages.***

Proactive

◆ Possess an affirmative action program, ensuring that whenever possible people of different cultures are included within the staff compliment.

◆ Develop, follow and make known the school's strong policy of tolerance to others.

◆ Have an active multicultural program.

◆ Develop a complex extra curricular program which allows, in fact strongly encourages, students to participate in more than one type of activity.

Reactive

◆ Respond to the incident as quickly as possible.

◆ Before taking discipline or other action gather as many "facts" and perceptions as possible.

◆ Using the age or ages of the persons involved determine the level of knowledge these individuals should possess concerning the school's policy and procedures on matter of harassment and bigoted activity.

◆ Is this a repeated or first time "reported offence" for the individual?

◆ You may use reflective activity and encourage the child to reply orally or in written form to a variety of questions such as:

  ◆ "Why did you do this?" (The usual response is "I don't know." This may actually be true BUT upon reflection they may be able to shed more light on the issue.)

  ◆ "How did it make you feel?"

  ◆ "How do you think the other person feels?"

  ◆ "What would you do if this happened to you?"

  ◆ "How would you feel?"

  ◆ "How can you make amends?"

  ◆ "In what way did your actions fail to meet the expectations of the school rules?"

  ◆ "What new behaviours or attitudes will you need to adopt so that this activity will not be repeated?"

  ◆ "How can the school help you learn better ways to handle your feelings about other students?"

◆ Determine how you may wish to involve the parents?

◆ What programs might be mounted in the school, taking into consideration, the school's and community's resources in this area?

◆ How, if appropriate, can this student be helped to become honestly more competitive?

◆ Who else may need to be involved?

◆ Determine how you might use restorative justice, conflict resolution and mediation in this or similar situations.

Why would this work

On the surface it appears that bigotry is simply a learned behaviour but actually it is a learned behaviour cum attitude. The difference is that attitude has a strong emotional component. What started out as cognitive learning quickly evolves into something more emotionally complex. The bigot's emotional response system is supported by fear, hate and anger. The bigot "sees Red" when he or she is bested by someone of a despised group.

• The program uses a combination of knowledge, to help reframe the cognitive memory system and interactive exercises designed to restructure the emotional memories.

- Leaders within the community should be involved in the overall school program. It is so easy for children to mimic elders and thus feel supported in their actions.

NOTE: In today's world. If we removed hatred based upon race, real or perceived religious beliefs, sexual orientation and greed we would have a very congenial planet.

NOTE: The suicide terrorist bomber is so filled with hate that they will sacrifice their life to kill members of another race or society. This is the ultimate bigot.

Case study

Some children and adults never get a chance to have a positive interaction with a person of another race, creed, colour etc. Alex, a 12 year old Caucasian, and a member of a touring boys choir was such a child. He was billeted at our house for two nights and shortly after he arrived he met Solomon my former colleague from Ghana, also a house guest. He immediately went to my wife and said. "Who was that?"

Very briefly, I was planning on putting down carpet in the recreation room that evening and at dinner I jokingly said to Alex that I was glad he was staying with us because I could sure use some extra help. He thought this was great idea and as soon as dinner was over there were five bodies, my two children, Alex, Solomon and myself, down on the recreation room floor taking up old carpet and putting down the new. Frequently Solomon and Alex worked side by side. Of course, Alex has long since left our lives, but it is my hope that the one evening of interaction he had with Solomon will have given him a new perspective on people of another colour. **But once is usually not enough.**

NOTE: The key message to be gained from the above case is that there was no discussion on how or why two races should get along but rather an opportunity for the individuals to work together on a project.

It is easier to engage the emotional brain of a child through activity than it is through language.

See:

- *"Emotional Memories."*
- *"Authentic Self Esteem."*
- *"Achieving a **Personal Best**."*
- *"It takes a Community."*
- *Restorative Justice case studies. Search Google – "Racial Conflict Fairmont High School" as an example*

3. "LEARNED AGGRESSIVE" BULLY

The family

When you have met with the family, has there been indications that they hold a **"Win at all costs attitude?"** This may be made evident by comments such as "We hope that nothing interferes with Johnny making a Major A hockey team." "We think he has a good chance of going pro." "That's the way life is, eat or be eaten."

Is the family successful within the community? If so, what has contributed to their success?

NOTE: It is also not unusual for such a family to derive their status within a community vicariously through the success of their child.

Gather an appreciation for:

- How the family members behave a sports events when their child is playing?
- Does the family encourage the child to develop skills?

NOTE: Many "Learned Aggressive" individuals tend to rely on size or a specific attack behaviour rather than acquiring a skill set to achieve their goals.

- How does the family interact with the coach, referee or/and others including the players, fans and coaches of the other team.
- Would you like to sit beside them during a game?
- How do the parents define their child's success? It is their way to assessing what is important.

Example: Our neighbour's daughter, Helen, was a very good ringette player and was one of the top two scorers in the league. The other leading scorer was the coach's daughter. In the last two games of the season the coach "short shifted" Helen so that his daughter would have a better chance of winning the scoring title.

Academic performance

I recently heard of a mother who told the Grade Two teacher, "You needn't worry about how well Johnny will do in school, because he is going to play professional hockey."

Students often:

- Try to determine how to get the maximum grades with minimum effort.
- May try to intimidate a good student to write or do most of the work for a good paper or report.

- Tend to dislike assignments or exams when explanatory work is required instead of regurgitation of factual material.

- May be kinaesthetic type learners.

Responses when called to task.

- "That's the way the game is played. There's no room for wusses."

- "You're nothing if you don't win."

- "The more aggressive I play the more I'll get noticed by other coaches, scouts etc."

Example: I think of the male high school student who deliberately crashed into the staff goalie in a noon hour student-staff floor hockey game. His reply when challenged about his unnecessary rough play during a friendly game was "I play the same way whether it's just a pickup game or we're in the league playoffs."

*NOTE: This child's social responsibility skills seem to be showing definite **signs of underdevelopment.***

School's responses

Although every school and community likes to have winning teams, there is a point when the focus on winning creates a mind set which is dangerous not only to the sports program but also to the mental development of the children involved. In life we don't win all the time. Sometimes we "crash and burn" and then we have to get back up and try again. **Skill attainment whether it be social, cognitive or kinesthetic is acquired through drill and a great deal of hard work. These skill development processes are the ones which** allow the individual to regroup and also establish some consistency in their lives.

The lives of people who solely or heavily depend upon always having a "**winning record**" are often riddled with unhappiness and frequently substance abuse.

The above statement does not mean that we should not encourage competition but rather the urge to compete should be coupled with considerable emphasis on achieving the highest possible skill level and developing solid life skills.

Proactive

- Try, where possible, to help all students take responsibility for being the best they can possibly become.

- Develop ways of evaluating the results of the game in addition to winning and losing. This could include a short debriefing at the end of the game. What did we really do well? What was the most exciting part of the game for each player? What did we do better than last game? What can we work on as a team for the next game?

- Teach skill development so that it becomes second nature to the child's approach to an activity.

- Try to build into each child's "attainment portfolio" a series of short and long term goals.

- Teach learning.

- Teach safe play.

- Help each student develop a healthy sense of self.

Reactive

The child may:

- Be directed to take anger management training.

- Be counselled on team work, specific skill development and playing within the rules.

- Be asked to reflect on how they see themselves, how others including team mates and classmates perceive them, how they could make a greater contribution to their own development and the development of others in the class. Many of these individuals are very narcissistic in their thinking.

- Need to become increasingly aware of his/her responsibilities to self and others.

Why may this work

Any time we can help a student or an adult become aware that they are much more than the clothes they wear, the car they drive or the amount of money they have to spend this weekend, then we have achieved a great deal.

This is not an easy task because we are living in a "**dumbing it down**" society. Children and adults alike tend to focus on short time frames, quick fixes and some kind of single measure score sheet. The brain doesn't grow and mature to its fullest potential in such a climate.

- See: *Self Esteem.*

- See: *Personal Bests.*

- See: *Addictive Substances.*

- See: *Social Development.*

- See: *Anger.*

Case Story 1

Marcia is in Grade 8, an average student and although school is not a great deal of fun she seems driven to compete in teams sports, primarily basketball and soccer. Her parents attend every game and cheer her on as well as verbally abusing players on both teams. If any of her fellow team mates make a mistake Marcia's Mum is immediately denigrating both the player and the coach for not involving her daughter in that play. Marcia's school is a small Junior High and her teams are infrequent winners at local tournaments. On one such weekend tournament Marcia told the coach and her team mates before the opening game that if they lost she wasn't coming back for any more games that weekend. The team lost and the coaches prepared the team for the next game on the assumption that Marcia would be a "no-show". Just before the game was to begin Marcia appears and says she is ready to play. The coaches say "Sorry, we weren't expecting you and we will play this game without you." Marcia leaves the dressing room in tears and the game begins. At the first timeout her father races across the gym floor and verbally assails the coaches and the team members. He says, "The team is crap , the coaches are crap and the only good player they have is his daughter" He won't leave and the referees have him escorted out of the gym.

In the social arena, Marcia has a few friends and her most recent exploit was to use MSN to try to get the team members to shun the daughter of one of the coaches. Fortunately, in this case, most of the girls replied that they liked Bailey and will continue to be her friend.

Case Story 2

Parental control in sports can take some bizarre turns. Timmy plays hockey on a team of 9 and 10 year olds and was a conundrum to his coach for although Timmy has above average skating and shooting skills he was never where the coach expected him to be. The riddle was solved when Timmy crashed to the ice after bumping into another player. As Timmy was being gathered up someone noticed a "hearing piece" lying on the ice. This is odd as Timmy was not deaf or hard of hearing. What was really happening was that Timmy's Dad was sitting in the stands with a small transmitter and was directing Timmy's play. Timmy was a kind of tiny robot hockey player.

Nothing further is known about Timmy but it is likely he gave up hockey as soon as he could.

4. "CONUNDRUM" BULLY

Know the family

It is impossible to know all that could be known about all families. In Canada where divorce ends nearly 30% of all 1st marriages, it is also known that even in the families that stay together there are always a few tensions. Some of these revolve around their children and children are being asked to choose between parents and or their wishes? Is one parent dominant?

All of the above and more can accumulate to become an enormous cognitive and emotional burden for the child's still developing brain. Any time there is an argument, they often wonder, will this lead to a marriage break up and am I somehow to blame. Most families are very good about hiding a substance abuse problem such as alcoholism, or a mental health issue such as depression or financial difficulties brought about by a job loss or a struggling business.

Often what you see is not what is happening. While outsiders may not know, the kids know or have a sense when things are not going well. Additional pressures include:

- What are the expectations that the parents have for the child? Are these realistic or an attempt to have the child live out a parental fantasy?

- How have the parents relayed these expectations to the child? Is the child being exposed to a kind of emotional blackmail such as you'll break my heart if ...?

- Why do the parents have these expectations?

- Is there balance in the parents expectations?

- Is there room for input from the child or other persons?

Academic Performance

- These individuals are often good students. They will, get into college, but they may not win many scholarships.

- Parental pressures and interests may be distracting the child from a solid academic performance.

- The child maybe experiencing stress as evidenced by being slightly more concrete in his/her thinking than you would expect for a student of this age and family background.

- The child may be showing academic preferences and skills that are not congruent with parental thinking.

Response to being called to task

- There is often an element of surprise. After all this student usually has a very positive school and community profile.

NOTE: School officials often find themselves in the awkward position of having to discipline a student who is a local idol. This is even more troublesome when the situation exists in a small community and the school official is an outsider. Local values can become part of the issue. In addition, the whole town doesn't know all the facts.

- The student may deny that there was any malicious intent in his/her interaction with other students.

- Some students acknowledge that they have been under some pressure and perhaps that has caused them to "cross over the line."

- Depending upon the prior relationship between the student and the school official, the student may become vigorously defensive or quite conciliatory.

School's Responses

Proactive

The students who most often fall into the "Conundrum" category are in their last few years of high school. They are caught between their natural desire for independence, a realization that they may not be able or want to fulfill the specifics of their parents wishes and are feeling pressured by their parents. The key to addressing the needs of this child is to realize that this child, even though they are from the right side of the tracks, is bullying other students and these actions must be addressed.

- Some educational, career and personal counselling is normally in order.

- It is usually wise to provide all student council members with leadership training. Some of the topics include, goal setting, meeting procedures, communications skills, group dynamics, responsibilities to the entire student population, use and abuse of power. The later of course deals with bullying.

- It is important for student leaders to understand how their actions can either enhance or undermine their leadership effectiveness.

- Student leadership can be an excellent means of building authentic self esteem.

- The need to have your counter bullying program well publized and hopefully understood by the community at large is vital when you know you will need to deal with children who for one or more reasons have a high profile.

Reactive

- You must call the student on his/her actions.

- It is essential that the counsellor seek out the reasons for this behaviour. Again it is important to note that children under stress or those who have been dominated to follow certain paths frequently are underdeveloped in the area of social responsibilities.

NOTE: It is possible that while such children may be popular in the community at large they are not well liked by a number who know them well. Often this group is largely made up of team mates. To combat this sense of dislike the child embarks upon a series of bullying activities.

- The high school coach could be asked to help these students from the following perspectives of team play, skill development and team leadership.

NOTE: The law of natural selection for athletes, There are many good, even above average, high school athletes but there are few exceptional athletes.

- Emphasize the need to develop skills in all aspects of life. Hard work and perseverance is required.

- These children need to take responsibility for their actions.

- Reflective assignments may prove very useful.

NOTE: Although the male tense has been used this issue is not gender specific.

- Male-female relationships could be adding to the problem.

NOTE: It is common for senior male students to be socially less mature than their fellow female students.

Why would this work

Once you can get beyond the parental expectations and the community idolization, then you have an increased likelihood of being able to help the individual take some level of personal control.

- The child is probably of good intelligence and has the capability of understanding the dynamics of the situation.

- This child may likely respond well to coaches.

- This child might respond well to administration or teachers with whom they have a working relationship.

Case Study – Mark, the kid with so much

Mark is a bully but he doesn't match the image of the stereotypical bully. This again proves that stereotypes can lead us astray when dealing with anomalies of the human condition.

Mark is the only child of Jack and Dorothy G. Jack, a former semi pro hockey player, owns and operates a successful business in a medium sized town. Dorothy, his high school sweet heart, was a "stay at home" Mum but now works as the office manager for the family firm. The family lives well and Mark, by local standards, has had the best of everything.

He is a tall, good looking, well built young man who excels at sports. He is the leading male athlete in his high school, plays centre on a local juvenile hockey team, pitches and plays third base for the regional baseball team and now, in this his final year at high school is the Student Council President. He is a good but not exceptional student and he had hoped to receive an athletic scholarship at the nearby university.

But Mark is a bully. He has history of being vindictive to kids who are over weight and when in middle school he was nasty to one or two children whose fathers work in Jack G's business. In this past year just when you would think he would take his leadership role seriously, it was noted his particular meanness to the freshmen male students. Also he can hardly tolerate Jim the top Grade XII student and takes every opportunity to put him down especially in Physical Education Class.

In the community Mark is seen as a local hero. His athletic prowess has been recognized ever since his days as a Pee Wee. On the day after a hockey game the talk in the coffee shop often centres on the "G" kid and how he pretty much controlled the game."

But close reflection of the game would reveal that Mark is not a team player. Other teams know this and they often will double team him knowing that he will try to score from a difficult position rather than pass to a team mate who is in the clear.

On another occasion a family friend relates the time he, his son, Mark and Mark's Dad travelled to the final game of a zone baseball playoff. In the last inning, Mark's team was down by two but when Mark came to bat the bases were loaded and two out. He struck out. If Mark had got a hit he would probably tied the game. He was "suckered" by a slow curve ball that broke well out side the strike zone. Mark's Dad was furious, "How could Mark let that fat farm kid make him look like an idiot". Mark never said a word but you could tell that his father's anger was very hurtful for him.

Mark's **mother** is very involved with her church and she has tried to involve him in this side of life as much as possible. He does sing in the church choir on those Sundays he is not playing sports.

But why does Mark bully?

Mark is a conundrum when you only look from the outside or simply at the surface. He is also a problem for the school officials because both he and his family have a high profile within the community.

He **seems** to have everything then why should he consciously or unconsciously need to bully others. Part of the answer might be found by checking out his attachment issues with his father. This may give one a better sense of his sense of self.

But for the most part he is defined by others including his father and probably by himself as being a good athlete. However, he is not a superb athlete. Although he has attended a number of hockey schools and baseball camps he hasn't attracted the sincere attention of any team scouts. He has attended two junior hockey team tryout camps but was cut mid way through both of them. This was hard for him to handle but very difficult for his father.

A summary of the possible issues.

Although Mark seems to be a naturally gifted athlete, it is possible he realizes that he is only average when assessed against the top provincial athletes in his age group. This is hurtful and disheartening and he sees himself as a failure in this father's eyes.

NOTE: It is not unusual for young men and women to be hurt if not shattered when they come to realize that their athletic skills will not continue to garner the recognition in the larger arena and higher levels of competition.

Perhaps the hero worship which was bestowed upon him by the local and school coaches and local sports fans gave him an unreal perception of himself and how he was were going to cope with life. Perhaps he is wrestling with the confusion about what he is going to do next and will he have his parent's support.

5. "STATUS BULLY" – BULLYS FOR LAUGHS AND "APPLAUSE"

NOTE: This person often doubles as the class clown, a "good ole boy", some one who sees school more as a social club than as a place of learning and a leader for similarly minded individuals.

Know the family

This family is often middle of the road. They are not strongly supportive of education but would be happy if the kid succeeded at something. While alcoholism is not necessarily a problem, social activities do involve the liberal use of alcohol. The child has grown up in a home where striving for success is more the exception than the rule. Parents:

- Are only moderately concerned with the academic success of the child.

- May contend that these "bullying activities" are normal "kids play."

- Recall doing the same thing when they went to school.

- Provide a fairly stable family environment.

- May discipline child with a short term grounding if problem is deemed serious enough.

Response to being taken to task

- Tries to include his "friends" in his defence.

- Doesn't think it's a big deal.

- Expects to strut out of your office with a smile on his face into the arms of his fans.

- Tries to shift the blame to the victim. "He's such a geek."

- Why are you picking on me? I wasn't the only one.

School's responses

Proactive

This is a very common and publicly visible form of bullying. It is more than simple malice. The bully in this case is getting a "**major hit**" from the applause he receives from his fan base.

The challenge here is to determine between what might be over exuberant fun and what is routine harassment. Check the kid out. It is highly likely he wants recognition, he wants applause. He does seem to have some "leadership" skills although they are misguided and inappropriate.

These are also the adolescents who tend to get into binge drinking on weekends.

In addition, to the bully himself there are a group of passive or somewhat active peers who are providing a support system. They must also be dealt with.

- Look around, do the school teams or economic groups provide an unhealthy form of cliquishness?

- How are these students viewed by most of the other students?

- Use a school survey on bullying to get a student perspective on the level of bullying activity.

- Distribute the results.

- Encourage the students to mount a poster program on social consciousness and responsible citizenship.

- Engage the drama club to develop some short skits and longer plays on bullying.

- Do information cum knowledge building on addictions and who are more likely to become addicted.

Reactive

- Who are the so called friends of this bully? Could they be split up or could their energies be channelled more productively?

- How can you give this kid applause for doing something constructive and responsible?

- Work at getting this student to make a meaningful and heart felt apology to the target of his actions.

- Add a significant, age appropriate, section on humour into the language arts curriculum.

- Can we overload his curriculum by focussing on his strengths?

- Work at improving language skills?

- Once again spend time doing reflective assignments with the student.

Why should this work

- You are trying to increase his sense of intrinsic rewards.

- You are trying to get him to realize the seriousness of his actions.

- Consider the possibility that either the bully or the victim or both are afflicted with ADHD.

NOTE: It is important that this student STOP taking the short route to a hit. Repeated activity of this type leaves him vulnerable to becoming addicted.

- See: *Social Skills Development.*

- See: *Authentic Self Esteem.*

- See: *Learned Bigoted Bullying.*

- See: *Addictions.*

- See: *ADHD.*

*NOTE: It is important to realize that this bully type probably causes as many children to contemplate or commit suicide than all other bullies combined. The primary reason is that the bullying is done in full public view, there is public acceptance of the bullying and the **victim has few avenues to obtain support from other students.***

Case Study – George and his friends: The local jokers.

George and his victim James lived in a small town. George was 4-5 years older than James but he took particular delight in harassing James at every opportunity. There are two reasons for this. George is developmentally delayed on the social scale and James over reacts at each encounter. The school is a K-12 school and about 75% of the kids are bussed in every day. This means that not only do bullies and their victims arrive at and leave school at approximately the same time they may also ride the same bus. This was the case of George and James. George teased and taunted James nearly every school day for about six years. He not only bothered his victim on the bus, but also in the hallways and then on weekends and evenings at the hockey rink or other community gathering places. For example, if James had a plate of chips George would knock it out of his hands. George and his "friends" would laugh and James would go ballistic.

In late July, 2000 James took his father's .22 calibre rifle, went out to a far corner of the farm and shot himself.

George and his buddies were never called to task, have probably thought that James was a little goofy and besides they were just having a bit of fun. Last note George and his pals are now well into heavy drinking and using street drugs to get their highs.

James's family are left mourning the loss of their beloved son.

The school division's response was that they had a zero tolerance policy on bullying. **But having a policy and doing something with it, are often disparate acts.**

NOTE: In the above, the male pronoun was used as this is the type of bullying is largely a male thing. Although girls are not above this type of harassment they tend to be somewhat more verbal and less physical in their attacks on their targets. See below: Social power bully.

6. "SOCIAL POWER" OR RELATIONSHIP BULLY

The movie Mean Girls is based upon Rosalind Wiseman's book Queen Bees and Wannabees. The title itself can lead to an increased understanding of the power struggles within cliques inhabited by teenage girls. Diane Davis a counsellor for Davis County Schools adds that the "most difficult" groups to be around are the school (council) officers, dance groups and cheerleaders.

There are cliques within cliques and the rules vary in accordance to the special and sometimes hidden reasons for the existence of the clique in the first place.

Know the Family

In a small town, a girl and her two friends bullied a classmate for twelve years. Finally in Grade XII just weeks away from graduation, the victim quit school. The three bullies were from affluent, influential families for the area. The mother of the leader was a member of the school board.

The questions are: Why was this bullying taking place? Why was it allowed to go on for so long? What resolution was attempted in the past, if anything? What role did the three families play in consciously or non consciously supporting their daughters in these activities? Some parents:

♦ Are bullies. Perhaps the teachers were afraid to address the issue.

♦ Are not emotionally close to their children

♦ Show their love to their children by giving them material things.

♦ Feel it is their duty to be community leaders to ensure their children have community activities but not necessarily strong personal values.

NOTE: Research on emotional attachment is suggesting that girls who are avoidantly attached to their parents but especially to their mother are often found at the centre of such dysfunctional cliques. The rationale may be that these girls want to form a family which they can control but invest as little intimate emotion in the process as possible because they have never experienced warmth and support within their own family.

Academic performance

It is common for relationship bullies to control or try to control the very top students. These bullies feel that they are **entitled** to be at the top of the class and will try to intimidate others to do poorly. Or they might befriend a top student solely for the purpose of controlling that person's academic performance. These students:

♦ Are usually in the top 20% of the class.

♦ Usually possess good language skills.

♦ May be experiencing some pressure from home to perform at a higher level.

♦ May force their victims to perform well below their capabilities.

School's Responses

Proactive

There is often a reluctance to develop and deliver programs on bullying, drugs or sex because there may be some local resistance. The local consensus may be that if we talk about it they will all start doing it. **Well folks, they are doing it now, so lets see if we can make things better.**

It is important to raise the profile of relationship bullying. Adopt a poster campaign, bring in speakers to target both the cognitive and emotional aspects of being socially conscious and having a strong social conscience. Discuss the topic of values which will allow one to appreciate the talents and presence of others.

Get articles into the local newspaper, have speakers available to speak at service club meetings, find ways to get parents to come to the school and become increasingly part of their child's education. Make sure that people know that "Sticks and stones may break your bones, names will never hurt you" is wrong **all to often dead wrong.**

- Conduct a student survey on bullying to determine what is really happening at your school?

- Involve as many students as possible in an active information program.

- Create an atmosphere whereby students feel a moral obligation to help each other.

- Create within your staff the desires and skill sets to assist students who go out on a limb to help a student in need.

NOTE: It is not enough to say that bystanders should take responsibility. These children need the intrinsic motivation, the skills and the knowledge that school support is available.

- Flood the school with information about the seriousness of the problem. "Once is not enough." **One day wonders** often make the situation worse because **brain change,** while it may benefit from a kick start, needs constant support. In addition, there is a tendency for school authorities to step away from the hard work of dealing with inappropriate behaviour such as bullying especially something apparently as innocuous as relationship bullying.

- Use drama and role play.

- Be vigilant.

- Create programs whereby students have increased school and social responsibility.

- Ban camera-cell phones.

- Try to control cyber bullying. Run staff meetings. Invite parents in for information sessions. The students already know about the techniques involved BUT THEY DON'T APPRECIATE HOW DANGEROUS THE INTERNET IS WHEN USED IN THIS FASHION.

Reactive

- Deal with these girls one on one.

- They are likely to deny what they are doing is intended to be personally hurtful.

- Have them read and comment on one of several books on the topic.

- Have them reflect in written form on what they are doing and why they are doing it.

- Have them reflect on how it felt, if and when, it had happened to them.

- Have them become actively involved on a restorative justice exercise.

- Have them study the *Prognosis for Bullies* (Appendix V) and consider the aspects of that prognosis which they don't want for themselves.

- Teach them leadership skills, conflict resolution and mediation skills.

NOTE: In this later case, if the girl shows limited social conscience then giving them the leadership cognitive skills may actually make her more dangerous.

Why this should work.

- The more information which is available to all students the more students will be empowered to speak out to defend themselves and others.

- Increasing a child's ability to feel empathy and social responsibility will cause some students to think,"May be I shouldn't be doing this."

- See: *Authentic Self Esteem.*

- See: *Attachment.*

- See: *Chapter 16 on groups.*

- See: *Chapter 23 on Creating Social Brains.*

Case Study

Mary Jane is a long time bully. She and her "pals" have continuously harassed and tormented Eleanor for most of the twelve years they have been together in their small rural village K-12 school. Mary Jane was not raised on the wrong side of the tracks in fact her family has always held responsible leadership roles in the community with her mother currently being a member of the school board and her father a successful farmer, who is very active in a service club and the Chamber of Commerce.

Mary Jane has never wanted for anything material, she has had dance and music lessons. She has competed in many festivals, travelled in Canada and the USA and always wears what passes for childhood and teenage fashion. But she is still a bully. She is seen as the ringleader and has made Eleanor's life so miserable that Eleanor, a good average student, has left school a few months before senior graduation. **Mary Jane is very typical of a relationship bully.**

While there is never moral justification for bullying there are always underlying reasons for the behaviour. Mary Jane is the second of three daughters. In fact, if Mary Jane had been a boy the third birth would likely not have happened. Mary Jane was born about 15 months after her older sister Patricia. Patricia was, fortunately for her, a beautiful and precocious baby. She talked early, walked early, performed well in music, dance and any other endeavour she attempted. She was a model student.

Mary Jane is by no means a failure. She has, however, lived in the shadow of her older sister. Of course she didn't realize early in life that her bigger sister could do things better and be allowed certain privileges simply because she was older and slightly more mature. She rationalized, in her own way, that her sister was smarter and **more favoured.** The music and dance experiences never yielded as many top place marks and in school she often heard, "Your sister, was so good at ....." Mary

Jane's self image needed a boost and Eleanor provided the avenue for such a boost. Eleanor was an easy target. She was a little over weight, has freckles and in the earlier years wore her older sister's "hand me downs". She had been an eager student and early in the school years was every bit as good a student, if not better than Mary Jane. Eleanor wanted to be friends with Mary Jane and the other girls but before long Mary Jane began the systematic process of isolating her and keeping the other two girls to herself.

Some additional reading

- *Odd Girl Out* – Rachel Simmons
- *Queen Bees and Wannabees* – Rosalind Wiseman
- *Reviving Ophelia* – Mary Pipher

7. "IMPULSIVELY AGGRESSIVE" BULLY

This is the explosive kid who always seems to have a chip on his shoulder

Know the family

Should you need to work with the family, be prepared for at least one of the parents to exhibit a volatile, defensive behaviour. (One school, when dealing with such a family, always has the police on alert.)

- At least one parent may exhibit depression, alcoholism or an another disorder.

- Parents have had years negative interaction with the school and are not going "to take it anymore" and may become quite aggressive.

- The family may be a re-constituted family and the child is having a tough time with his/her new parent. Birth parent may defend child.

- Mother may give off "vibes" of being abused.

- On the other hand the child's anger may be the result of a brain injury. In this case the parents may be a great help.

Student's Response when taken to Task

The child may be volatile by nature and explode in your office or may repress anger, "flat line" and become studiously if not defiantly uncommunicative. The child may even appear under control and participate in a discussion but beneath the surface can't wait to get out of your office to **"beat the crap"** out of someone.

In the progression of bully profiles, this individual generally displays serious levels of cognitive and social underdevelopment and emotional instability.

The child's response will likely depend on the situation at hand, the stress level of their life at present and their relationship with you.

NOTE: When I am giving workshops I stress over and over again the necessity for you to be able to establish a working relationship with both the parents and the students.

There is no single formula or rule for solving these problems. It is an inexact science but having a working relationship with either the parent or student or both can be of immense value.

- Child may be aggressively paranoid about the unfairness of your accusations.

- Child may, if he or she trusts you, provide you with background information on why they are acting like they are and actually ask for help.

NOTE: It is uncommon for a child to display this type of behaviour based only on recent developments. Recent triggers may "tip the balance" but the brain's neural structure has been developing for some considerable time.

- Child, depending upon age, may assign blame to the victim. There can be a host of possible reasons, some real, some perceived and all enlarged by the child's imagination and volatility.

School's Responses

Proactive:

- Is there a safe place within the school for the student to go to when he/she feels intensely angry. **A punching bag is not recommended.**

- Are there intensive and extensive anger management programs available in the school or community?

- Are these students being taught to monitor their mood changes?

- See: *Anger management.*

- Have staff been trained in dealing with excessively angry students?

- Are there specialized training or treatment programs available (which may include medication) or does the school wait until the anger gets out of control and then the student must be dealt with as a serious discipline problem?

- What internal structures can be modified to create a more positive dynamic for the student? These might include change in curriculum, coaching on learning techniques, a period of time when the child is involved in strenuous exercise or quiet meditation.

Reactive:

- Keep calm but be firm. Anger begets anger.

- Is there evidence of mental disorders?

- Determine what additional professional help including medical attention may be called upon.

  NOTE: This does not mean that the student's behaviour is excused or excusable because there is a medical reason for the child's anger. But rather means that you are prepared to explore every possibility of creating an internal and external environment where the student can react to challenge without being distracted by angry outbursts and whereby teachers and other students can operate in safety.

- Is ODD or ADHD or FAS an issue?

- Know the child. Know the triggers.

NOTE: When the child is calm there is greater likelihood of success.

- Assess the child's language skills. Does work need to be done in this area?

- Can you or another staff member teach the child a personalized anger management plan?

NOTE: The ultimate measure of success would be for this angry individual to be able to honestly apologize to his victims.

BRAIN FACT # 72

It is highly unlikely that any brain which is hyper vigilant or emotionally engaged in anger will be able to easily enter into a cognitive learning or rational discussion.

Why would this work

The process is to help the student build skills which will, over time, change the brain's reaction to a variety of triggers. This is a slow process. Anger is not simply a cognitive approach to a situation but rather includes a complex number of unfavourable emotional memories.

There are no guarantees

- If you are able to prove to the child not only by your actions but also by the child's own observations that success is possible, the child may be more willing to buy into the program.

- If the child is coming from a hostile dysfunctional home, there may be need for a cooling down space each and every day. Use of quiet music, low lights and being able to be alone may help get the child off to a day of learning.

- If the child is deeply frustrated by his lack of academic and other successes he is likely experiencing an anxiety attack almost every school day.

- See: *Anger and Anger Management*

- See: *ADHD, Depression, FAS*

- See: *ODD*

Case study

In our school there were two Bob Smiths and they became known as big Bob and little Bob. Big Bob had an anger problem. He was the oldest son of a military officer who was the base discipline officer. Officer Smith demanded respect, was obsessed with power and had a problem with alcohol. He didn't leave his work at the office but instead brought it home to his wife and three children. He routinely disciplined his sons by going a couple of rounds of boxing with them.

Big Bob grew up first fearing his father and then later trying to avoid him. He learned early that he could never please his father, he wasn't athletic and he had pretty much given up on school. In fact he was putting in time until he could leave home. Although he didn't work very hard at his subjects he nevertheless took criticism badly. Every low grade was an insult. Every time he was caught loitering in the hall, he took this as an attack. In class he would mock students when they asked questions and he kept some of his teachers on edge. His anger was always evident from the sneer on his face, to the abrasive and abusive way he dealt with those not his friends and about once every couple of weeks there was fight with another student.

8. "PERSONAL POWER" BULLY

While all bullies are driven by a need to dominate others for one or more reasons, the Personal Power Bully is compulsively driven to control at least one person. **An example** of this bully is the boy/girl friend or spouse who is excessively jealous of their partner and becomes enraged if this person is seen talking to another, unable to account for all time for which they are separated etc. This person becomes even more dangerous should the couple split up. These people are the stalkers, the ones who completely disregard a judge's restraining order or will commit murder in order that their former lover person doesn't take up with another partner.

In the high school setting these are jealous controlling boyfriends or girlfriends or throughout the school obsess on their victim or wait around the corner for their victim to appear.

In addition these people **will plan their attacks,** will set goals such as stealing a certain amount of money, or destroying their victims property or coercing them to do things that are clearly wrong. There is much more!

Know the family

It is extremely common for there to be severe dysfunctional factors within the family environment. Even in families which have not been interrupted by separation and divorce, there is often alcoholism or an abusive parent and a pattern of inconsistent and severe discipline. It is highly possible that the child has not bonded with either of the parents. This is an environment where bullying begets bullying in a very significant manner.

Children from broken or reconstituted homes often live with a deep sense of emotional or physical insecurity.

- Generally only one member of the family will speak at a parent-school interaction.

- The dominant adult, often the abusive spouse, tries to control all aspects of the interview including you.

- The dominant parent frequently blames the spouse for failing to "bring up the kid right."

- If alcoholism is an issue there is usually a great deal of denial.

*NOTE: There is **no socio-economic or vocational group which can be excluded** from the above. Parents who are repressing anger, suffering from depression, living within unstable homes all create environments which support this type of bully.*

- Parent(s) may threaten to sue or physically assault school officials.

Example: I was in such a meeting where the father offered to go outside and settle the issue with the principal.

Example: A female cousin, who was a headmistress, in England confronted an angry father who was carrying a length of chain and was going to "tune up" his child's teacher.

Example: My dental hygienist's father was an elementary school principal who at least once threatened by a shotgun toting parent and on another occasion was physically attacked by a parent.

Academic performance

Some students may be so out of synch with the curriculum that they see your school as just one more frustrating or even threatening experience.

They and their parents have minimal expectations about your school and education in general. There is absolutely no guarantee the age-grade education system we use meets the needs of a significant number of these students.

Children growing up in dysfunctional homes or communities can be developmentally delayed.

- Weak language skills.

  NOTE OF EXCEPTION: Occasionally students in this category are academically gifted and are bored into defiance. Academically gifted students who are made to conform to a curriculum or classroom structure which not only does not challenge them but actually may de-motivate them can become troublesome students. Whether or not these children would resort to physical violence would depend on how their giftedness is managed.

  Furthermore, there is no guarantee that giftedness translates into exceptional social development.

- Weak social skills except with students of their own "kind."

- Many of these students do not see a significant future for themselves.

- Many of these students do not find the curriculum meaningful.

- Their work, if done at all, is of poor quality.

Response to being taken to task

Most of these kids are old pros at being taken to the Principals office.

- There is likely to be defiance.

- They will want to know who turned them in.

  NOTE: Treat the above query with great care. If these bullies get the idea that their victim or the victim's parents reported the bullying they will endeavour to seek revenge on the victim.

- The student may even try to dominate you.

- There will likely be denial and even some paranoia like statements.

NOTE: Counsellors and psychotherapists find these individuals frustrating to involve in a development program.

NOTE: Deal with these kids one on one.

- They are unlikely to show any remorse

  NOTE: Their level of low social conscience and perhaps some narcissistic traits prelude consideration for others.

Some may even confuse the situation by threatening legal action.

School's Responses

Proactive

- Recognize this deviant behaviour as early as possible. Pre-kindergarten may not be too early.

- Engage the child into a behaviour moderation program. Reward or discipline with privileges. Be prepared to continue a behaviour program throughout the child's school life.

Example: A pre-kindergarten child kicks every other child in the group. When asked why he did so, he replied "I don't like them."

NOTE: Most of these kids started to make their presence known in Kindergarten but because we didn't appreciate the seriousness of their condition nor anticipate the final outcome schools have traditionally been reluctant to put the time and resources into trying change their dysfunctional brains. In addition, when children move to the next grade or the next school the behavioural program is often dropped.

- Be prepared for the long haul.

- You might want to create a student handbook of Bully Case Studies. The combined works of the Creative Writing Class or the Journalism Students coupled with assistance from the senior Psychology class under the direction of an interested staff member could make this a dynamic school project.

An example might be. A case study specific to teenage relationships that are destructive. What are the dynamics? Why is it difficult to close down the relationship? What might be the outcomes of such a relationship?

NOTE: The sexual act causes the release of oxytocin within the female and vasopressin in the male. Oxytocin plays several roles one off which is bonding to the sexual partner which leads them to be reluctant to leave him (perhaps also out of fear), be willing to defend him or even believing that she can reform him.

Teenage girls and even older women may come to believe that they are treated badly because it is something they have done ie. they deserve to be beaten, threatened, dominated and humiliated.

In the male, the bonding actions takes another form. Vasopressin increases aggression and causes the male to become protective and possessive about the female. This can lead to physical, emotional and sexual abuse.

All too frequently insecure adolescent girls find themselves in a sexual relationship with a dominating insecure male. The neuro-chemical activities in both their brains doom this relationship from the start.

Reactive:

When preparing to meet with Personal Power Bully have a plan. This is a child involved in or bordering upon serious criminal activity.

- Refer again to Confronting the Bully.

- Be situation specific.

  NOTE: Consider the age, mental maturity and your previous encounters with this child. Realize that this child has a deep emotional commitment to his/her behaviour. There may also be a mental disorder such as Conduct Disorder at play.

- It is usually useless to consider sensitivity training.

- This child may respond to high activity Cognitive Behavioural Training or Resick and Schinke's Cognitive Processing Therapy, (CPT) or some adaptation of these.

  NOTE: Therapy which is passive, is unlikely to work. Their language skills and cognitive processing skills are usually too limited for discussion to make impact. Furthermore you have to reach their amygdala.

- Determine if there are other contributing factors such as ADHD, FAS, Depression etc.

- If so, try remediation which addresses these issues.

- Might this person be showing some signs of Oppositional Disorder or Conduct Disorder.

- Determine if there is someone else within the community who might be able to help this child.

- Is there an alternative school which may be able to provide the attention needed?

- Try to determine the status of the child's authentic self esteem.

- You may consider the use of professional therapies which are both cognitively and emotionally focussed.

Why would this work

Who knows!

- The secret to dealing with problems of any kind but more important a problem of this significance is to try to find "windows of opportunity" and deal with one or two aspects of the problem. Sometimes that allows the troubled student enough confidence to take calculated risks.

- The brains driving most of these children are much more concrete and less abstract than the brains of other children of the same age. Therefore activity is critical.

- See: *ADHD, FAS and Depression.*

- See: *ODD and Conduct Disorder.*

- See: *Authentic Self Esteem.*

- See: *Social Conscience.*

Case study

Rod is a Grade XI is a student in a public school located in the upper income area of a mid sized city. His father is a well known personality having played professional hockey on the NHL and is now the owner of a successful sports business. He was a tough, aggressive player who usually played as checker on the third line. Although he moved to three or four teams throughout Canada and the USA, the family residence for most of Rod's early school years were based in a large Canadian city. For about eight to nine months a year Rod's mother was left to look after him and his older sister.

Rod's relationship with his father is a complex mix of hero worship, long periods of absence, an unnatural sense of responsibility and a lack of closeness even when his father was home. A couple of examples may help explain the above. When Rod's father would leave for a hockey season, he would, in a macho manner, say, "Rod, I want you to take care of your Mum and sister while I am away". Rod as a child could never really understand what his Dad was saying, but in his mind he had some responsibility and a sense that his mother needed taking care of but when his Dad returned, Rod was unceremoniously dumped from his position of authority. Over the years his Dad used his influence to get Rod on a couple of hockey teams which were actually for boys far more talented than Rod. Since Rod hadn't worked to get on the teams he felt no need to work at staying on the teams and his skill level did not improve.

Finally the coach of his school hockey team cut him from the squad for two reasons one Rod wasn't a very good player and secondly he was so disruptive that an assistant coach had to be on his case continuously.

In school he is argumentative, obstructive and has selected several students to bully on a daily basis. His father blames the school for these problems and says this was never a problem when Rod attended elementary and middle schools in the larger city. However, the mother has, on separate occasions, indicated that actually there were numerous problems in both of his former schools. Rod is particularly rude and obnoxious in classes where the teacher is female.

Rod's has had the same girlfriend for the last two years who is not a member of the school's "in crowd" and not from a well to do family.

Rod also has a small cadre of friends who will do Rod's bidding for him such as the time last Summer when Rod gave money to one of his buddies to get another student drunk. If someone not called 911 when this student passed out on the street he would probably have died of alcohol poisoning. Rod showed **absolutely no remorse** when confronted about this situation.

His friends stay with him, in part, for the perks. There are free tickets to games, weekend parties at Rod's family cottage, Rod's family profile and Rod drives a pretty neat SUV.

In closing Rod's father gives strong evidence of being a bully, who thrives on his profile in the city and is not about to let some school teachers tell him that his kid has a problem.

9. SOCIOPATH BULLY

This bully is the most complete bully and lives virtually without social conscience. They are self absorbed, self convinced and are willing to commit any act for self gratification without concern for consequences and with no concern for the victim.

Know the family

Be prepared to have to deal with some of the most challenging families in your school system. Sociopath bullies are all too often the product of **highly dysfunctional** families where **physical**, social and sexual abuse are common place. Alcoholism and other drug abuse, reconstructed families, single parent families, foster care, abusive relationships, depression are common place. It is unlikely that the parents will be willing or able to provide assistance. There may also be social workers, the police or probation officers involved.

NOTE: The very fact that a child is or has been in foster care should raise a red flag. This does not mean that the foster care the child is receiving is/was bad or other wise wanting but rather that the child has had to be removed from a home which was/is incredibly dysfunctional. The emotions built around living in that home, being removed from the home and being placed with strangers are often deep and filled with angst and fear. However, in spite of all of this foster care is at the minimum better and hopefully a dynamic powerful force for good.

These are conduct disordered children.

Academic performance

- Limited language usage. **It has been shown that these children are often two to three years behind their peers in language.**

- Limited range of "meaningfulness."

- Limited interests and limited sense of the future.

    NOTE: However, there are some who are sufficiently gifted to be able to manipulate the system to their advantage.

- These children will almost never risk in classroom setting.

Response to being called to task

- Anger.

- Display of plenty of "street cunning."

- Indifference to activity.

- Completely unable to understand why there is any concern.

- Feels justified.

- May threaten or appear to threaten the authority figure.

School's responses

Proactive

This is an extremely difficult situation to manage. There are few windows of opportunity. **These children trust very few adults.** Most of the adults who have played important roles in their lives have betrayed them often in abusive or intensely neglectful manner.

- Incredible information can be found in *Without Conscience* – Robert Hare or *Trauma and Juvenile Delinquency* – edited by Ricky Greenwald

- Try to find an area of strength which can be built upon within the context of the school system.

   NOTE: The challenge for the school is to find the right challenges for the student.

NOTE: Although they possess a near psychotic sense of self, they are very careful to avoid structured environments in which they might fail. They present a dichotomy for on one hand they may torch a school, beat up someone, steal a car or get involved in selling drugs and/or unsafe sex but are usually afraid to try writing an essay or solving a mathematics problem.

- Traditional psychotherapy tends not to work. The experts tend to focus on rigid rote memory activities with rewards based on privileges.

Reactive

- Professional help should be sought.

- Removal to an alternate setting.

- Provision of teachers and other professionals who can care for these kids.

- Recommended treatment for ADHD, ODD, PTSD and anger if deemed appropriate.

- Intensive work on language.

   NOTE: It is not simply a matter that the child's language skills be brought to a level which will allow them to be able to handle academic subject material. It is important that their language skills be enhanced so that those doing therapy can engage these students in dialogue. Many of these children possess very immature conceptual capabilities. These concepts include fairness, responsibility for others, long term responsibility for self, the future and similar matters which most of us take for granted.

- Provide training/education which is "real" and appeals to their concrete manner of thinking.

- Be prepared for a long, slow rehabilitation process.

- Use non-monetary extrinsic motivators.

- Look for ways to "break up" the gang.

NOTE: Some of these children are so starved for attention and love that success has been achieved by giving them responsibilities to look after plants and animals. In selected cases they have been given responsibilities to assist in the care of special needs children or children who have been bullied.

Why might this work

We cannot shirk our responsibility to these children. The facts are very clear. Untreated, these children will have a better than average chance of becoming career criminals. Over 60% of these bullies will "do serious time". Garbino reports that over 80% of teenagers on death row are conduct disordered. It is costly to keep them locked up and it is scary to have them roaming the streets.

- They are trainable. The emphasis is on **TRAINABLE.**

- They do like material goods, the trick is to have them mature to the point where they will delay gratification.

- Medications might alter their behaviour to the point that can connect with their cognitive processes.

- See: *Authentic Self Esteem.*

- See: *ADHD, FAS, ODD and PTSD.*

- See: *Conduct Disorder.*

- Listen to Elvis singing "In the Ghetto."

- **Case Studies.** Please read *Lost Boys* – James Garbino.

CHAPTER 30
CYBERBULLYING

To research this topic I called upon two experts, Bailey, a female middle school graduate, and Bill Belsey, the founder of the website: www.cyberbullying.org

The computer and INTERNET have created a vast new means for the world to communicate in an instantaneous manner. Children, definitely pre-teens and up, have mastered the technology with ease and often use it with reckless abandon.

This is the 21st century extension of the telephone, the electronic bulletin board of recent past, of blackboards and hall bulletin boards, washroom graffiti and other manual means of "spreading the word."

Not everything is bad in fact most is AOK and is likely to be intellectually enriching.

Here is what I have learned:

1. **Adults have lost control.** The technology is beyond them. Parents are complaining to the schools about their children's inappropriate use of the home computer. What can the schools do except assist in a variety of ways to increase the parents understanding of the technology?

2. Many children are completely unsupervised when they are using the home computer. Even though a parent may not be as computer literate as their child, the parent still has the ability and the responsibility to observe what the child is doing on the computer and how much time the child is spending on the computer. Parents can also learn about how you can easily switch from one site to another.

3. Young children are incredibly vulnerable to the perversions of some adult users.

4. Children are using photo enhancement technology to appear older and more risque as they prepare their blogs. Others are simply doing their best to present a sexual image which is well beyond their years.

5. Many of these children do not realize that once a picture is placed on a website or blog or in a communication with a "trusted" correspondent that picture may be traded, sold or used in a defamatory way or even as blackmail. The picture is forever and may be manipulated into an unlimited number of "poses."

6. Digital photography removes the censorship that once existed with photo labs.

7. Some children are controlling their conversations with well known friends. Some of these are using aliases to disguise their real identity. Others are entering onto chat rooms where there is absolutely no control.

8. Fifteen year old girls are carrying on dialogue with older guys many time zones away or may only appearing to be many time zones away.

9. Grades are suffering.

ELECTRONICS – A MEDIUM FOR BULLYING

Cell phones, e-mail and hateful websites have given bullies a new venue for denigrating their targets. These include:

♦ Camera-cell phones have been used to take pictures of the targets in the washrooms, shower and change rooms and distribute these images instantaneously throughout the school. These same images can easily be placed on websites.

♦ Students are digitally altering photos to further embarrass their victims. Head shots are being superimposed on porno images or even animals.

♦ Instantaneous e-mail servers are being used to anonymously send out denigrating bulk e-mail for the sole purposes of hurting a specific person. In other cases threatening e-mail is being directed to specific students.

Example, my neighbour's son was the victim of such an attack. An unknown person threatened to cut him up with a razor blade the "next day" at school. In this case a suspect was quickly determined, the police seized his computer and found the offending message and a number of others.

NOTE: This was a very disturbed teen from a middle class dysfunctional home and was known to the police as they had been called to the house on two occasions after he had attacked his mother.

♦ Hateful websites use altered photo images, hateful language, defamatory statements, threats to the targeted persons or other persons who may associate with the victims.

♦ Most schools and police forces are not equipped to effectively deal with this blatant intrusion of privacy and the legal barriers which restrict prosecution.

♦ A number of schools are attempting to assist the parents by teaching evening programs on kinds of programs the children are involved with.

In addition parents are:

♦ Encouraged to keep computers out of the children's bedrooms.

♦ Encouraged to monitor the children's time on the INTERNET.

♦ To work at keeping an open relationship with the child concerning INTERNET activity.

♦ To involve the child in other activities so that the INTERNET is not all consuming.

♦ To discourage children from releasing personal information including names, photos, age and address to unknown persons.

NOTE: All of this is good and proper advice but teenagers have a keen sense of independence and a low sense of their own vulnerability. On a recent TV news cast teenage boys were quite dismissive of suggestions such as those above. In addition, if only certain parents are keen on intervening and others not keen, it won't take long for teens to migrate to the homes where supervision is lax or non existent. Relationship between parent and child is critical.

CHAPTER 31

VICTIMS – WHO ARE THEY?

Victims are the pawns in the bullies need for power and unconditional control. Most, but not all, have not chosen this role. They have been selected by the bully because they offer the aggressor a safe and sometimes profitable venue. They do and will suffer untold physical and emotional pain. They will feel shunned and excluded by the population at large, they may withdraw from actively pursuing their own goals and may settle for surviving at a minimal level for the rest of their lives. Others may over achieve and become highly successful all the while believing that driving a Benz is great retribution for pain suffered. Still others may get themselves into positions of authority and do one of two things. On one hand they may become incredibly ruthless and on the other may work hard to make sure their employees are treated fairly and encouraged to succeed.

VICTIM SUBSETS

1. **Children whose Brains are NOT in Survival Mode.** These include children who:

   - Spend a limited amount of time watching TV and playing video games but rather are able to occupy themselves, reading, playing a variety of card, board or backyard games with friends.

   - Their parents are active in their daily living. These children are regularly exposed to good behaviour. They verbally and socially interact with their parents, they eat and vacation together as a family. They are likely to have emotionally bonded with one or both parents.

   - They know that their parents have expectations of them and will help them reach these expectations but will also discipline them fairly and consistently when certain expectations are not met.

   - They interact with playmates whose families possess similar values as their own.

   - They have not needed nor have they learned the necessity to be on guard or super vigilant when interacting with others. **Aggression, for them, is not an automatic means of resolving disputes.**

   NOTE: A participant in one of my workshops exclaimed after hearing this exclaimed "Good heavens, these are the kids I and the people in this room are trying to raise."

2. **Those children who are alone or lonely, these include the child:**

   - Who is the soul member of a specific race, creed, colour in the school.

   - Who by his/her nature is highly introverted or shy and has few social skills.

   - Who has a complexion problem, has skin condition that causes body odor, is overweight or underweight, has an illness that prevents him or her from participating in certain activities, has a learning disability or a speech defect etc.

   - Who gets upset easily and cries or "goes ballistic" in even minor crisis situations.

   NOTE: These children seldom, in most schools, if ever receive the support of the general student population.

3. **Those children who lack basic defence mechanisms.** These children:

   - Tend not to fight because they have been taught that it is wrong to fight.

   - Are often the progeny of over protective parents.

   - Tend to not have quick replies to their tormentor, nor do they try or are able to use humour to diffuse the issue.

4. **Those children who are seeking attention.** These children:

   - Are often attention deprived and will seek out attention no matter how unpleasant that may be.

- May behave, dress or appoint themselves in a manner which may be seen as unusual although they may think they are making a personal statement.

- Frequently have low social interaction skills

- May be somewhat masochistic and actually enjoy being selected for negative attention.

- Have low social monitoring skills and may unknowingly act inappropriately in the presence of a bully.

- May claim they have been physically or verbally assaulted for the sole purpose of getting another child into trouble.

NOTE: Some of these children deliberately put themselves in the out group and although this is not an offense, they should be offered assistance to ensure their safety.

5. **Those children who are at odds with a dominant culture within the school.** Examples include:

   - A small number of children from one economic bracket attending school where most of the children are from families of a decidedly different income bracket.

   - Gay or lesbian children attending a school or living within a community where intolerance is high.

   - Children who are not athletic attending a school where athletics, particularly team sports, is a principal focus.

   - Children who are physically too small or too large or have some physical deformity which attracts attention.

   - Children who move to a school where inward migration is not usual.

   - Children who are from a racial group that is new to the community.

6. **Those children – adolescents who have been victimized at home or in a relationship.**

   These include children who:

   - Are socially underdeveloped.

   - Have limited authentic self esteem.

   - Are emotionally dependent on and fearful of their love partner (This is more common among insecure high school females).

   - Are abused emotionally, sexually and physically by their love partner.

7. **Those children who are being victimized and in turn are victimizing others.**

   These children are:

   - **Victims cum bullies.** And may be both in the same time span but, of course, in different venues.

CHAPTER 32

VICTIMS – WHAT CAN WE DO FOR THEM?

The long term prognosis for persons who are or have been victims of school yard bullying is, in general, not good if they haven't been able to access some assistance. That is why we should be concerned. Many lives are being and have been wasted both literally and figuratively.

The quick answer is: We must be:

♦ Concerned about loss of the child's learning and growth potential.

♦ Concerned about the child's mental and physical well being.

♦ Willing to help the child overcome their feelings of helplessness, unworthiness and hopelessness.

♦ On guard to help the child deal with thoughts of either suicide and homicide.

> *NOTE: A thirteen year old boy wrote in his final note to his parents the following words. "I often thought about killing them, but I am a good person." He then went and shot himself.*

NOTE: In virtually every high profile school or workplace violence situation the perpetrators of the crime were the VICTIMS NOT the BULLIES.

NOTE: A significant proportion of children placed in alternate classes for violent children are the VICTIMS NOT the BULLIES.

NOTE: There are very few victims who have not harboured thoughts about killing their tormentors.

UNDERSTANDING THEIR THOUGHTS AND FEELINGS

It is critical that we take a quick look inside the life of a victim. We need to understand their pain. **They:**

♦ Live a life of fear which may present its self as anxiety attacks, anger, stress, hopelessness, depression, sleeplessness, poor or reduced academic performance.

♦ **Very Important: Honestly believe that adults will NOT be able to help.**

♦ Develop a low sense of self. Often turn inward and blame themselves for their predicament.

♦ Are usually alone in their pain. In fact, others see the **victim as a "loser and a loner"** and they try their best to stay away. The victim becomes a leper.

♦ May be trying to deal with other problems such as a learning disability, ADHD, a speech or hearing affliction, weak social skills or predisposition for depression. Bullying may be the final straw which makes life completely unbearable and suicide becomes an option.

♦ Are afraid and/or too embarrassed to tell their story to their parents.

STRATEGIES FOR ASSISTING VICTIMS OF BULLYING

1. Believe the victims story. (If in doubt, check it out but do it later.)

2. Create a school contact and a safe haven. Every child needs to have access to a safe "human haven." Every staff member can be such a person.

3. Make it "cool" to support a victim. We need to rewrite teenage "cool" so that it is **"cool"** to be a responsible citizen. See: *Appendix IV.*

4. Counter the presence of "self blame"– it is not (at least 95% of the time) the victim's fault. Victims are almost always incredibly ashamed of being a victim. Teach Optimism.

5. Emphasize throughout the school the value of human dignity. Many teachers are justifiably worried about how stress and weak social development detracts from academic learning. In fact the grand total of academic learning will rise exponentially if the students are able to **feel safe** and pool their efforts toward the learning process.

6. Monitor children for behavioural changes. Sudden downward changes in school attendance, performance or behaviours is usually a tip-off that the child is being stressed and the stressor may be a bully. Put an **All Points Bulletin** on the kid to see what might be happening.

7. Provide the victim with support both in school and out of school. Parents need help working with their child and they also need to be able to interface with the school.

8. Teach assertiveness skills, use of humour, conflict resolution and mediation skills

9. Repeatedly inform all students that reporting incidents is not tattling. Student safety is the Number ONE criteria. See: *Chapter 16.*

10. Help all students to develop a solid sense of authentic self esteem. Authentic self esteem is not given to anyone but is earned through developing certain cognitive and emotional skills.

11. When the victim uncharacteristically lashes out, make sure **the entire story is understood** before action is taken. Being a victim is somewhat akin to being "**nibbled to death by a duck**". One day that duck will bite a vital nerve or bite one time too many. The tormentor probably did not do anything unusual but it was the one thing the victim could no longer tolerate.

12. A victim's situation is highly stressful. **Victims feel that no one can help them.** Provide the victim with counter stress techniques and another game plan.

13. Bullies bully, as they consciously and non-consciously see it, to level the playing field. Victims may resort to carrying some kind of weapon to level their own playing field. We must be proactive in dealing with the victims so that they don't rationalize that the only solution available solution is take matters into their own hands

14. Develop a school plan which ensures that the incidents of bullying are being dealt with as quickly and as thoroughly as possible.

LONG TERM PROGNOSIS FOR VICTIMS

What might be the long term prognosis for persons who are or have been victims of school bullying?

The following is a list of possible outcomes and examples. This cannot be a definitive list because there is not a definitive group or person living amongst us.

1. Some people **seem to be unscarred** by being bullied. This is seldom completely true although a vast number of people are able to forge ahead and become extremely successful and believe that the best defence is driving a Benz. But even the inner worlds of these individuals may carry around an unusual amount of personal insecurity.

2. The **shame** of being bullied may last a life time. Recently I watched a documentary on Chinese migration into Canada in the early 1900's. A distinguished gentleman recalled that shortly after arriving to Canada as 7 year old boy he started school and within days was chased by two larger boys who caught him, knocked him down and then urinated on him. The shame of that event was so deeply ingrained that even 80 years later he sobbed when relating the story.

3. Victims who become leaders may be super sensitive to the dynamics of the workplace but others will run the continuum of concern to indifference of employees personal needs to outright persecution of specific workers.

4. Many never reach their potential for several reasons. They leave school prematurely, they feel inadequate and fail to seek out other growth opportunities. For some, the experience has left them suffering from a mental illness such as depression, alcoholism and/or another drug addiction.

5. Many live the life of the perpetual victim in fear even though the old bullies are long gone. It is not uncommon for these individuals to enter into relationships where they are overly dependent on the other person. The vulnerability of their dependency leaves them open to abuse.

WHY SHOULD WE BE CONCERNED?

1. The answer appears to be very obvious. As educators, parents and leaders we have a responsibility to ensure that all children have the opportunity to maximize their potential. It is in our best interests to have people who are intellectually and emotionally well endowed living with us as friends, lovers, neighbours, co-workers, employers and casual acquaintances.

   We need to create and maintain safe schools and communities.

2. Within our schools there are victimized children who are operating in a dysfunctional manner and are curtailing your efforts to help all children to grow.

3. Victims, in larger numbers than are ever officially recorded, are committing suicide. Tim Field has written a very disturbing book called Bullycide which high lights case studies of children who have killed themselves as a result of being bullied. Please don't read this book alone.

4. Data is showing that approximately 15% of all students have been bullied at some point in their school life. These are not isolated incidents.

5. There is every likelihood that your child or the child of another family member or friend is currently being bullied.

   All children are precious gifts who deserve the opportunity to develop to their fullest potential intellectually, emotionally and socially.

CREATING AND IMPLEMENTATION ACTION PLANS

In this last section you will have the opportunity to explore a range of human dynamics, environmental and administrative matters which are designed to help you become increasingly able to deal with bullies and similarly dysfunctional students.

CHAPTER 33

ASSESSING SCHOOL AND COMMUNITY

The school, its students, their parents and the community at large are linked together in such a manner that they impact on each other on a continuous basis.

- The school is by its mandate an organized administrative structure.

- The children are required to attend school in accordance to the laws of the land.

- Parents have a large or small stake in the school depending upon their interest in their child's academic and social growth.

- Lastly, the community at large may or may not be much concerned with the school. If the community is not supportive of the school then the school becomes relegated to the status of an institution which is located within the community, somewhat like a jail.

Of course there are **continuums** for each of these groups.

- Schools may range from well organised, vibrant student growth centres to institutions of near total chaos.

- Students run the gamut from being excited, secure learners to angry frustrated individuals who hate being there.

- At one end of the scale parents may be enthusiastic, interested and supportive and at the other end display aggressive indifference.

- The relationship between the school and community is a complex array of finances, history, traffic, student mess and noise, age of residents, size of school, jurisdictional issues, intercommunications etc.

To help look at theses matters further lets look the groups in more detail.

THE CULTURE OF YOUR SCHOOL

A. What is the Status of Learning?

- Do parents have realistic and optimistic expectations for their children?

- Do parents actively assist their children to meet these expectations?

- Does the community support education?

- Is local business and industry supportive of education?

- Do students, as a group, have a commitment to becoming engaged in the learning process?

- Do teachers sincerely feel they are making a difference in children's lives?

- Are the administration and teachers supporting each other in the development of a positive school culture?

- Do the students feel a sense of ownership of their school?

- Is there a dominant sports or other culture within the school?

B. What are the Student Groupings in your School?

Most of today's schools are a mix students from a wide variety of races, cultures, skin colours, economic backgrounds, developmental histories and support systems. Although we may feel that all students should be treated equally, we must always be aware that the needs and wants of all students are not equal.

- What is the nature of racial groupings?

- What is the relationships between various racial groups?

- Are there two or more distinct economic groups?

- Are there rural-suburban-urban geographic splits?

- Are there inner city-suburban splits?

- Is there a presence of gangs?

- Is there an influential student group which dominates the general student population?

- Do you see students grouping along ethnic or other defining characteristics?

- What roll do student cliques play in your school?

C. What is the feel or emotional tone of your school?

Example: For a number of years part of my job was be a high school liaison officer for a small college. This meant meeting a great many counsellors, teachers, administration and of course students in many different high school cultures. The difference in the emotional tones of the individual schools was striking. Almost without exception the emotional climate was consistent throughout the school from the hallways, to the greetings extended or not extended by the administration, to the conduct of the students in the presentation room and the teachers in the staff lounge.

It is critical that the emotional health of the school **not be overlooked.**

- What is the level of school pride from the staff perspective?

- What evidence is there that the students feel a sense of school pride?

- How does the community at large feel about the school?

- Is this a school which attracts and retains dedicated teachers?

- Do most students make a serious attempt to take or feel ownership of the **"their"** school?

- Do students feel safe within the school, its grounds or transportation system?

- Do the teachers feel they are respected and able to make significant individual contributions to the school? (Or is it a job?)

D. What are the integral forces which positively contribute to your school's culture?

Often schools will become self defined as academic or some thing else and this mind set becomes inculcated within all who are associated with the school. However, this single mindedness is often erroneous and excludes a significant proportion of the students.

Example: One school declared itself to be an academic school and repeatedly discouraged its graduates from considering college diploma or industrial training programs even though over 50% of the graduates did proceed to this level of training.

1. **Is your school considered to be an Academic School?** If so:

   - How do you insure that the vast majority of your students are given the support to handle the programs?

   - What provision is made to accommodate students with dyslexia, ADD or simular problems?

   - Are you able to accommodate students who have a special area of giftedness but encounter difficulties in other areas?

   - Is there an assumption that because this is an **Academic** school that **bullying will not be an issue? Wrong Assumption!**

   - Does your staff have a tendency to over focus on the academic preparation of students and be less concerned with their social development?

2. **Does your school have reputation of being a school where athletics have a dominant profile?** If so:

   - Do one or two teams dominate the school program?

   - Are equal opportunities provided to both male and female teams so that all may develop their athletic talents?

   - Are there individual sports programs such as tennis, archery, track and field etc?

   - Are sports programs solely evaluated on wins or losses or on skill development, team play and general athletic deportment?

   - Can the coaches and physical education staff be counted on to assist the administration in dealing with an anti bullying program?

- Is there a good working relationship between the coaches and other staff concerning maximizing the academic and athletic performance and social development of all students?

- Is there a balance in the recognition of students for their achievements, in athletics, academics, leadership, arts and music or any other program which the school offers?

  NOTE: A failure to have balance sends the message that the school values one program or set of programs over all others. Balance is not easy to achieve and maintain.

- Are there opportunities within the school for every student to be able to excel in something?

NOTE: A significant proportion of bullies excel at very little or at least do not excel in areas where parents or others may expect them to succeed.

3. **What is the status of the Music programs in your school?**

   NOTE: There has been much made of the Mozart effect and how listening to Mozart or similar music has the potential for enhancing brain performance. The research shows that listening to Mozart does increase the potential for increased performance in spatial reasoning but only for a relatively short period of time.

   NOTE: The discipline of learning to play a musical instrument enhances ones ability to concentrate, to stay focussed and receive stimulation in the pleasure reward zone.

   NOTE: Recent research is showing that ability to distinguish between tones may prove to be useful to children as they learn language.

   NOTE: There tends to be a strong correlation between being involved in music program and solid academic performance. In one school all students on the honour role were also active within the music program.

Are:

- Music students given their due recognition within the school environment?

- Students from all economic backgrounds able to participate in the music programs?

- The music programs flexible enough to accommodate the musical interests of most interested students? Skill development and personal enjoyment must always be a key requisites.

4. **What is the status of your school's Art and Drama programs?**

   NOTE: Art and Drama should be seen as integral subjects in your school. There are three essential reasons. These courses:

- Are highly meaningful to a goodly segment of your students.

- Provide opportunities for certain students to have their place in the sun.

- Are one of the few spots into the entire curriculum where students can be reflective and connect with their emotions.

   NOTE: Please do not insist on placing students into these courses who have not expressed an interest. But also ensure that these programs are not downgraded in the eyes of the "macho" students. There are within this group, persons who have the interest and basic talent but are too afraid to let this side of their self be revealed.

   NOTE: Both art and drama can be used very effectively as means of establishing communication links with students of all ages but especially students in their early years.

5. **The friendly nature of the building?**

   The next time you enter your school, stop for a minute or so, look around, listen, smell the air. What messages are you receiving? How institutional is it? How home like is it? Our brain reacts one way in one environment and another in the other.

   NOTE: How many readers have ever seen inside a jail? I was a day visitor at a "Correctional Centre" many years ago. Three memories are etched in my mind. The starkness of the place, the steel doors locking behind me and being left alone with about 80 inmates in a large cage like room while I gave a college liaison talk. Jails are the ultimate institutions.

   NOTE: One school had a large entrance way and decorated the edges with real living room furniture. It worked. The presence of a living room helped calm students coming into the school.

6. **The friendly and helpful nature of all staff?**

   At the risk of appearing glib it is not uncommon to find that the attitudes of the staff parallel the physical appearance of the school. This would lead to a high degree of congruency between the institutional look of the school and the way staff and students interact.

Example: A number of years ago, on parent's day, I sat in on several of my children's classes. Two phrases come to mind **non inspirational and non interactive**. On my way out of the school I encountered the principal and mentioned something about the low level of student teacher interaction. His reply was "That's the way we like it at ...." This school has the classic old "academic" look about it". To be fair there were a number of exceptional teachers who engaged their students in highly interactive ways.

7. **The internal cooperative and collegial nature of staff.**

Another dimension of the corporate culture of a school is the way the staff are united in meeting the expectations of the school as a whole. United can have two meanings such as the teachers are rigidly following the dictates of the administration or united means that the staff are collegially working as a synergistic, multi disciplined team to achieve goals which are in the best interests of the students.

Some teachers have a very rigid and narrow perspective of their role and some of these could be classified as bullies who will usually offer little to the collegial culture. In fact they may actively attempt to sabotage it. See: *Appendix I.*

School leadership is probably one of the most challenging jobs in today's work place.

E. Internal forces which negatively impact upon culture of school.

◆ **Rancour between various bargaining units.**

The various bargaining units that represent school staff can significantly enhance a school's chances of being dysfunctional. If your school is to have an effective **anti bullying program all staff members** must be able to work together in a cohesive manner.

Support staff, teachers and administration all need to have the same training, need to be empowered to take action and lastly can expect to be supported by their supervisors.

NOTE: Many custodians have an excellent track record working with difficult students. Support staff in the offices are generally available throughout the day in specific locations to provide a emergency refuge for students in trouble.

◆ **Historical grievances.**

It often seems that history that is remembered is that history which should be best forgotten. Grievances and slights from days long gone are so overburdened with emotions that any attempt to find rational solutions will tax the talents and patience of nearly all administrators.

◆ **Feeling of defeatism.**

It is very common for teachers and other staff working in schools in the inner city or in other areas where education is not valued to routinely feel a sense of depression, they feel they are banging their heads against the wall and no one cares. It is natural. When one is feeling down there is a tendency to shut off the left side of the frontal cortex and limit oneself to thinking in a more global manner. Hence the thought processes are much more inclined to be all negative.

Two possible solutions. Look for the successes and review the Learned Optimism writings of Seligman.

◆ Sensing a lack of support from both the board and/or the community.

Example: I became aware of a school located in a logging community at the top end of a beautiful island. The loggers earn good wages, but the isolation and lack of local amenities leaves the older population dependent upon alcohol and the teenagers are using drugs. The school and community centre are routinely vandalized. To the credit of the teachers they are doggedly determined to make a difference.

◆ Limited student development services and related support resources.

F. Parental Interaction

◆ Level at which parents are engaged in other aspects of school life. See: *Appendix II.*

◆ Degree of parental confrontation with teachers and administration.

◆ Willingness of parents to become engaged in student remediation.

NOTE: In Raising Cain (p32) A parent is quoted as saying. When "I (a successful corporate consultant) walk into a school building I can feel my chest get tight. It's a place that is up to no good. I had a difficult time in school over stuff I had no control over. What I learned in school was that in some essential ways that matter to other people I didn't measure up."

NOTE: It is difficult for most of us who work inside the education system to realize that not all that we do is appreciated or beneficial to the people we are attempting to serve. The gentleman mentioned above goes from age 38 to age 8 when ever he enters a school building.

NOTE: Schools can develop a kind of corporate group think and become like politicians who have been in power too long, they tend to believe their own press and they tend to lose touch with those they are supposed to serve.

NOTE: Some school staff develop a "them against me" or a "them against us" circle the wagons attitude.

G. People Strengths

It takes a community of committed people to raise a child. All of whom are willing to make an emotional connection with that child.

Gabor Mate writes "Our children will heed our leadership only if we can reattach them to us." Children and adults who are devoid of emotional attachments tend to be numb to their inner self and fearful of the outer world.

We need:

♦ Staff members who are extremely interested in creating a safe and educationally exciting school for their students. They must care! Kids will know!

    Example: My cousin's daughter B... was attending a Grade 3 class in Paris and suddenly her work began to fall off and the teacher suggested that unless B's work improved she would have to repeat the grade. When questioned about this unusual performance our little scholar told her mother. I don't like the teacher, she isn't fair. She picks on Raphael (who was the only black child in the class). When the matter was fully discussed, B... went on, worked harder, passed Grade 3 and became the top student in her Grade 4 class.

♦ Staff members who are willing to review their approaches to learning and seek innovative ways to reach students.

♦ A student council which is concerned and focussed on providing quality social/educational experience for all students. They must be able to think and act beyond themselves or their immediate clique.

♦ A student council which is concerned and knowledgeable about the issues of troubled students and counterproductive student behaviour.

♦ A student body which is willing to cooperatively accept the challenge of increasing the safety and welling being of all their fellow students.

♦ An administration that focuses on the quality of learning and student development.

♦ Parents who are concerned and willing to assist the school in meeting its objectives. These parents may have to be re-invited and re-orientated to the school.

♦ A parent - teacher body which is dynamic, creative and able to initiate, develop and deliver programs which in turn increases parent participation in school programs.

♦ Community leaders who are willing to use their positions to garner additional support to strengthen school programs including an anti-bullying school program.

♦ People in the community willing and able to contribute to school programs such as, music, drama, various alternative athletic activities, co-op work placement, job skills training etc.

♦ Able "gutsy" kids who will take on formal and informal leadership roles. These kids need your support. They need to have the school to have a "new feel" an inclusive "group think."

    Example: The other day Atley, another honourary grandchild, who is in Grade 7 was at his locker and observed a couple of his classmates taunting another classmate who has a skin condition which is really problematic. He told them to take a hike and they did. The boy who was being tormented was extremely grateful and he thanked Atley.

♦ Respected people in the community who will provide mentoring to students who have difficulty attaching themselves to a role model.

♦ Representatives from "social services," "health" and police forces working with designated school personnel to try to ensure "At Risk" students are not falling through the cracks. Jurisdictional barriers have to be broken down.

♦ Service clubs, sports organizations and other groups within the community which could provide venues and support for a variety of school programs. This could be mutually beneficial.

CHAPTER 34

STAFF DEVELOPMENT – ANTI BULLYING

IDENTIFYING BULLYING ACTIVITIES

This is a multi step process:

1. **Be vigilant.** It is important to be on the look out for activities that seem "out of place."

2. **Determine if inappropriate behaviour is bullying.** Monitor and check to see if there is a pattern of inappropriate behaviour or it is a one off event. It still needs to be dealt with in some manner.

3. **Check power balance.** A key to bullying is a power imbalance.

4. **Repetition.** The activities are repeated.

5. **Realize that there are many types of bullying.**

Some indicators are:

♦ Students who have **very little in common** are repeatedly in some kind of interaction.

♦ A **larger child is seen jostling** a smaller child and laughing.

♦ You observe **unidirectional name calling** or taunting.

♦ You observe an **"accidental bumping"** in the hallway and then you see the same action repeated later in the day and then the next day. Often this seems to happen only when the "bumper" is in the company of a group of friends.

♦ You see a group of students encircling someone who is **not normally part** of their group.

♦ You observe a group of students leave a lunch table or work station and move to another area just when another student attempts to join them.

♦ You see a student who is **normally "uninvolved" suddenly lash out at another student.** This could include swinging a back pack, a chair or making a stabbing motion with a pen etc. This child is often a victim who has taken too much.

♦ In your classroom you observe that one student is routinely the **receiver of snide/hurtful remarks** from one or two others in the room who are not his or her friends.

♦ You observe graffiti on the washroom walls that is extremely demeaning and/or threatening regarding another student.

♦ A student is unaccountably absent from school.

♦ A student seems to be increasingly distant from other classmates.

- A student comes to you and either complains of being bullied or reports that another student is being bullied.

- You repeatedly hear words like "fag," "queer," "wuss" being directed at a student by another or others who are not of the same social group.

- You observe members of a sports team or club harassing other students in certain sections of the hallway or in the parking lots.

- It is not unusual for a gang to take up ownership of an entrance way and exact various kinds of vengeance on people who trespass into this area.

- Female students being molested, groped, receiving verbal abuse with sexual overtones.

- The "after physical education" shower activity contains overtones of abuse and harassment.

- You notice that certain students are avoiding physical education by feigning illness or injury or simply skipping school.

- You learn of initiation rituals (hazing) for certain teams or clubs.

- You observe the unusual occurrence of a person or persons from another class loitering near your classroom door and meeting up with one of your students. Their relationship does not seem friendly.

- You observe that a student who is not in the "in group" is more moody and detached than normal

- You observe that a student who is an "outsider" has ripped, muddy or wet clothing when the clothing of others seems to be OK.

- Parents raise concerns about their children's clothing being torn, their school supplies being stolen or broken, their children coming home hungry because some one has stolen or spoiled their lunch, or children rushing to the bathroom upon coming home because they are afraid to use the washrooms at school.

- **Students who are rude, oppositional or otherwise problematic for you as a teacher are also likely candidates to bully one or more students.**

- If you have observed the parents acting in an anti or unsociable manner there exists a reasonable possibility that their children will bully. It is not uncommon for a son or daughter be modelling the behaviour of one or both parents.

- You confront a person on a bullying matter and they lie about the act, even though you or another responsible person were right there, or if they may try to deflect the act by say "It was just a love tap." **They are revealing two basic characteristics of a bully ie. no respect for the truth and insensitivity to the pain or hurt they cause others.**

- When you read a student's poetry or prose and there is a theme of Gothic, hatred or dark thoughts including suicide there is an urgent need to refer that student for counselling or therapy. This may be depression brought on by being victimized. Better to be safe than sorry.

- Some victims become fixated on destroying their tormentors. This information may appear as a preoccupation with violence and revenge in writings or art work. (**All too often the victim becomes further victimized by the system and the bully perpetrators are left to go free.**)

- Students from one racial group taunting (or more) students of another racial group.

- Seemingly popular students target a less popular student for no apparent reason.

- **You observe children whose parent(s) have power or status in the community "lord it over" a student of a "lower status."**

- When you observe academically weaker students mocking or intimidating "stronger" students in your class. Take time to observe any interaction in the hallways or at the lockers. The intimidation might become physical, homework might be stolen or damaged, projects ruined or the better student may be coerced into helping the other student cheat on tests or exams.

- Students reporting being the target of cyberbullying.

- An inappropriate amount of cell phone use, especially camera cell phone use after a physical education class.

- A student (or parents) report the existence of a website which contains demeaning material about themselves or another student.

- You learn of children being photographed while using the washroom.

CHAPTER 35
POLICIES AND POLICY MAKING

It is usual practice for schools, school districts or divisions, religious organizations, government departments and corporations to develop policy. The purpose of policy and policy statements is to ensure that the organization will proceed with consistency and in accordance to a certain set of beliefs, goals and standards.

From a purely administrative perspective policy makes life easier as it gives consistency and perhaps efficiency to corporate operations. If people follow policy and procedures derived from policy everything goes well or at least according to a plan.

If individuals within the corporation or organization fail to follow policy they can be disciplined as severely as the policy allows.

NOTE: However, efficiency and effectiveness are not synonyms. A policy driven organization may be efficient and consistent but not necessarily effective if its stated goals, objectives and procedures of the organization are not congruent with role it is expected to fill.

Example: A political party or a school system which professes that it operates against a backdrop of certain principles may be extremely ineffective if these positions are not in keeping with either or both the thoughts and needs of the population as a whole. Principles are **man made** and can be very misguided. **However, policy can be fraught with other difficulties.**

- Policy is sometimes seen as being sacred, as if it was determined by a divine force. Such policies have a **"written in stone"** quality.

- Policy is usually not reviewed regularly for its relevancy although it may be added to on a frequent basis.

- Frequently policy is written in a "broad brush" manner and tends to set into place a "one size fits all" processing of actions or transgressions.

  NOTE: The human condition as found within schools, unlike the manufacturing of nearly consistent widgets, does not present itself with any degree of uniformity.

- Policy may not support the institutional mission or goals.

- Policy may be written to cover future eventualities based on recent crises.

- Some organizations fall back onto their policy statements in times of crisis. They respond, "We have a policy on that." and sometimes will expand with "We followed our policy."

  NOTE: Policy in this context becomes a convenient shield. School boards may still find themselves liable should it be shown that the policy was applied infrequently, unevenly and that there were few, if any, supportive programs attached to the policy.

- Policy proliferation can occur. What is a right number? Is the policy document so comprehensive that every possibility is theoretically covered and nothing is left to chance or administrative judgement? Is there an overlapping of policies? Are policies contradictory? Can current policies be easily misinterpreted? Are the policies reactive or proactive? Are there policies that do not focus on the goals and objectives of the organization?

POLICY STATEMENTS WHICH DEAL WITH VIOLENT AND AGGRESSIVE STUDENTS SEEM TO FOLLOW SEVERAL TRENDS

Zero Tolerance

1. The **"zero tolerance"** policy, was originally put into place to reinforce the concept that violent and aggressive acts within a school complex can and will not be tolerated. Fair enough! Student safety was and is an essential entity in schools and school jurisdictions. "Zero tolerance" was intended to treat all transgressions of a particular category in a consistent, firm manner and to send a message to the students.

   However, it has been found wanting in a number of key areas.

A. It inhibits able administrators or discipline committees from assessing independent acts and taking steps that are situationally appropriate. Examples include:

- Suspending a six year old Grade 1 student for six weeks for displaying a pen knife he found either on the school grounds or on his way to school. This seems excessive!

- Suspending a female teenager because she had inadvertently brought a butter knife to school. OK, a knife is a knife. But is it always dangerous? The Supreme Court of Canada has just ruled, that the Sikh ceremonial dagger called a kirpan is not a weapon and may be worn by students providing it is concealed in the child's clothing.

- Suspending a student for fighting and assault with a weapon. The incident arose when a student who had been bullied and taunted grabbed a chair and attempted to do damage to his tormenter. The bully/tormenter was not punished for his actions.

- Expelling a student who had inadvertently picked up her mother's lunch bag which contained a paring knife. She immediately reported the error to a teacher but was expelled anyway.

These situations would normally be considered outside of the original intent of a **no weapons** policy or the **banned substance abuse** policies.

B. A second question has been raised in Canada and the USA deals with the uniformity of the application of the "zero tolerance" policy.

- Some studies are showing that teenage males from visible minorities are more likely to be suspended/expelled than other students even though the offences are the same.

- Or, on the other hand, schools may not enforce the policy at all. The case of 13 year old boy who shot himself on the family farm after 8 years of relentless bullying was the outcome, at least in part, of a school system which had a zero tolerance policy on bullying but was seemingly unable or unwilling to enforce the policy.

C. A third concern, deals with the nature of or lack of programs for those individuals who are now suspended from the school but who may be able to return to the school at some future date. The concern is not that the action may not have been

warranted but rather what must the student do during the suspension period and how will that student be re-integrated into the school system.

NOTE: Some political leaders are promoting programs of increased incarceration for juvenile offenders. While this will leave the public safer from being victimized by these individuals for the short term there is absolutely no guarantee that warehousing dysfunctional youth with other dysfunctional youth will net the sought after long term positive results. Unless these same politicians will actively support "brain change" programs within the juvenile detention centres the revolving door concept will continue forever and ever.

The concerns are:

- A student who is suspended from regular classes without there being an alternate program in place will be further behind in his or her studies upon return school than they were upon suspension. The literature would suggest that it is highly unlikely that such a person will have gained new skills which will help avoid future discipline action.

- Students who are failing and who commit a serious transgression which leads to suspension are unlikely to be terribly upset. The only exceptions may be those students who are serving court ordered community sentences and one of the conditions of the sentences is attendance at school.

  Personal comment: I often feel that the courts are abusing the school systems in these later cases. For unless there is provision within the justice system to support additional services at the school and for the student of record the school becomes an under funded and under skilled detention centre.

- Without a program in place one can rest assured that students who are serious trouble makers within the school before they were suspended will be even more so after spending copious free on the streets.

- Are the students allowed to be readmitted to the school from which they have been suspended?

D. A fourth concern. Is the discipline action been taken for the right reason.

- Is this a "safe school" issue whereby a violent student is removed because he or she is a threat to others including, teachers and students, and perhaps to themselves?

- OR is this part of a camouflage action to convince the parents and others community that the school is indeed a safe place.

E. A fifth concern is that schools with a "zero tolerance" policy may not be proactive in establishing and delivering diversionary or remedial programs for students who are identified **"At Risk."**

F. An additional concern. If a zero tolerance on bullying exists at your school or within your district does it apply only to students?

Conflict Resolution and Mediation - At the other end of the spectrum.

2. Some schools, districts or divisions attempt to place the burden of managing student behaviour on the shoulders of the students.

- They have policies and programs in place to provide the students with conflict resolution and mediation and restorative justice skills with the purpose of having the students taking responsible for managing bullies on their own. **These should be seen only as several dishes on the menu not the entire menu.**

- Some school districts have a policy of disciplining students who do not report incidents of bullying.

GENERAL GUIDELINES AND THOUGHTS FOR POLICY MAKING

1. Avoid making policy statements for every possible contingency.

2. Avoid the urge, to impulsively, create a policy to cover future eventualities based a recent incident.

3. Annually review your policies to determine:

- Do they meet existing school goals, objectives, school and student needs?

- Should they be expanded to cover situations which are now more prevalent?

- Are the support programs in place and working?

- Is the policy easy to administer?

- Are there policy provisions which empower administrators to act in accordance to circumstance?

- Avoid creating policy solely to meet limited expectation of **special interest groups.**

- Be sure that policies are being utilized. **It is unpleasant being investigated or sued for not following policy.**

5. Ensure policies are being philosophically and financially supported.

6. Ensure that all within the school system are fully aware, within capability, of the policies and procedures.

   NOTE: However, it is impossible to believe that the six year old mentioned earlier could comprehend the school policy on "weapons."

7. Ensure that there is an appeal system in place.

   Examples of situations for which mitigating exceptions should be considered:

- Child with a mood disorder such as depression or Bipolar disorder.

- Child under severe stress due to the death of a close relative or friend or the divorce of parents.

- Child whose medical condition is known and normally controlled by medication.

- **Child who has been the victim of repeated bullying and finally loses control.**

- **Child who has an exemplary record and transgresses on one occasion.**

- **Child's transgression does not match the reason for the policy.**

CHAPTER 36
CREATING PUBLIC AWARNESS

(This chapter is written to assist you in putting together information for the general public. It is a summation of many other sections of this book and may be modified or used verbatim for community development purposes.) See: *Appendix II.*

Bullying is a community matter and to address the issue fully all members of the community must be challenged to take a share of the responsibility for resolving the problem. **Schools however have, by default, assumed a lion's portion of the task.** They have done so because bullying is interfering with the safe operation of the schools and the opportunities for all students to reach their academic potential. In addition, schools are becoming increasingly aware that their role has expanded to significantly include both academic and character development. Families, the church and the community at large are no longer able or willing to focus on the unity of the community or the concept of the common good. The school is now the only common element for all facets of these mini societies and leadership must emanate from this place. That does not mean that all other groups should not be held responsible

The first step in sharing responsibility is to create awareness.

A. **Chapter 4 dispels many of the myths about bullying. The following few are listed to help refocus the reader on some of the misconceptions which pervade the minds of our citizens. These include:**

  1. Bullying is simply a pair of kids settling a dispute.

  2. Bullying is "kid stuff." They'll grow out it.

  3. Bullying is simply hurting someone physically.

  4. Bullies can't hurt you by verbal abuse.

  5. Rumour mongering only hurts the supersensitive.

  6. Bullying is limited to kids and teenagers.

  7. Bullying is only a male thing.

B. **A vast majority of school yard and community bullies continue on to become adult bullies. Why would they not? As adult bullies they are often:** See: *Prognosis for Bullies, Appendix V.*

  1. Spousal abusers.

  2. Parents who neglect their children.

  3. Parents who physically, verbally, emotionally and sexually abuse their children.

  4. Persons who show a disregard for the law, are inconsiderate of the safety of others and over focus on their immediate personal needs.

  5. Bosses who psychologically harass or on occasion sexually harass their employees.

  4. Coaches who terrorize their players and who may encourage hazing of rookies.

  5. Workers who taunt or play dangerous, **practical "jokes"** on fellow employees.

NOTE: Most such employees are marginally competent or highly incompetent. In any case, they are costing their employer through their incompetence and by reducing the productivity of other employees.

  6. Parents and others who teach bigotry, racial hatred and gender intolerance.

  7. Teachers and other educators who use unethical classroom practices to "control" students.

C. **Real life facts about bullies.**

  1. The vast majority are control freaks suffering from social development deficits and not infrequently some psychological disorders.

  2. A high percentage of bullies have an under functioning reward zone in their brain and frequently become substance abusers.

  3. Most bullies are highly manipulative. A goodly percentage will create a public persona which belies their true character. Many **display** high self esteem.

4. Bullies are "bad" marriage partners. **You never want you son or daughter to marry a bully.**

5. Bullies commit criminal acts, up to 60% of school year bullies will have a criminal record by age 25.

6. Bullies teach their children to disobey the law and social customs.

7. A bully's self centredness makes him or her a lousy neighbour.

8. **Bullies kill people either directly or indirectly.**

9. Bullies seldom if ever take responsibility for their actions.

D. **The help you may need.**

1. Increased resources to mount an anti bullying – Responsible Citizen Programs. (This is an Australian term.)

2. Increased training for teachers, coaches, administrators/managers on dealing with bullies.

3. Increased means to communicate the anti-bullying message to the community.

4. Increased awareness of the current research findings on issues related to bullying.

5. Skilled personnel who can deal with Mediation, Conflict Resolution and Restorative Justice.

6. More early childhood support to deal these issues before they become large and complex.

7. People lobbying the governments. **"An ounce of prevention is better than a pound of cure."**

8. Increased arts, music and sports facilities.

9. Jurisdictional integration of the relevant agencies.

E: **Who do you need?**

1. Politicians who care about the people of their community and who are prepared to support programs which will meet the needs of all persons. **This means leadership not political expediency.**

2. Business and service club leaders to lend their voices and influence to relevant projects.

3. Coaches and youth workers who are capable, tolerant and flexible.

4. The entire school staff trained and committed.

F. **Possible topics for presentations.**

1. "You don't want your daughter to marry a bully."

2. "Bullying can be stopped if we work together."

3. "Creating responsible citizens is a full time job."

4. "Put our money into parenting and early childhood **education-not jails.**"

5. "Bullying is costing you money."

CHAPTER 37
SUMMARY AND CONCLUSION

Bullying behaviour is a human condition which is focussed on survival.

A. In its **simplest format** it is the outgrowth of some inappropriate learned behaviours.

B. In its more **complex configuration** it is an agonizing blend or learned behaviours, neglect, physical, emotional and sexual abuse, addictive tendencies and a range of negative developmental and genetic influences.

To have a bully stop this personally and socially destructive behaviour we have to understand at least nine key components of the problem.

1. What is driving the person to bully? In other words what intrinsic and extrinsic benefits does the bully receive from this activity.

2. What genetic and environmental influences would support this level of aggression?

3. What has the child learned at home, in the community and in school which supports his/her bullying activities?

4. What cognitive and emotional developmental deficits does the child possess at this moment which will impede remediation?

5. What cognitive and emotional strengths does the child possess which would support growth by actively participating in a therapy program, to become a responsible citizen.

NOTE: In #s 4 and 5 we must also consider the child's age, levels of cognitive and social maturation, language skills, sense of meaningfulness, safety and trust.

6. What other resources can the home, the community and the school bring to the table which would result in the desired changes in the child's behaviour?

7. We must estimate the gap that must be bridged between the child's current behaviour and the new "default behaviour" we want the child to adopt.

8. The behaviour may be due to mental illness or mood disorders.

9. Lastly we avoid the temptation to apply one remediation process to all children when the causes of these behaviours lie some where on the continuum between A & B above.

In closing I want to end with a list of 15 scenarios where the remediation runs from quick and easy to complex and protracted.

Scenario # 1

Cognitively aware and emotionally sensitive children suddenly realize that they are are dealing unfairly with a sibling, a playmate or a classmate. They know this is not what their parents have taught them, they feel uncomfortable and decide to change their behaviour.

This can happen but do not rely on it happening with great frequency. These children have high levels of social consciousness and social conscience and are mature enough to develop a new pattern of behaviour.

Scenario #2

Another person such as a peer or an adult raises the matter that a child's behaviour is inappropriate, it is making him/her look bad and it should stop. The child has similar strengths as #1 above and makes a determined effort to relate with others in a more positive manner.

Scenario #3.

Another person usually an adult takes the child aside and makes comment about the child's behaviour. The child seems somewhat, taken back, confused and uncertain about what to do next. The child may ask for help or be receptive to help in order to adopt new behaviours which will be mutually beneficial to him/herself and those with whom they have contact.

These new behaviours must be taught, coached and monitored to ensure they become permanent fixtures of the child's life style.

Scenarios 1-3 are the easy bully situations to resolve.

only different but, in the bigoted person's mind, are causing him or her grief. The word **"they" takes on a new meaning**. See: *The Learned Bigoted Bully.*

Scenario # 6

Approximately a third of all males and about a sixth of all females are genetically predisposed to being more aggressive than average. Fortunately not all these folk will be overly aggressive each and every day. If the frontal cortex develops according to plan and the child's environment has not been one of abuse or neglect then these children will cope quite well.

Boys, more so than girls, will expend inordinate amounts energy physically jockeying for space. They are continually bumping each other and often would not be aware **at the outset** that they are repeatedly bumping and bothering someone who is not bumping back.

They have migrated into some bullying activity and until someone draws their attention to it or they are required to reflect on it they would be oblivious to it. Now the challenge is to get the behaviour stopped.

If they are cognitively aware, emotionally sensitive and sufficiently mature they may be able to contain their unappreciated exuberance with a minimum of external support and maintenance.

Scenario # 7

Lets take scenario #6 a bit further. Perhaps these boys are deliberately causing harm and embarrassment to another person. Now you have a different problem to address. In the child's mind there is a definite reason to torment the target, there is enjoyment in doing this and perhaps the child is achieving certain goals. The resolution now centres around the reasons, alternate means for enjoyment and other ways to achieve his/her goals.

Scenario #8

Girls can be ever bit as aggressive as boys. In fact in their early years little girls are physically as aggressive as their male playmates. Later on their aggression takes the form of language and emotional attacks such as shunning, exclusion etc. This aggression tends to get overlooked because the physical elements are missing. There is little blood, few bruises and seldom broken bones.

There are however many hurt feelings, leaving many girls with their personal self worth so damaged that they contemplate or actually commit suicide.

The challenge for teachers and other caring adults is to recognize the activity and to accept it as an intense form of aggression and react to it.

Scenario #4

A young child is heard being verbally abusive to a child of another race. Before you bring in the race relations team in and initiate a course of racial sensitivity, you might want to sit down with the child and discuss the terminology, where it was learned, what it means, why it is hurtful and how it makes this child appear. When young children use denigrating language they are not always aware the impact of the terms especially if they have been heard at home or on the local streets. You might have success in having the child clean up his/her language and you might try using activities such as cooperative games so that the children learn to play together as equals.

Scenario #5

This scenario is similar to #4 above but the child is a bit older. This child has obviously learned the language but also has picked up the emotional nuances around racism. In addition, the child is prone to amplifying the emotional response when the normal bumps and annoyances common place in the classrooms, hallways and playing fields occur.

The solution becomes much more difficult because the disaffected student begins to internalize the differences between races in negative ways. These people are not

Again the resolution now centres around the reasons, alternate means for enjoyment and other ways to achieve his/her goals.

NOTE: People who study female aggression are reporting an increase in physical aggression. One of my honourary grand daughters was recently deliberately cross-checked and threatened with a hockey stick in an intramural floor hockey game. Repeatedly we hear of teenage girls **swarming and beating their victims** *before stealing their jackets, shoes, cell phones, etc. at malls and schools.*

Scenario #9

Consider the information in scenario # 8 and add to it girls desire to dominate others for the following reasons. They want to gain additional control over their lives, they have limited empathy for their victims, relationships are not for intimacy and sharing but rather to be used for personal gain and a means to attain and maintain power. See: *Relationship Bullying.*

Scenario #10

Some children and adolescents bully even when there doesn't seem to be any reason for them to do so. Their families seem stable, they are doing OK at school and they seem to fit in well with their peers.

They may stop bullying if you ask them to. Or they may become more secretive with their bullying. They may even go on the INTERNET. In my opinion it is usually unwise to ask them to stop unless you can help them deal with some of the issues which are driving this misbehaviour and you can help them develop an alternate plan of behaviour. See: *The Conundrum Bully.*

Scenario #11

There is a fallacy that pervades the educational and workplace world. It is simply this, the human is a rational cognitive being and educational and behavioural change programs should operate from that premise. Wrong! A considerable portion of our thoughts and behaviours are heavily influenced by emotional memories.

A child who is obsessed with anger or fear will not be able to respond to cognitive based programs until such time as the counter emotions have been addressed in some fashion. The bully who is explosively angry is extremely unlikely to respond to rational requests or demands for change. See: *The Impulsively Aggressive Bully.*

Scenario #12

Children who have suffered brain trauma due to hits to the head, accidental crashes from automobile accidents, falling off their bikes, falling downstairs or out of trees etc or brain cysts, tumours or strokes can exhibit impulsive behaviours which are well outside the normal range. Telling them to stop is not going to work. It is necessary to treat the cause and then help the person create new behaviours.

Scenario # 13

Children who have been severely abused may have cognitive deficits, an over focussed cingulate and a hyper vigilant limbic area. Their high levels of mistrust, low levels of emotional sensitivity and their tendency to obsess on certain individuals and immediate gratification makes them difficult children to treat. Their under functioning frontal cortex is further made less relevant by over activity in the inner brain regions.

Therapy must in most of these cases must pay attention to the needs of the inner brain and then work outward.

Scenario #14

The addictive nature of bullying must be recognized and dealt with using some, although perhaps modified, programs that are used to treat teen and adult drug misuse. Recent studies on the later show that family intervention to be extremely beneficial. The key aspects are support, alternate lifestyle and the development of a social network.

Scenario #15

Communities are often very tolerant of bullying behaviour. Often this is due to ignorance and/or an unwillingness to take responsible action.

ADULT BULLIES WITHIN OUR SCHOOLS

INTRODUCTION

Seldom do I give workshop without one or more participants commenting on or asking about the adult bullies within our schools or school systems. As sad as this comment is, it is the reality of bullying. Many bullies don't fade away into the sunset once they reach some mythical age of maturity. Many live on to become bullies in the workplace including all professions such as medicine, religious ministry and unfortunately education. The workplace bully is everywhere. Even scholastic achievement does not eliminate the bully. Universities and colleges have their fair share of people who take advantage of both undergraduate and graduate students and some of their colleagues.

Within the K-12 System. The Adult bullies work their "magic" in a number of ways.

Some students:

- Are repeatedly graded more favourably than others for work of the same or even inferior quality.

- Are singled out for disciplining even though their behaviours are no worse than those of other students.

- Have unnecessary attention drawn to their learning difficulties.

- Are singled out for ridicule because they are considered outsiders by their peers.

- Are denied special assistance even when this assistance is being funded by an outside source.

- Are repeatedly ridiculed in school activities for which they do not possess a natural talent.

  Examples include: Obese children who have limited agility or endurance in physical education classes, the underweight child who doesn't have the strength for certain activities, the child whose handwriting is terrible because of a coordination problem, the child who can't draw to save his/her soul, the child who can't carry a tune, those who find certain academic subjects extremely difficult or the child who has ADHD or ODD.

- Are "denied the ear" of the school secretary, principal, teacher, counsellor, custodian, bus driver simply because they are not deemed to be worthy of attention.

Reasons why education may be an attractive vocation for a bully.

- This level of control provides the individual with an ego boost.

- The desire to be seen as an expert by others.

- The opportunity to control a group of subordinates (children) behind a closed door.

Indicators that a staff member may be a bully.

If:

- This teacher repeatedly sends students to the office for discipline while other teachers seem to be managing the same students with routine classroom procedures.

- This teacher frequently complains that the administration and system do not support him/her.

- This teacher gets into power struggles with bright able students.

  Example: One such example concerned the extremely bright high school student who was, and still is, profoundly deaf. Two of her male teachers grew large bushy moustaches which interfered with her ability to "read lips." Not only did they refuse to shave or, at least, trim their facial hair, but would teach to the chalk board and on one occasion gave an oral exam. The family had to, at considerable expense, move her to another school which was very responsive to her needs. She now holds two university degrees.

- The principal has favourite teachers and assigns classes and extracurricular duties based upon favouritism rather than technical competence or student needs.

- The principal or teacher refuses to use the services of a special needs consultant or teacher because they feel threatened or simply do not want to give up control.

- The teacher who ridicules certain students with the hope that he/she can draw other students to his/her side.

- The person knowingly has skill deficiencies but uses bullying tactics to camouflage these deficits.

- The teacher undercuts a colleague by making negative comments about that colleague to students.

- The person is very rigid or literal when applying school regulations to students but is very lax, if not contrary, about following similar regulations for him/herself.

The bully in the staff room usually does the following:

- Quietly or openly ridicules a colleague for going the extra mile for a difficult student.

- Repeatedly finds fault with the skills of the administration. Tries to divide staff into camps.

- Is very gracious and complimentary to senior administration when ever they are in his or her presence.

- Finds it difficult, if not impossible, to acknowledge the accomplishments of fellow colleagues.

- When required to be involved in professional development, disrupts the facilitator, talks to others and ultimately declares the event to be a waste of time.

- Refuses to support anti bullying programs.

- May try to get new teachers on side.

- Will try to off load work onto new teachers.

- May make rude, suggestive and bigoted remarks about colleagues.

- May make unwanted sexual overtures to another colleague.

Surviving the bully in the staff room: Not an easy task. Suggestions include:

- Keeping them out of your head.

- Avoiding being on any committee or work assignments with them. Should good fortune not be on your side you will end up doing most of the work and they will end up getting most of the credit.

- Keep your authentic self esteem intact.

- Study the bully. Get to know their strengths and weaknesses. Manipulate their strengths to your advantage. You can almost always appeal to their vanity.

- You may choose to go head to head with the bully in private. It is usually unproductive to skewer the bully in a public forum. However, there are occasions where this has worked.

- Keep your focus. Make sure your accomplishments are made known to those significant persons.

- Take classes. Rekindle a hobby. In other words, do things that are self affirming.

- Utilize the services of the teacher's association for counselling or skill development.

- Keep your sense of humour

- You must always see yourself as the winner. Rely on your authentic self esteem.

NOTE: A teacher in one of my workshops remarked, after I had uttered the truism that most bullies get their just rewards at some point in their life, **"Yes that may be true but it usually doesn't happen soon enough."**

To minimize the negative affects of bullies on your staff try to avoid hiring them.

This is easier said than done. But there are some "tell tale" traits that will surface during a careful job screening. Most bullies host some serious insecurities, they have a history of frequent job changes, may be overly glib discussing how they handled discipline at their last schools, or how they fostered collegial relationships. Some referees may be loath to comment poorly on a former colleague but you may rephrase the question this way. "Could you comment on "XYZ" or would you rather not do so. A no comment is sometimes worth a thousand words. The referee may make a comment such as. "I am not sure of the state of his/her marriage". This may be an offhanded way of saying the marriage is in trouble and your candidate is the principal contributor to the breakup.

General questions might include:

- How would you handle a student who has Oppositional Defiant Disorder?

- If your class had a number of special needs students how would you attempt to meet their needs as well as the needs of the other students? The person's answer may shed some light on their ability to be flexible but still have high expectations for all students OR it may reflect disdain for those who can't keep up. Sometimes you will get comments such as "I don't believe there is any such things as dyslexia, ADD, Learned Helplessness etc." Sometimes the candidate is not so blatant with the statements such as above but will by tone of voice or body language convey messages that belie the verbal statement.

Selecting Leaders

Recruiting and choosing good leadership for schools and educational systems is critical for the entire educational enterprise.

Educational leaders unlike many other leaders in business and industry supervise/manage a highly educated workforce who work in an arena of complex variables and multiple outcomes. **Good educational leaders are worth their weight in gold.** Sadly, in our all too superficial world, we often pay nearly illiterate people to play sports or otherwise provide some level of entertainment, unseemly large amounts of money.

- A bully in an administrative position often is a "Kiss up and kick down" type of person. This management style has much to do about **ME** and much less about students and staff.

- There is a need to research the candidate's background to the extent as limited by the law.

- It is important that the selection committee be able to distinguish between assertiveness and aggressiveness. Candidates who are assertive are able to give of themselves, focus on goals and bring people together to achieve these goals. Administrators who are aggressive drive rather than lead.

- It is important to listen to the tone of the answers, observe the body language and count the (I)s.

- One might want to follow up on answers which include "Cleaning Up a School" and getting rid of "Dead Wood Staff." What were the conditions of the school which required cleaning up? How did you go about it? What is your definition of an underperforming staff member? After you have put this school into good running order, why do you want to come to a new school?

- What new programs were initiated in schools administered by this person. How were they implemented? How was resistance overcome? Why were these programs necessary? How successful are they now?

NOTE: Bullies have weak track record in laying out projects, gaining people's support and input, supporting the people charged with implementation, providing feedback and taking a project to completion.

- Ask the question, How important is it to be liked? If the candidate replies to the effect that "I am not here to be liked, I am here to get a job done," there may be a hidden message. The proper answer has to do with respect, trust and leading people to where they want to go.

- Ask the candidate how they would use all the resources currently available or potentially available to meet the needs of their staff and students.

NOTE: Some bullies in authoritative positions have diverted grant monies and services from the designated student to other students, have refused to involve learning specialists and refused to seek other outside assistance.

- Ask the candidate how they would see themselves working through a normal school day. Does the answer parallel your vision of seeing this person being highly interactive with students, teachers and support staff? **Remember Mirror Neurons! Walking the talk is important.** Principals and vice principals set the tone for the school. What tone will this individual impart? Attitude filters down from the top.

Note: What impression was left by the principal who refused to autograph a graduating student's yearbook? What impression was made by the vice principal who chastised a graduating student who was returning her textbooks late even though she had permission to do so by another senior staff member?

The work environment of a school administered by a bully.

◆ Staff tend to work independently.

◆ Students become aware that staff do not work as an integrated unit and will act accordingly.

◆ There exists an undercurrent of tension. Students respond with an increase in misbehaviour.

◆ Staff are less likely to refer to the school as "our" school.

◆ Staff are less inclined to be active in professional development.

◆ Staff do not volunteer for special assignments.

◆ Staff are unsure which of their colleagues can be trusted and will be supportive.

◆ School is run by a set of inflexible rules which may not meet the needs of special situations.

◆ Staff meetings tend to be lecture style information sessions with little opportunity for staff input

◆ Staff report that good programs developed by a previous administrator are being ignored.

Staff survival within a school where the supervisor is a bully.

◆ They come, do their job and go home. They keep a low profile.

◆ They refuse to let the bully get into their heads.

◆ They involve themselves in a range of out of school activities.

◆ They take additional classes for professional or personal development.

◆ They hope to find a better work location.

*NOTE: Barclay, a vice principal Grades K-8, was the very **antithesis** of the bully administrator. He attracted staff and students to him and they readily sought him out for assistance and support. He knew his students. One Saturday he encountered two of his very young charges in the local mall. He called them by name. After this brief encounter one of these "now opened mouthed" scholars exclaimed. Mr. C.... knows our names.*

NOTE: As a contrast a former physical education teacher is now the principal of a small high school. He has so overloaded his staff with persons with a physical education background that the school is now deficient in staff competent to teach senior mathematics, history and science. It is common for an administrator who is a bully to avoid hiring staff who are more intelligent and/or skilled than he or she is.

Helping the administrator or teacher who is exhibiting bullying behaviours.

The over riding goal would be to help these individuals become more effective in their roles as defined by their profession or their employer. This is not an easy task and this one is filled with pitfalls. But there are courageous administrators and others who will accept the challenge.

NOTE: There is the old joke that goes as follows. How many psychiatrists is needed to change a light bulb? The answer is one but the light bulb has to want to change. This story raises the dilemma of trying to get people to change a behaviour that has served them well for many years. The odds of change are better if the individual realizes that things are not going well and perhaps help is needed. Nevertheless, it must be remembered that bullying is addictive and the new behaviour must provide comparable emotional rewards.

Example: An acquaintance worked as a train dispatcher which included getting trains on the right tracks etc. He was also an alcoholic. After some near mishaps his company came to him with an ultimatum, take a year's leave of absence and undergo alcohol rehabilitation or be fired. He chose the former, was successful in returning to work and he eventually retired from the company. This example is provided to re-enforce two key brain facts. Addictive behaviour is difficult to change unless there is a strong incentive to do so.

SCHOOL AND PARENTAL PARTNERSHIP – BUILDING BETTER SCHOOLS

"Any activity that involves parents....enhances ownership in the education process and directly contributes to the achievement of children."– *Mary Ellen Imbo, Principal. Westwood Elementary School, Broken Arrow, Oklahoma*

The key word is ownership and ownership glues together cognitive and emotional energy. Emotional energy is absolutely critical. When parents use words like "**my** school," "**my** children's school," "**our** school," "**our** teachers at our school or our teachers" they are expressing a solid emotional connection between themselves, the building and personnel which comprise their school.

Wording that indicates another relationship is the repeated replacement of **OUR with THE**. This implies a more distant relationship such as one might have with large discount stores which tend to be impersonal, inconsistent in the provision of service and are non engaging. In fact many seem to send the message if we have what you want, good, if not take a hike. These are not the images or characteristics we want for our school.

Time split

In a normal year each child spends 1100 of his/her 8760 hours directly devoted to classroom activity with the remaining 7600+ hours more or less under parental control. In other words 7 of every 8 hours of a child's school life are spent outside of the school's jurisdiction or influence. Children whose parents take an active interest in their educational and social well being are indeed fortunate. They will be influenced by their parent's positive and supportive teachings/guidance on almost a continuous basis. The trick is to bridge the gap between home and school so that parents and teachers are collaborating for the benefit of the children. Very few teacher preparation programs allot time to this topic.

Parent and school interactions

Parental involvement within schools (teachers-administration) runs the gamut from "**Alright too much already**" to healthy involvement, to indifference **and perhaps to even hostile non involvement.**

A review of the literature reveals a range of parental groupings and their willingness to be actively engaged with their child's education. The following four groups have been identified for illustrative purposes.

1. **The intensely over involved parents.** These parents want the very best education for their children and if their children are attending a private school, they have the added incentive of trying to get value for their dollar. Their desire for involvement includes volunteering for virtually every possible activity. This can be overwhelming. Some teachers feel intimidated by these ever present and some times interfering parents. This intense involvement often puts a strain on the school's organization as they need only so many chaperones, so many lunch providers or lunch room monitors, classroom readers, so many fund raisers etc. In some schools the volunteer pressure is so intense that selection decisions are made by lottery.

   While the parent volunteer is a welcome addition to a school's resources, there is a cost involved. Training, at some level, is required and coordination is essential. In some cases experienced volunteers can be of service here.

   Parents, at this level, are acutely aware of how their children are performing, so this is not the issue.

   NOTE: There can be a down side to this from the child's developmental perspective. The complex nature of a person's overall development requires that children experience the joys and disappointments of making some of their own decisions. From their good decisions they can take personal ownership of what they have accomplished. From their wrong decisions they can develop an appreciation of the value of good decision making and the ability to take responsibility for their actions. Parents can't be there 24/7 for the rest of their lives.

NOTE: It is now being noted at some universities the super keen parent is also actively engaged in the child's university life. This includes visits to the professor's and Dean's offices.

2. **The reasonably involved parents.** They attend every open house, parent-teacher interview, all student activities when their children are involved and they keep in contact with the school on an as needed basis. They will likely volunteer for one special activity a school year. They also keep close track of their children's school performance and welcome notes, e-mail and other communications from the school. But because of family, work or children's recreational obligations time is a scarce commodity. They earnestly and caringly do what they can do.

3. **The indifferent parents.** Education is not a high priority. They will rarely attend school functions as there always seems to be something else which needs their attention. This could include a televised sports program, a special TV series, bingo or couple's night at the bar etc. It is common for older children to take their younger siblings to school for registration purposes. These children quickly pick up on their parents attitudes and generally let their academic endeavours and social development slide to finally they are in deep trouble.

4 **The hostile non-involved parents.** These parents are very much divorced from the school-child environment. They are incredibly lax about their child's school attendance, academic performance, behaviours and are loath to become involved in any aspect of the child's school activity. In fact they often can become very defensive, even hostile when they are required to deal with their child's misdemeanours and/or lack of performance. A frequent comment is "What the hell do you want me to do with him/her?"

SCHOOLS NEED

Parent volunteers

Parents are:

♦ Often required as chaperones for dances, field trips, music and drama recitals etc.

♦ Needed as classroom assistants for special projects including community history or cultural activities.

♦ Needed to assist in areas where they have an interest or skill such as music, drama, crafts or athletics.

♦ Required to serve as leaders in parent-school organizations.

♦ Required to assist children in reading and similar language skill areas.

Parents are not:

♦ Needed to be ever present in their child's classroom unless there is a critical life-death health issue.

♦ Being helpful if teachers see them as spies rather than helpers.

♦ Being helpful if they seek leadership on a parent advisory committee to promote a single issue agenda item. This focus has included initiating action to dismiss an administrator or teacher.

Parental involvement that gets results

Parents who:

♦ Ensure the child has a proper diet and gets an adequate amount of sleep.

♦ Read to and plays with children.

♦ Teach their children a variety of games.

♦ Teach and model socially responsible behaviour.

♦ Monitor and control children's involvement with television.

♦ Set up study areas for their children which are essentially devoid of distraction.

♦ Ensure that child's use of the computer and INTERNET is appropriate.

♦ Provide organizational and ancillary help to the children as they do their homework.

♦ **DO NOT DO CHILD'S HOMEWORK.**

♦ Call teacher on emergency matters and make appointments to work out other issues.

♦ Hold high expectations for their children and help their children develop the necessary skills.

♦ Keep up to date with events and directions taking place at the school.

♦ Attend all open houses, student-teacher conferences, special events etc.

♦ Keep school informed of issues which might be interfering with children's progress.

♦ Keep an open communication line between self and children.

♦ Volunteer for one or two activities per year.

♦ Give the children room to develop a learning relationship with the teacher.

Parental responsibility is a massive undertaking which requires commitment and self sacrifice.

Teacher skills which complement parental involvement. Teachers who:

- Have strong interactive skills which allows them to respectfully explain the child's successes and failures.

- Feel personally secure and welcome parental involvement.

- Are able to empathetically connect to the parent so that both can work as colleagues.

- Give clear information on homework assignments and the preferred manner for parental involvement.

- Is able to communicate educational issues with a minimum of jargon.

- Learns words of greeting in the mother tongue of the parents especially parents who are recent immigrants.

    NOTE: While this might seem irrelevant or even silly, teachers who do this help "break the ice" when meeting the parents and also reveal their own vulnerability. Many immigrant parents can be overwhelmed when entering the school of their children. For often, in their home country teachers are seen as absolute authority figures and parents are not welcome in the schools. In addition, if language is a barrier an interpreter may be needed or beneficial.

- Tries to think of ways that the parent might become involved in the school even in a very small way.

Schools where parent involvement is low.

There are at least five factors which lead to limited parental involvement.

1. **Large schools.** The bigger the school the more impersonal it may become and the more difficult it is to coalesce the necessary energy to create an active bonding between parents and teachers. Even the size of the building may inhibit collegiality within the school itself, little alone extend an inviting message to parents. There is even a greater challenge when the school is a high school. Parental involvement tends to drop off from a participatory perspective even though there may be an increase of concern about high school graduation and future education.

2. **Urban schools particularly inner city schools.** Families tend not to stay at the same address for extended periods of time. Families are also configured in a multiplicity of ways and change is frequent. Education will have a reduced importance when students and their families need to spend considerable energy on feeling and being safe in their homes or community. Many homes are not conducive to providing places for students to study or even get a requisite number of hours of sleep. Parent(s) even if they did want to become involved with their children's education, frequently don't have or feel they have the skills, the money, the necessary transportation or even the clothes which would let them be comfortable in school. **For the most part schools and teachers are intimidating to these parents.** (This may not be readily apparent to the teacher who is repeatedly confronted by angry aggressive or frustrated parents.) In truth, unless the parent has a mental health problem, these parents may intentionally work themselves up into a state of aggravation in order to feel comfortable meeting with the teacher. Many of these parents may be reliving memories of their own, less than happy, school days when they enter their children's school.

3. **Suburban schools and their mobile population.** There are many who sleep and eat in their suburban houses but in the truest sense do not live in the community. Many households are comprised of two income earners, who travel some distance to their work, whose church affiliation (if they have one) is in another part of the city, their children may play on sports teams or take music lessons also at some considerable distance from the physical location of their home. In addition, their children may travel to schools far beyond easy walking distance. In my small subdivision, there are home schooled children, others are bussed to a Christian school about 25 km away or to French Immersion, middle and high schools most beyond easy walking distances for younger children and the remainder go to the nearby elementary school. All of this reduces the number of children who live next door to each other and walk to the neighbourhood public school together. This also reduces the number of parents who casually interact in the normal course of daily events surrounding the neighbourhood school.

4. **Rural schools and great distances.** The continued decline of families living in the rural areas plus the decrease in family size has meant, the eliminations of the one-room schoolhouses, the virtual elimination of the small town high schools and the general improvement of roads which allows for easier transportation of children over longer distances has collectively changed the physical connection these parents have with their children's schools. The continued consolidation of school districts, divisions and boards further changes the delivery of education into "**more efficient units**" but causes further alienation between home and school.

People from small towns and farming communities who have "hated" the folks from the next town or at least been intense rivals at the hockey rinks or football and baseball fields are now gathered together under one school roof even though many of these community teams and rivalries still exist. Parents will squabble over where the graduation ceremony will be, what the rotation might be and who gets to go first. Some parents may have to drive nearly 50km to attend a school function only to meet someone who has travelled 50km from the opposite direction. What do they have in common? These folks don't meet in the coffee shops, grocery stores and most other gathering places. They are strangers to one another. The informal energy of good parent-school organizations will be difficult to establish.

But if one were to fly over or drive through one of these new enlarged school jurisdictions one might assume a sameness throughout the region but that assumption would be wrong. There are pockets of religious affiliation, ethnicity, economic disparities and historical differences including the expectations they have for their children.

5. **Special Needs or Alternative Schools.** There are any number of factors which inhibit parental interaction with this type of school. The student catchment area is usually such that most of the students are bused considerable distances. When their child is assigned to one of these schools many parents feel somehow defeated, this is the end of the road, their hopes and dreams for their children may never materialize and they have great difficulty becoming emotionally connected to this place of last resort. If these are their feelings and in large part I believe they are, then the school has a major challenge to make the necessary connection with the parents. Each child and each parent has special needs and they can benefit from a coordinated home-school program.

General Solutions

There must be complete acceptance within the school that parental involvement is critical and that the school and the community are co-dependent for mutual success. The school must try to cultivate a supportive relationship with parents and while on the surface this may be seen by some as yet another drain on the school's resources it is in fact a **net sum gain**.

NOTE: Even university Presidents are no longer recruited and hired solely on the basis of their scholarship and administrative skills but are also considered on their ability to interact with the local and national community for the purpose of fund raising and institutional development. While this does not imply that public school principals must be "on the prowl" for operating funds, it does mean they should always be seeking opportunities to legitimately raise the school's profile and interact with the local community.

◆ Look for opportunities for parents to personally benefit from being part of the school. This could include computer, language, nutrition, exercise, high school completion classes etc.

◆ Develop leadership skill sets within the staff on the effective use of parent volunteers.

◆ Help teachers who are reluctant to share their "space" with a volunteer.

NOTE: Some parents may already have many of these skills and these people may be co-opted in assisting teachers and volunteers alike to effectively use volunteer help.

◆ There must be a sensitivity to the needs and prior experiences of all parents who venture inside the doors to volunteer their help or simply to enquire about the progress of their child.

◆ It is important to know the economics and traditions of the various sub-communities within your catchment area. This knowledge may provide you with the background so necessary to build bridges between disparate groups of people.

◆ It is important to balance the maintenance of student safety with volunteer services.

NOTE: Lawyers, insurance companies and news media have collectively raised the paranoia about student safety to such a height that in many districts volunteers including grandparents are not even allowed to come to hear children read. If your school or school division has a policy in place which prohibits the use of volunteers unless they have undergone a criminal record check you have a situation which has delivered the kiss of death to your volunteer program and your school will be grossly less effective for it. Most volunteers will not subject themselves to the cost and indignity of such a check. You must try to come up with an alternate solution.

◆ Many volunteers may not see themselves being part of such groups as the PTA or a Parent Advisory Committee but rather want to utilize their time and skills performing specific tasks with students. **Different strokes for different folks.**

SPECIFIC IDEAS

Large Schools

◆ Re-acquaint yourself with the history of parents and your school. Has there been changes?

◆ Determine the needs you may have. Tutors, mentors, co-op work placement opportunities, specialists in the arts, drama, sports, hobbies, clubs etc.

◆ Are there segments within the school population where parental involvement is virtually negligible. Why is this so? What could be done by yourself or community workers to help bridge the gap? What services can you provide which will encourage these parents to be part of your school?

◆ Do you have an "Evening Extension Program?" Is this affordable to the parents of your students? If not, could funding be found to make it affordable?

◆ How could you use volunteers on Career Days, Drama Nights, Music Festivals, Track and Field days etc.

Urban - Inner City Schools

◆ Get the grandparents involved if at all possible.

◆ Set up a clothing exchange room and have it manned by volunteers.

◆ Have a coffee room lounge.

◆ Honour differences. Regularly have persons from different ethnic groups visit classes to talk about and showcase dress, food, art and music.

NOTE: One school wanted the community's First Nations Elders to become part of their school but the people wouldn't come. Finally some wise person put a sofa just inside the front entrance along with a coffee pot. It wasn't long before the elders started coming, first to sit and visit by the front door and then finally venturing into the school to tell their stories and enhance the student's knowledge of First Nations culture. Part of their reluctance may be due to certain cultural traditions but part may be due to the legacy of Residential Schools.

◆ Develop a community kitchen which need not be in the school. (Many mothers do not have the skills, in some cases nor the pots and pans etc. to prepare inexpensive but nutritious meals for their children. In addition food purchased in the small corner stores or grocery stores within inner city tends to be more expensive than food purchased in the larger stores in the suburbs. Community kitchens have allowed people to buy food more cheaply, often in bulk, and share the expense of preparation. Is this a school responsibility? Technically the answer is no, but until most children come to school with full stomachs learning will not take place.

◆ Engage volunteers to help with the breakfast and lunch programs.

◆ Engage the mothers on high school completion programs.

◆ Position the social service and public health offices for this area in your school.

◆ Use volunteers for reading assistance and tutoring help.

NOTE: In August 2005 Christine Penner, a vice-principal at St Johns High School in Winnipeg visited 459 homes of her new Grade Seven and Grade Eight students. Her hard work paid off when 150 parents, instead of the usual 15-20, attended the first parent teacher evening. Over 20 new volunteers are now engaged in school programs.

Suburban Schools

It is likely the skill level of the volunteers in this area will be greater than perhaps in the inner city schools. However, this need not always be the case. In my area, there is a great multicultural mix with may homes housing three generations and at least one parent being a professional or a business owner. The other parent may or may not be as well educated but will be working and it is the grandparents who are tending the children and are not fluent in English.

◆ As mentioned earlier suburban families often do not see themselves as members of the local community. Perhaps the school can offer coffee times so the stay at home mums can bring their pre-school children for play and access to books etc. Some of the grandparents might also welcome a chance to meet other grandparents who share the same first language.

◆ Pot luck suppers or BBQ's can be arranged so that families can stop at the school on a given night for food and friendship. Food speaks a universal language.

◆ Some volunteers may have the skills and interest to be event organizers. The events should be low key and with limited expense but inviting to other parents to come and be comfortable within the school.

◆ Provide parenting classes, one or two evenings on children's brain growth, childhood nutrition, INTERNET usage, language development, cooperative learning, safe schools etc.

Rural schools and great distances.

NOTE: The small high school, which services the rural area where I grew up, now has a catchment area of at least 3600 square kilometres (1400 square miles) and broad range of ethnic and economic diversity. In addition, there are only two elementary schools which are feeder schools.

Suggestions:

◆ School staff meet with parents and others in various geographical/community regions. For example: Within the catchment area above, there are at least five distinct communities that have halls or recreation centres which would provide meeting space for the school staff to interact with parents and others in the community. Again food is always a great ice breaker and these communities are renowned for their pot-luck suppers or BBQ's.

◆ The staff should have the opportunity tour the area and get a deeper appreciation for the life style of their students.

◆ Curriculum tends to be very urban focussed. This is often not meaningful for rural children. Perhaps there are volunteers in each community who could provide expertise on local history, economics, science, language etc. that teachers could incorporate into portions of the curriculum and projects.

◆ If the staff travel out to the various communities by school bus they may experience for the first time or once again the life of a student who travels great distances each day.

NOTE: After a while riding a school bus becomes boring at best or fearful and dangerous at worst. It is common for bullies to torment their victims during the bus ride and some of these bullies have even threatened the bus driver. Bus drivers have also been harassed by the parents of these misbehaving students.

◆ In addition to establishing better communication links with the parents and others, it is also important to deal with school programs, teacher-parent expectations including a safe and caring school.

◆ The possibility exists for localized student and parent support groups or homework clubs or small PTA grouping being established.

Special Needs or Alternative Schools.

Each one of these schools has its own student and program configuration. In addition, if the school focuses mostly on students with behavioural problems, many of these problems may be the offshoot of dysfunctional parenting or dysfunctional homes. For the most part these parents are not inclined to be actively engaged in their children's education. But do not lose hope. There may be a volunteer, such as a grandparent, who is able and willing to work with these parents to build relationships that would allow them to be comfortable working with teachers and others in the school system.

On the other hand if the school caters to children with learning disabilities then there may be another level of interest. **Know your students. Form strategies on how to interact with these parents.**

Suggestions:

◆ **Visit the homes.** The person or persons who do the visitation must in some way be closely connected to the development and delivery of the students's program. They will likely become the principal contacts that the parents have with the school.

◆ Try to build into the child's program a project which could be of interest to the parents.

◆ Wherever possible involve the parent in the child's program. This may also allow for the parent to receive training on certain learning or behaviour management strategies.

◆ Consider the formation of parent support groups which are either directed by staff or are mutually supportive or interactive.

◆ Support the parents in their attempts to gain special diagnosis or treatment for their children. Some times the external bureaucracy or personal lack of resources simply overpower these parents.

◆ Tailor each program to the specific needs and strengths of each child. BUILD FROM STRENGTH.

◆ Every time there is progress let the parent know.

◆ Don't expect to hold BIG parent nights at least until you have done all the ground work.

ADOLESCENT SHALLOW SELF ESTEEM-
AUTHENTIC SELF ESTEEM CONTINUUM

ACTIVITIES/EVENTS/ PEOPLE/THINGS	SHALLOW SELF ESTEEM	INTERMEDIATE ZONE (THE GREY AREA)	AUTHENTIC SELF ESTEEM
Failure	Blames others.		Accepts responsibility.
Dress Style	Current Fashion.		Tasteful.
Peer Pressure	Meets group standards.		Makes independent decisions.
Alcohol/Drugs	Very susceptible.		Able to say No!
Personal Effort	Works to minimum standards.		Works to high standards.
Risk	Reluctant to take calculated risks.		Accepts risk as a challenge for growth.
Future	Lives for the **moment.**		Lives in the present. Plans for the future. Conscious of the past.
Sports	Winning is everything.		Performing well and improving is important.
Personal Entertainment	Movies, Mall, Video, TV hobbies, books.		Some TV, movies, a few friends, creating and doing neat stuff.
Peers	To be used for personal gain.		Friendships to be enjoyed and developed.
Adults	A necessary evil. Keep at a distance.		Not a threat. Seek advice and support.
Most important	Being in style, being "cool," being in a group, doing "fun" things.		Enjoying life. Being AOK with Self. Being in charge of Self. **Being (Brain) Cool.**
Material Possessions	Requisite for success.		By products of success.

BEING COOL—THE CHILD/TEENAGE DILEMMA

BEING COOL: PERSONALLY FOCUSSED	BEING COOL:BEING IN CHARGE BEING OTHER FOCUSSED
It's Cool to:	**It's (Brain) Cool to:**
Get smashed!	Protect and grow your brain. (You'll never get another!)
Wear "Cool," "Faddish" Clothes	Being proud of who you are. Dress tastefully
Shove people around.	Help another student. Hold a door open.
Put other students down.	NOT be a Bully. Report a Bullying Incident.
Make fun of students who try to succeed.	Encourage others, even your competition to succeed.
Smoke.	Treat your body as a temple.
Model the behaviours of media personalities.	Model your thoughts and actions on people who have made great contributions to society.
Be sexually active.	Follow "Safe Sex" practices.
Strive to have a really a"Nice Body".	To "Exercise and Sweat." Build skills.
Not try. Laugh at those who do.	Try your best. Acknowledge large and small successes.
Go with the flow.	Make individual decisions. Act on knowledge of "Right and Wrong."
Have extensive body piercing or body art	Learn conflict resolution and mediation skills.
Ignore your parents.	Talk to your parents. Benefit from their experience.
Have weirdly coloured hair, wear "Cliquish" clothes.	Risk challenging yourself, letting yourself be vulnerable to challenge.
Strut and Boast.	Develop authentic self esteem.
Drive an expensive car to school.	Drive a car that you have rebuilt yourself.
Be a "junk food" junkie.	Prepare and eat nutritious food.
Shun other people.	Be friends with people of other cultures. Strive to build your leadership skills.
Befriend others for selfish reasons.	Treat people with respect.
Select friends who are like minded.	Enjoy being with your friends. Rekindle old friendships and form new friendships.
Use offensive language in public	Be sensitive to the presence and needs of others.
Use drugs for "HIGHS."	Further develop your skills to get authentic HIGHS
Drive while impaired and be proud about it.	Be responsible. Be a designated driver.
Spend your free time at the mall or arcades.	Volunteer at seniors homes or homeless shelters.
Ignore others in hallways, doorways and side walks.	Say hello, please, thank you and you're welcome.

APPENDIX V
PROGNOSIS FOR BULLIES

1. **Criminal Record:** Between 35 and 60% of school yard bullies will have a criminal record by age 25. This is the result of these individuals not developing or being able to develop the necessary levels of social consciousness and social conscience that would empower them to live in a socially responsible manner. Their obsession on immediate gratification inhibits their ability to project into the future. Their crimes may range from petty theft, theft with a weapon, assault, murder, molestation, fraud, uttering threats, extortion, stalking, insurance fraud etc.

2. **Low Workplace Skill Level including being the Boss:** A significant percentage of bullies are reluctant to spend the time or energy building the skills necessary to be productive in a complex, integrated work environment. Since these individuals are reluctant to take calculated risks they don't challenge themselves to develop proficiency in both interpersonal skills and technical skills. The area of interpersonal skills is often their greatest weakness.

3. **Unsuitable Marriage Partners:** Adult bullies are prone to infidelity and spousal abuse. The prime reasons rest in their obsession with domination, immediate gratification plus anger management problems, lower than average ability to emotionally connect with another person and a array of personal insecurities some leading to paranoia.

4. **Increased Likelihood to Commit Date Rape:** Bullies are accustomed to getting what they want. A sexually aroused male (teenage or young adult) bully will likely over focus on his own desires and ignore the wishes and feelings of his female date. They are more likely to operate on a "my way or the highway principle." In a similar vain these same males may also resort to using emotional abuse as a means to dominate and control their "girlfriends."

5. **Increased likelihood to commit driving offenses:** These might include excessive speeding, driving with reckless abandonment, driving while impaired and similar offenses. Again the reasons lie with the person's obsession with their own personal desires and limited concern for others.

6. **Addicted to several Chemical Substances:** Bullying is an addictive behaviour but after awhile the bully's brain may experience neural adaptivity and the temptation to use chemicals which produce greater highs may be too strong to resist. An alcoholic bully as either a spouse and/or parent is not be a "pretty sight."

9. **The Bully – As a Coach:** These persons obsess on winning at the expense of skill building, team play and the athlete's physical and psychological development. They coerce players to play outside of the rules including injuring other players. This coach may actively support hazing rituals, intimidate players to play injured and physically, emotionally or sexually abuse players. The damage caused can be severe and last a life time.

10. **Be held in contempt by most people who know them.** They are disliked, distrusted, despised by most of their peers. Many of their victims want to kill them and some of them do.

11. **Develop Anti Social Personal Disorder, aka. Sociopath or Psychopath:** These individuals are the most dangerous and destructive of all human kind. The crimes they commit are heinous and done without any remorse what so ever. These individuals are virtually incorrigible and many will spend most of their adult lives in jail.

12. **Less likelihood to complete secondary or post secondary education:** Those who do receive a diploma or degree usually underperform in the work place if all aspects to their performance are considered.

7. **A bothersome, if not, terrifying neighbour:** As a neighbour this person would have little regard for your property, your privacy, your psychological if not your physical well being. Children of bullies have been known to play loud music and bounce basketballs outside of the bedroom window of a dying man, drive the family automobile with their parent's consent before they had a driver's licence, ride their bicycles over their neighbour's lawn even the part that was freshly seeded. Bullies have pounded on the walls of their neighbour's house, yelled obscenities at their neighbours and told the community police to take a hike, in a manner of speaking.

8. **A dreadful parent:** They model dysfunctional behaviour and create a unhealthy stressful (often including neglect and abuse), environment for their children. These parents take little or no responsibility for their children's actions. School officials are frequently, if not constantly, dealing with the child's misbehaviour or limited academic success and the bombastic outbursts and threats of the parents. These are also likely to be the hostile, aggressive parents who will attack sports coaches, referees/umpires, parents of other team members and players of either team. The children are candidates to become bullies themselves.

APPENDIX VI

PROFILING THE BULLY—A FACT SHEET

Each bully brings to the "table" a common pattern including a need to control, a lack of social conscience, an extensive amount of self absorption, a learned or acquired contempt for others and a track record. However, if your goal is to bring reconciliation to this problem through remediation then you must get the "facts."

The remedial success depends on addressing the specifics of this individual's behaviours, attitudes and knowledge base. The following is designed to give the school a draft format for information gathering.

1. **Nature of the bullying event(s).**

- Nature of bullying activity. What was happening? Did it match one or more of the types? If so in what ways?

- What are the age and size differences between individuals?

- Your observations and/or reports of repetitive bullying activity.

- The location of incident(s).

- The presence of others and their contributions or interventions.

- Information which supports your sense of the "rationale" for the behaviour.

- The stated reason for the bully's actions.

2. **Academic and attendance records.**

- Attendance patterns of both the bully and victim.

- The strengths and weaknesses of the bully.

- The strengths and weaknesses of the victim.

- Family support for both students' school activities.

- Behaviour in normal classroom activities.

3. **Identified deficits or problems areas which are identifiable when bully is confronted such as.**

- Anger.

- Bigoted beliefs.

- Immature humour.

- Excessive aggression.

- Low sense of empathy.

- Limited understanding of issues.

- Limited sense of truth.

- Limited sense of responsibility.

Possible reactions to child's behaviour.

♦ Family support for bully's actions.

♦ A resource of potential support. Grandparents, coach, minister/priest, teacher, counsellor, youth worker.

7. **Input from other teachers, counsellors and social workers which may be helpful.**

8. **Analysis of the bullying behaviour – other possible reasons.**

♦ Attachment, ODD, ADHD, Depression, Learning disabilities. etc.

♦ Child has experienced neglect and multiple abuse. Previously bullied by other students.

♦ Previous family dissolution and reconstitution.

♦ Substance abuse within family such as alcoholism.

♦ Dysfunctional family environments, family disconnected from community.

♦ Frequent school changes.

♦ Family holds bigoted views.

4. **Other school infractions.**

♦ Previous visits to the principal's office. What was tried? What success was achieved?

♦ Altercations with other students and staff. Frequency? Causes? Remediations? Successes?

5. **School activities, if any.**

♦ Extracurricular activity(ies) in which the bully is involved.

♦ Extracurricular activity(ies) in which the victim is involved.

♦ Is there any overlap? If there is overlap are there problems?

6. **Families of both the bully and the victim:**

♦ What is the connection to school? Nature of previous interactions?

♦ Did previous encounters lead to some resolution?

♦ What is the current stability of family constellation? Can either or both parents be helpful?

HELPING THE PARENTS OF BULLIES

The parents of children who bully are placed in a very awkward and sometimes delicate position. This is embarrassing! This is threatening! This may be a challenge to their very way of life. Sometimes they may see it as an answer to a prayer as they may desperately want help.

However remember, many of these parents are in "survival mode" or are bullies themselves.

A. A RANGE OF PARENTAL RESPONSES.

1. **Denial.** "This is definitely not something my kid would do."

2. **Extreme defensiveness.** "This is simply another case of the school singling out my child".

3. **"It's no big deal."** Kids have always bullied. "They'll get over it."

4. **Shock.** "Oh my ...!" This can't really be happening to me?

5. **Assuming blame.** "They are telling me that I haven't raised my kid right." "They are blaming me for my kid's behaviour."

6. **Assigning blame 1.** "It is the kids my child hangs out with. They are the one's who are causing the problem."

7. **Assigning blame 2.** They assign the blame to the victim. "He/she just ran off to the teacher over some little incident. I know the whole family, they are just ...."

8. **Overwhelmed.** "What do I do now?" "I've got my hands full already and now this."

9. **Plan to straighten out the school.** Extremely hostile, antisocial individuals will go ballistic and may resort to threats and intimidation.

10. **Take excessive punitive measures with their child.** This usually does not make things better. The child's behaviours may be primarily due to the parents previous attempts at discipline which have been excessive, erratic and seldom with any developmental follow up.

11. **"OK, what can we do now?"** Some parents get there quickly but many do not. This is an extremely difficult part of the process.

The key here is the relationship that exists between the school and the parent. If the relationship is open and full of trust then the parents are more likely to accept that the school wants to achieve the best for both children.

B. EXPLANATION OF RESPONSES.

This is an emotionally charged time. Much of the literature points to environmentally acquired insecurities and tensions. In addition, many learned behaviours and attitudes have evolved from the home. Furthermore, many parents may be reliving their own unhappy student experiences.

C. HELPING PARENTS HELP YOU SOLVE THE PROBLEM.

This is often a challenge for a variety of reasons. Again the **essential ingredient is relationship building** and the key is trust. While the school would like the problem to be solved immediately, the school must realize that the forces at play are many, varied, long standing and are not prone to be resolved by quick fixes. Lastly quick fixes seldom have longevity.

1. Involving the parents may **appear to slow the process down.** However, you must remember that the children are under your direction for only 5-6 hours per day. The remaining number of hours they may be in the care of people who are contributing to their dysfunctional behaviour.

2. There is no guarantee that any punitive or remedial action taken by you alone will stop the problem from reoccurring. This is particularly true if the

parents view their child's action as being of little consequence or in line with their thought processes.

3. Provide the parents with information about bullying including the **Appendix V Prognosis for Bullies**. They may be still operating with a lack of information. Stress that you want to help them avoid the headaches and heartaches of having a child who experiences serious troubles because of bullying activities in late adolescence or adulthood.

4. **Address the goals and procedures of the process you are about to undertake. Stress long term growth and success.**

   ♦ Provide the parents with resource assistance. This may include parenting groups, involvement with community resources through continuing education, family life centres, recreation groups or committees that are keen on fostering human growth. Additional resources may be this book as well as other books, videos etc.

   ♦ Provide the parents with the facts about bullying, most specifically the possible outcomes, such as criminal records, drug addiction, teenage pregnancy, school failure etc.

   ♦ If restorative justice is a possibility, then an appropriate amount of pre-mediation and coaching may be necessary. It is important to note that it is common for children who are resistant to change to **buy into the language of restorative justice** but not be willing to incorporate any of the principles into their day to day behaviours.

   ♦ Engage the parents in supporting any academic remediation that may be deemed necessary.

   ♦ Not all bullies are academically challenged. Some are troublesome because they are bored out of their tree. In such cases every effort must be made to challenge them academically or vocationally for the purpose of having them gain a sense of achievement.

   ♦ Depending on the nature of the indiscretion, school counsellors, peers counsellors and student mediators may be engaged.

   ♦ Assigning the child to an alternate school setting may be required. The curriculum should be a combination of academic skill building and behaviour modification. In order for the behaviour modification classes to be effective, language skills usually must be enhanced plus a range of activities whereby the student can gain a sense of positive emotional involvement.

   ♦ Employ the services of others in the community, such as the police departments, social services, addictions counsellors, responsible members of the church community, and other leaders who may be able to add substance to the program. **Mentors have proven to be invaluable.**

5. **Actions to avoid.**

   ♦ Premature face to face interaction between the parents of the two students. This all too often leads to heated verbal charges and counter charges and, on occasion, physical attacks. It is very difficult to reach any middle ground in these disputes.

   Example: In a recent case the father of the bully invited the other father to come outside and settle the issue in a man to man fashion.

   ♦ Premature reconciliation between the bully and the victim. The victim is usually at a disadvantage and the bully will see this as another opportunity to further control the victim.

   NOTE: It is sometimes possible, when dealing with young children, to patch up their differences quickly. However, this must be monitored closely to ensure that the patch has permanence. New behaviours seldom become permanent without monitoring and coaching.

   ♦ Shielding the bully because for some reason they hold a special status in the school or in the community. This has happened when the bully is also a star athlete and has had athletic scholarships pending. Bullies must accept responsibility for their actions.

   NOTE: There have been instances where the victim has been suspended from school in order that a court order made against the bully be followed.

6. **Assure the parents that your actions are based on the following principles.**

REACT

R – **R**epair harm done. Reparation (Step 4)

E – **E**xpect the best from others. Everyone has great potential and worth.(Step1)

A – **A**cknowledge feelings/harm done. Acknowledgement of seriousness or the action. (Step 3)

C – **C**are for others. Creating a community of caring people.(Step 5)

T – **T**ake responsibility for behaviours/feelings. Taking charge of a life of positive acts. (Step 2)

A BRIEF GLOSSARY OF TERMS

Brain Model Please make two fists and bring them together so that your finger nails are touching. This represents the two hemispheres of your brain. Where your finger nails are touching could be thought of as the corpus callosum. Just above the corpus callosum approximately where your first knuckles are is a ridge (fold) called the cingulate which runs from near the front of the brain to the back. The space behind the second fingers would contain the amygdala, basal ganglia and other parts of the limbic system. The space occupied by your thumbs could be considered to be the prefrontal cortex and about two thirds of the space along the back of your hands could considered the temporal lobes.

Neurochemicals

Adrenaline is the body's version of the brain's noradrenaline. Adrenaline is released by the adrenal glands at the command of the limbic area to assist the body when in its fight or flight response. Technically adrenaline is not a neurotransmitter, but it plays a major role in stress and aggression.

Dopamine is a neural transmitter of the excitatory kind. It is essential for keeping the brain focussed, firing the brain's reward system and a host of similar functions. A breakdown in the production of dopamine will lead to Parkinson's disease.

Neurotransmitters there are over 70 of these neurochemicals which influence functioning at the synapses. They have familar names like histamine, noradrenaline, serotonin, dopamine, GABA and others.

Noradrenaline is the brain's primary stress and excitatory neurotransmitter.

Serotonin is a neural transmitter which falls into the category of being a neural inhibitor. Its job is to balance out some of the activity of more excitatory neural transmitters. A shortage of serotonin may lead to depression, an over focussed cingulate or violent behaviour. It is the second "S" in SSRIs such as Prozac.

Brain Regions

Amygdala is probably the most influential part of the brain. It monitors nearly all incoming messages, assesses these messages for safety, threat or uncertainty and also stores most of one's emotional memories.

Cingulate is primarily concerned with helping the brain change thought processes. An over focussed cingulate results in a number of obsessions in thoughts and deeds including worrying, continuous checking, Oppositional Defiant Disorder and aspects of Post Traumatic Stress Disorder.

Hippocampus is also part of the screening system but is also an integral component of the long term memory process. Stress negatively affects the hippocampus which of course affects the brain's capacity to create and recall memory.

Orbital Frontal Cortex is located just behind the eyes and is responsible for most of the communication between the Prefrontal Cortex and the Amygdala.

Prefrontal Cortex is the term applied to the cognitive region of the brain that occupies the area behind the forehead. This is the executive management section of the brain.

Temporal Lobes are those portions of the cerebral cortex which are located on each side of the brain. They are some what pistol shaped and start just behind the ear and proceed forward until one's cheek bone. They are critical for managing mood and anger. In addition the Wernicke's area is located to the back, just behind the ear.

Brain Functions

Brain (The) is a composed of 100 billion neurons, several hundred neurochemicals and perhaps 500+ trillion synapses. A good proportion of the brain is dedicated to biological functioning and basic survival but these and other parts can become engaged in a whole range of other things such as reading which is not a natural brain function. The brain is very adaptable and plastic.

Mind (The) is in a simple way what you see or get when the brain is operating. The mind is the outcome of days, years of experiences, of activities and making connections between all the knowledge the brain has processed. The mind represents how the brain is internally wired. To change the mind, the brain must become configured in a different manner.

Mirror Neurons are scattered throughout key parts of the brain such as the pre-motor cortex, and the centres for language, empathy and pain. They fire not only when they are performing an activity but also when they perceive some one else performing that activity. They are critical to a child's learning including accents, patterns of behaviour, physical motion, mannerisms and much more. They require us, as teachers, to walk the talk.

Neuro network is a number of synapses firing together in response to stimulation. An integrated neural network would be able, for example to combine the process of mathematical multiplication to the solving of a physics problem. Or a person with a reasonably complex integrated neuro network would be able to make intelligent decisions when driving on icy or wet road surfaces.

Synapses are the points of interchange between one neuron and another. Synapses that are used frequently become, as it were, hardwired and extremely efficient. Synapses, once established, can only be broken down by disuse, disease or brain injury.

Behavioural Terms

Punishment Punishment operates on the theory that young people must experience pain in order to grow into responsibility. *Marshall p.46*

Discipline Discipline means to teach rather than punish. Discipline should be a positive way of helping and guiding children to achieve self control. *Marshall, p.68*

A RESOURCE LIST

Relationship Bullying, Alternative Aggression – Adolescent Girls

1. *Reviving Ophelia: Saving the Selves of Adolescent Girls*–Mary Pipher

2. *The Shelter of Each Other: Rebuilding Our Families*–Mary Pipher

3. *Odd Girl Out: The Hidden Culture of Aggression in Girls*–Rachel Simmons

4. *Ophelia Speaks: Adolescent Girls Write About Their Search for Self*–Dara Shandler

5. *Queen Bees and Wannabes: Helping Your Daughter Survive Cliques, Gossip, Boyfriends and Other Realities of Adolescence*–Rosalind Wiseman

6. *Girls Circle.* See: *www.girlscircle.com*

7. *The Ophelia Project.* See: *www.opheliaproject.org*

8. *Girls Incorporated.* See: *www.girlsinc.org*

Resources on Aggression including Male Adolescent Aggression/Bullying

1. *The Explosive Child*–Ross Greene

2. *Real Boys and Real Boys Voices*–William Pollock, (Two Books)

3. *The Boy Named It, The Lost Boy and A Man Named Dave*–David Pelzer (Three Books)

4 *Lost Boys, Parents Under Siege*–James Garbino (Two Books)

5. *Bullycide: Death at Playtime*–Neil Marr & Tim Field (Very Disturbing Material)

6. *Raising Cain*–Dan Kindlon & Michael Thompson

7. *Primal Teen*–Barbara Strauch

8. *The Bully, the Bullied and the Bystander*–Barbara Coloroso

Other references to help with understanding and program development

1. *Change Your Brain Change Your Life, Healing ADHD*–Daniel Amen (Two Books)

2. *DSM-IV-TR*–APA

4. *Emotional Intelligence*–Daniel Goleman

5. *Owners Manual for the Brain*–Pierce Howard

6. *Different Brains, Different Learners*–Eric Jensen

7. *Punished by Rewards*–Alfie Kohn

8. *Putting the Brain into the Classroom*–David Halstead

9. *Six Pillars of Self Esteem, How to Raise your Self Esteem*–Nathaniel Branden (Two Books)

10. *Discipline Without Stress*–Marvin Marshall
See also: *www.AboutDiscipline.com*

11. *Reading Connections*–Mary Howard
www.readingconnections.net/message.html

12. *The Anger ToolBox*–Tricia Irving and John Taylor Smith, www.skylight.org.nz

13. *Revised Olweus Bully/Victim Questionnaire*
See: *http//:vinst.umdnj.edu/VAID/TestReport.asp*

14. *Bullying Questionnaire* : www.state.de.us/attgen/main_page/teachers/bullquesti.htm

15. *Why Zebras Don't Get Ulcers*–Robert M. Sapolsky

16. *Answers to Distraction*–Edward M. Hallowell and John Ratey

18. *Trauma and Juvenile Delinquency*–Edited by Ricky Greenwald

19. *The Resilience Factor*–Karen Reivich and Andrew Shatte

20. *WHY IS EVERY ONE SO CRANKY?*–C. Leslie Charles

21. *Without Conscience: The Disturbing World of the Psychopaths Among Us*–Robert Hare

22. *Cognitive Processing Therapy*–in Ricky Greenwald's book

23. *The Optimistic Child*–Martin Seligman

24. *The Developing Mind*–Daniel J. Siegel

BRAIN POWER LEARNING GROUP
ONE AND TWO DAY PROGRAMS

David Halstead is one of North America's leading speakers and facilitators in the area of applying the latest neuroscience to the world of learning. In *The Bully Around the Corner: Changing Brains – Changing Behaviours* David combines three knowledge sources: the neuroscience that deals with brain development, his own national and international experiences as a teacher, counsellor and administrator (in six countries and four continents) and the observations and questions of the thousands of people who have attended his workshops. The end result is this definitive book on bullying and the brain.

David's is also the author of *Putting the Brain into the Classroom – 39 Brain Facts and 231 Teaching Strategies* is now in it's forth printing and is being used by educators in Canada, Australia, New Zealand, Singapore, United Kingdom and the United States, a co-author of a comprehensive career development program and a contributor to a contributor to the *Praeger Handbook of Learning and the Brain*, Greenwood Publishing Group.

Educational Workshops include for Grades K – 12:

Applying Neuroscience to Teaching and Learning

The Nature of the Brains of Bullies

The Dynamics of the Middle Years Brains – Learning and Behaviour

Neuroscience and the Gifted Child

Adolescent Brains: Maturation and Social Pressures

College Presentations and Workshops include:

Applying Brain Research to Increase Student Effectiveness

Bullying in the College University Environments

How's Your Memory or Have you Forgotten? Brains Secrets for Better Memories

Embracing Change: Overcome Resistance by Understanding the Brain Brain Fitness

Business and Industry Workshops

Accelerated Learning in Company Training Programs

Embracing Change: Overcome Resistance by Understanding the Brain

Violence and Bullying in the Workplace

DAVID HALSTEAD CAN BE CONTACTED AT:

Toll Free in Canada or USA at: 1-888-562-0132

Telephone 204-261-8483 Fax 204-269-7466

e-mail: halstead@mts.net or Website: www.brainpowerlearning.com